A GREAT FEAR

ATLANTIC CROSSINGS

Rafe Blaufarb, *Series Editor*

Gabriel Paquette, *Area Editor*

A GREAT FEAR

Luís de Onís and the Shadow War against Napoleon in Spanish America, 1808–1812

Timothy Hawkins

The University of Alabama Press
Tuscaloosa

The University of Alabama Press
Tuscaloosa, Alabama 35487-0380
uapress.ua.edu

Typeface: Caslon

Cover image and design: David Nees

Library of Congress Cataloging-in-Publication Data

Names: Hawkins, Timothy, 1967– author.
Title: A great fear : Luís de Onís and the shadow war against Napoleon in Spanish America, 1808–1812 / Timothy Hawkins.
Description: Tuscaloosa : The University of Alabama Press, [2019] | Series: Atlantic crossings | Includes bibliographical references and index.
Identifiers: LCCN 2018026900| ISBN 9780817320041 (cloth) | ISBN 9780817392130 (ebook)
Subjects: LCSH: Spain—History—Napoleonic Conquest, 1808–1813. | Spain—Foreign relations—1808–1814. | Onís, Luis de, 1762–1827. | Spain—Colonies—America.
Classification: LCC DP205 .H38 2019 | DDC 940.2/73098—dc23
LC record available at https://lccn.loc.gov/2018026900

For Margaret, Nathan, and Philip

Con todo mi amor . . .

Contents

List of Illustrations ix

Preface xi

Acknowledgments xiii

Introduction. Chasing Shadows: French Subversion in Spanish America 1

One. Francophobia and Spanish America 17

Two. On the Edge of the Abyss: The Spanish Legation to the United States, 1807–1809 41

Three. Luís de Onís: From Cantalapiedra to Philadelphia 57

Four. The Spanish Diplomat versus the French Emissary, 1809–1810 75

Five. Onís on the Offensive, 1811 101

Six. Fighting Napoleon in Totonicapán 124

Conclusion. Spies and Shadows 145

Appendix 155

Notes 169

Glossary 213

Bibliography 217

Index 229

Illustrations

MAPS

Map 1. The Spanish Empire in the Caribbean Basin, circa 1810 xiv
Map 2. The United States, circa 1810 xv
Map 3. The US-Spanish frontier in the Gulf of Mexico, circa 1810 xvi
Map 4. Plan of Philadelphia, 1797 70
Map 5. The Alcaldía Mayor of Totonicapán, circa 1810 127

FIGURES

Figure 1. Portrait of Luís de Onís 59
Figure 2. "Boney at Bayonne blowing a Spanish bubble" 63

Preface

As is the case with many second books, this project had a long gestation. The original idea for this book arose in the mid-1990s when I was deep into the research that eventually resulted in an earlier work, *José de Bustamante and Central American Independence*. As I explored the Guatemala City archives for information on the Spanish kingdom's response to the imperial crisis of 1808, I took note of the frequent expressions of concern on the part of local officials about French subversive activity. In some cases, the colonial administrative records included names of suspected French agents. Additionally, prosecutors who brought cases before Guatemala's various judicial institutions often emphasized links (or at least sympathy) between local malcontents accused of acts of disloyalty and foreign conspirators. The possibility that a French espionage network had in fact operated in Central America intrigued me, especially since the archival evidence left little doubt that Spanish officials governed as if one existed. Consequently, while my first book would make mention of the Guatemalan cases, I became convinced that a second project—devoted to the origins, impact, and larger context of Napoleonic subversion in the Americas—was warranted. Fifteen years of following the *emisario francés* (French emissary) back and forth across the Atlantic has led me to this point.

I completed most of the research for this book in Spanish archives. The Archivo Histórico Nacional (AHN) in Madrid in particular stores the bulk of the diplomatic correspondence and government records used here. Documents from the Archivo General de Centroamérica (AGCA) and the Newberry Library are central to the case study at the heart of chapter 6. The George A. Smathers Libraries of the University of Florida, notably the Department of Special and Area Studies Collections, provided access to valuable material from its East Florida Papers and the Papeles de Cuba holdings from the Archives of the Indies (AGI). Details about the southwest borderlands came from holdings in the Latin American Library at

Tulane University and the Bexar Archives of the University of Texas. A visit to the Archivo General de la Nación (AGN) in Buenos Aires allowed me to explore the unique history of the Río de la Plata in the decades following the French Revolution. Microfilms of the National Archives' Notes on the Spanish Legation provided a major source of information about both the American and Spanish diplomatic posturing during this period, as did the Thomas Jefferson and James Madison Papers. All scholars of the period owe a debt of gratitude to the librarians and archivists working at the National Archives, the Library of Congress, and various state archives, who provide public access to such valuable historical material through publications and online websites.

Acknowledgments

Numerous family members, friends, and colleagues supported me as I worked to bring this decade-long project to completion. The History Department at Indiana State University (ISU) was an ideal professional home during this period. A number of grants from ISU's research funds provided critical financial reinforcements for my trips to Spain and Argentina, while a Summer Library Grant from the University of Florida enabled me to spend two weeks at the Smathers Library. Chapters 4, 5, and 6 in particular benefited from the critiques of panelists and participants at the scholarly conferences where they were first exposed to public scrutiny. In this respect, I wish to recognize the thoughtful comments and valuable advice I have received over the years from Richmond Brown, Alvis Dunn, Laura Matthew, Blake Pattridge, Jordana Dym, Christophe Belaubre, and John Savage. Special thanks to Lyman Johnson and Mark Burkholder for helping me to work through my evidence and refine my argument—especially that one time over lunch at the Acme Oyster Bar in New Orleans. I am grateful to Bill Nelson for the care he took in preparing the maps used here. I would like to express my appreciation to Wendi Schnaufer and the staff of the University of Alabama Press for their editorial assistance and unwavering support. Finally, I would like to recognize Alabama's anonymous readers for the time they spent reading, reviewing, and evaluating this manuscript. Their guidance and suggestions were invaluable.

Despite so much support and my best efforts to craft *the* perfect book, I am ultimately responsible for any errors of fact or interpretation found herein.

Map 1. The Spanish Empire in the Caribbean Basin, circa 1810 (Timothy Hawkins).

Map 2. The United States, circa 1810 (Timothy Hawkins).

Map 3. The US-Spanish frontier in the Gulf of Mexico, circa 1810 (Timothy Hawkins).

A GREAT FEAR

Introduction

Chasing Shadows

French Subversion in Spanish America

> We must inform all priests and their assistants that reports have arrived which confirm that the French have entered Andalusia and that the Intruder King has sent emissaries, including four destined for this kingdom, to deceive, seduce, and win over to his authority the inhabitants of the Americas.
>
> —Isidro Sicilia, archdeacon of the Guatemalan Metropolitan Church, May 23, 1810

Between 1808 and 1812 Spanish officials loyal to the deposed King Fernando VII inundated Spanish America with warnings about Napoleonic emissaries, spies, agents, and other foreign provocateurs. While local governments ruled over subjects who offered frequent and passionate displays of loyalty to the Bourbon monarchy, colonial authorities nevertheless found their administrative policies and defensive measures shaped by a profound anxiety over French-inspired insurrection. Officials responded to this perceived threat by publicizing regular bulletins about suspected cases of espionage, offering rewards for information leading to the capture of spies, threatening severe punishment to *afrancesados* (Francophiles), and exhorting the public, often via the clerical establishment, to be on guard against revolutionaries. They instituted severe restrictions on travel, prohibitions on the use of Spanish American ports by French ships, and increased scrutiny of the transit documentation required of all foreign vessels. The governments of individual colonies called for the creation of new militia forces, sought funds—either through forced loans or *donativos patrióticos* (patriotic donations)—to outfit existing units with the most up-to-date equipment, and stationed veteran troops in strategic areas to guard against surprise attacks. The heightened bureaucratic alarm even produced dubious institutional changes in a number of colonies, as both military courts and ad hoc tribunals of loyalty emerged to investigate and adjudicate suspected cases of *infidencia* (subversion).

Not surprisingly, the climate of insecurity that descended on Spanish America after 1808 also affected the governed. While Spanish officials searched for evidence of subversive French activities within their communities, some colonists challenged the legitimacy of local authorities who were tainted by French associations, however innocuous those connections might be. Others began to question the nature of the political relationship between Americans and Spaniards, for it was now possible to doubt the viability of an empire whose metropolis seemed likely to fall into the hands of a foreign conqueror. Whether it was used to depose an intendant (provincial governor) in Chiapas, smear the reputation of a viceroy in Buenos Aires, or demand the creation of an autonomous governing junta in Mexico City, this fear of the French—more clinically, Francophobia or more colorfully, the "tricolor scare"[1]—encouraged numerous challenges to the political status quo at a troubled time in the history of the Spanish empire.

Indeed, Napoleon Bonaparte's shadow, that is, the threat of French intervention, proved to be a destabilizing factor in the period between his overthrow of the Spanish Bourbons at Bayonne in May 1808 and the subsequent consolidation of full-fledged independence movements across Spanish America. Nevertheless, while the foundations of Spanish sovereignty were certainly compromised in the wake of this unprecedented coup, the empire remained largely intact for another decade. In a 2007 essay addressing the geopolitics of Latin American independence, Rafe Blaufarb revisits a question first raised two decades previously by Timothy Anna. Namely, why did Spanish Americans not take the opportunity to seize independence during the critical period between 1808 and 1812, when Spain was overrun by French armies and was, arguably, at its weakest state?[2]

The present book addresses this important question and offers a hypothesis for why the process of independence proved to be so slow and controversial in the region. By concentrating on the four-year period between 1808 and 1812, the analysis that follows covers a narrow but critical phase in the thirty-year imperial crisis that culminated in the collapse of Spanish authority in the Americas. Arguably, this crisis began in 1793 when Spain entered the first European coalition against revolutionary France. This fateful decision was followed by fifteen years of military defeats and political failures, a sequence of punishing events that prevented the Spanish crown from defending itself in 1808 when it became clear that Napoleon intended to assume control over Spain and its empire. The French emperor's decision to replace the Bourbon monarchy with his brother Joseph Bonaparte brought the Spanish state to its knees. The adoption of the Bayonne Statute fractured traditional political institutions, sparked a six-year war against the French occupation that consumed the entire Iberian Peninsula, and shook the stability of Spanish America. Yet, despite the near collapse of the metropolis, the Spanish colonial bureaucracy survived. Not only did it remain viable in the face of intense pressures, but in a number of cases imperial officials became energized to confront the challenges facing them.

Paradoxically, the climate engendered by the French threat appears to have had a short-term stabilizing impact on a region discomforted by European events. Napoleon's shadow gave the Spanish administrators focus; it united them behind a common cause; and, for a time, it drove them closer to their subjects. So long as the French remained the enemy, the campaign developed by colonial bureaucrats to protect the empire retained wide popular support. Thus, when anticolonial movements broke out in earnest in Caracas and Buenos Aires early in 1810, Spanish officials were able to respond rapidly and effectively to the new emergency. Francophobia allowed the empire to weather the worst of the metropolitan crisis and, at the same time, to overcome the first signs of colonial unrest. As a result, the forces that ultimately produced the end of Spanish rule in the Americas could not combine effectively until after 1814.

Little direct proof of Napoleon's efforts at subversion in Spanish America in fact exists, though enough circumstantial evidence survives to establish an outline of his principal objectives. This study, however, does not seek to confirm the existence of such operations. Instead, I argue in the pages ahead that the *fear* of French intervention mattered far more than the reality, for colonial officials and their subjects believed implicitly in the threat posed by Napoleon and his agents—the infamous *emisario francés*—and reacted accordingly, with real and unexpected consequences for the empire. In the absence of actual local or regional unrest, the loyalist governments in the Americas nevertheless operated as if they were under siege. With Napoleon in control of Europe, colonial authorities had every reason to believe that he would shift his attention to the far side of the Atlantic and seek to destabilize the Spanish empire. Far from an abstract concern, Napoleon loomed large over the region, and his shadow could be felt on an almost tangible level. In a very real sense, he already existed there by proxy: via local converts to his cause, foreign spies and subversives, cruising French warships and corsairs, and even, potentially, French armies. This imminent danger required an appropriate defensive response from representatives of the Spanish Crown. As their collective strategy developed, however, the relationship between the colonial bureaucracy and its subjects, between the rulers and the ruled, changed in a way that had negative consequences for long-term imperial survival. The official reaction to the threat of French intervention increasingly led Spanish authorities to view their subjects with suspicion, as potential enemies rather than allies in the struggle to preserve the empire. Over time, this climate of fear eroded the legitimacy of the Crown among Spanish Americans, a process that contributed to the unraveling of the empire by the 1820s.

More fundamentally, this work argues that a more complete understanding of the breakup of the Spanish empire requires a consideration of the wider geopolitical struggles underway in the Atlantic World during the first two decades of the nineteenth century. The collapse of the Spanish empire did not occur within a vacuum. Multiple external forces shaped the response of Spanish officials to the imperial crisis and the subsequent colonial rebellions. At the same time, proponents of independence also found their desires and actions channeled by external forces beyond their control. The entire region was shaken by the disruptions caused by the French Revolution of 1789, an event that produced more than two decades of war that ultimately entangled all the traditional European powers as well as a new nation, the United States. As any timeline of Latin American independence suggests, Napoleon's overthrow of the Spanish Bourbons in 1808 was one among many globally consequential acts resulting from his reign.

Above all, this account seeks to understand the nature and consequences of the Spanish reaction to a four-year campaign by the French emperor to manipulate the political destiny of Spanish America with spies, agents, and other foreign provocateurs. In the process, some details of these subversive operations will emerge from the shadows. At the same time, the narrative also affords a glimpse into the emergence of the United States as a major Atlantic power. Perhaps ironically, this young republic served as the primary springboard from which France sought to project its influence into the Spanish colonies. While Spain prioritized the Napoleonic threat, no less problematic for the preservation of Spanish rule in the Americas was the unrelenting pressure from its expansionist northern neighbor. The often-conflicting interests of two states that shared a long border separating their respective possessions in North America contributed to the gradual disintegration of Bourbon authority over the empire at a time of already great political strain.

A work largely set in the eastern United States and whose primary antagonist is Napoleon might seem an odd basis from which to launch an exploration of the early years of the Spanish imperial crisis. However, a different stage and new actors can inspire fresh perspectives. Most of the traditional historiography on this subject seeks insight into the period either through an analysis of the internal dynamics that set anticolonial movements in motion or through a dissection of the personal motivations of revolutionary leaders. At a fundamental level, it seems logical that one should look within the colonies themselves to explain the motivations that precipitated movements for independence. At the same time, it is important to understand Spanish American independence as a multicausal event with transatlantic dimensions. During the critical period from 1808 to 1812, the primary existential threat to the Spanish empire was external, defined by French aggression against Spain and Napoleonic policy toward its colonies. While 1810 marked the beginning of internal rebellions against Spanish rule in such strategic colonies as New Spain (modern-day Mexico), Venezuela, and the Río de la Plata (modern-day Argentina), these movements had conflicting causes, motivations, and goals and largely proved ephemeral. Only after 1812 did concerted and sustained campaigns emerge in Spanish America with independence as a clear objective. While these later manifestations frequently claimed inspiration and direction from their predecessors, such ties were often tenuous. Arguably, the strongest link between the 1810 revolts and the 1812 versions was that the colonial authorities treated both in exactly the same manner—as something to be eliminated at all costs. By 1810 an official Spanish response to rebellion had already emerged. The inspiration for this counterinsurgency strategy was the Napoleonic emissary.[3]

As such, this work suggests that a more complete understanding of the breakup of the Spanish empire requires careful examination of the besieged nature of the colonial bureaucracy between 1808 and 1812. In particular, I maintain that the earliest movements for autonomy and later independence in Spanish America were exacerbated, if not set in motion, by specific measures taken by the colonial officials to defend against external threats during this four-year period. To be sure, the colonial officials on the front lines of Spain's imperial crisis feared rebellion, especially as the political consensus within the empire began to unravel in the wake of Napoleon's symbolic decapitation of the Spanish Bourbon dynasty. However, they expected that unrest would be imported following contact with various foreign contagions rather than emerge organically from within the colonies. There was precedent: notable examples of recent European interventions included the disastrous French occupation of the island of Hispaniola from 1802 to 1803 and the botched British invasions of Buenos Aires in 1806–1807. Even American-born troublemakers like Francisco de Miranda, who tried but failed to inspire a revolution in his native Venezuela in 1806, were viewed as carriers of a French revolutionary virus.

These cases demonstrated that thousands of miles of ocean could not protect the inhabitants of Spanish America from the tremendous political upheavals that transformed Europe during the wars of the French Revolution. Until the collapse of the Spanish monarchy, however, the Hispanic world had managed to avoid any significant sign of social unrest or revolutionary sentiment. Thus, when the unsettling news from Bayonne spread across Spanish America over the course of the summer of 1808, imperial officials began to prepare for what was widely expected to be the primary consequence of the disputed transfer of the throne to Napoleon's brother: the invasion and conquest of the American colonies by French forces.

Within eighteen months, the loyalist government in Spain and its colonial representatives had instituted a patchwork defensive strategy for the region built on counterintelligence and counterespionage operations. This approach, which demanded overt demonstrations of allegiance to the crown, also afforded local governments extra incentives to question the loyalty of Spanish subjects.

By 1810 official fears that Spanish America was in imminent danger of invasion began to subside in light of the stubborn resistance by Spanish loyalists to the French occupation of Spain itself. Nevertheless, within the colonies the preoccupation with defense did not disappear as the military threat from Europe diminished. Rather, it quickly developed into an obsession with subversive activity. In the uncertain political environment created by the imperial crisis, Spanish officials convinced themselves that Napoleon had turned his attention away from direct conquest in favor of a subtler assault on the integrity of the empire. In the wake of multiple and repeated warnings regarding the activities of spies, provocateurs, and other agents that reached colonial capitals between 1808 and 1810, the French became linked in the public imagination to the growing levels of unrest, discontent, and autonomist sentiment in a number of Spanish colonies. While some areas still appeared uninfected by the revolutionary contagion, colonial authorities had few illusions that the empire would continue to avoid the consequences of subversive activity. As a result, many officials persisted with their aggressive counterinsurgency policies. In some cases, these measures evolved into a broad-based militarization of society and its civil institutions. Before long and with little encouragement, the Catholic Church also began to contribute its vast resources, bureaucracy, and propaganda tools to the discovery of foreign espionage networks. Although the French threat remained the ostensible reason behind the deployment of these measures, once the independence movements began in earnest in certain parts of Spanish America colonial authorities could not simply set aside these policies, particularly as they seemed an appropriate response to the new challenge. As a result, to the chagrin of many loyal subjects, much of the counterinsurgency infrastructure remained in place in the colonies well beyond the liberation of Spain in 1814.

Despite the expectations of the Spanish colonial government, the antisubversive measures that emerged during the imperial crisis proved awkward to execute and, in certain cases, counterproductive. While colonial administration in theory was highly centralized under the Spanish Bourbons, the actual implementation of defense regulations depended heavily on the active participation of provincial and local officials. The direct authority of viceroys—or captains general—did not extend far beyond the outskirts of their capitals, and when governors issued kingdom-wide decrees they could never confirm that their orders were fully carried out. The concept of a central power with the ability to enforce its laws and impose its will on the entire area under its jurisdiction (or, to put it differently, of a police state consisting of a complex web of bureaucracy with sensitive links between the government and the people) was not part of the late colonial experience of Spanish America. Difficult terrain, poor communications, entrenched local interests, and a small, overextended colonial bureaucracy all limited the extent to which these authorities could exercise their power. Consequently, the official preoccupation with foreign subversion went a long way toward encouraging the kind of instability that the government hoped to avoid. Colonial officials confronted Spanish Americans with questions about their loyalty to the Crown at a time when evidence of widespread opposition to Spanish rule remained unsubstantiated. Just when Spain needed the support of its empire the most, the obsession with France turned the colonial bureaucracy against its own subjects and undermined the foundations of loyalty to imperial rule in the Americas.

This study examines the challenges faced by the Spanish colonial bureaucracy during the four-year period following Napoleon's 1808 coup by concentrating on the activities of Luís de Onís, who served as Spain's senior representative to the United States from 1809 to 1819. This diplomat played a critical role in the evolution of the anti-French defensive strategy in the Americas. More than any other official in the Spanish colonial bureaucracy, he kept the colonies sensitized to foreign threats and worked tirelessly to substantiate the alleged link between the Napoleonic emissaries and the first outbreaks of rebellion against Spain. The loyalist ambassador to the United States regarded himself as the de facto supervisor of the entire colonial bureaucracy, even though he held no such official charge. This was a presumptuous yet also understandable position to take at the time, one he assumed above all by virtue of his location. Divided into many semiautonomous jurisdictions, headed by viceroys, captains general, and other governors who jealously guarded their privileges, the empire was not nearly as manageable as officials in Spain would have wished. Based in Philadelphia, Onís took advantage of a favorable geographic position that enabled him to communicate and strategize with colonial officials who were in relative proximity to his base of operations. With the loyalist government in Spain distant and besieged by Napoleon, colonial officials could not expect consistent and coordinated policy from the metropolis. In this environment, despite multiple obstacles to effective organization of the system responsible for colonial order, Onís sought to ensure that the bureaucracy operate as cohesively as possible.

The ambassador also found himself at ground zero of the foreign threats against Spanish America. By 1809 it was apparent that the United States served as an ideal staging area for French subversive activity in the Americas. As a result, between 1810 and 1812 Onís waged a clandestine and oftentimes personal campaign to neutralize French efforts aimed at undermining the Spanish empire. At this time many Spanish officials considered France a more immediate and dangerous threat to the integrity of the empire than the nascent autonomist/independence movements in the colonies. As someone who supported this position, Onís took advantage of his presence in Philadelphia to ensure that the primary battlefield in Spain's war with France over these American possessions became the United States.

Onís undertook to lead this campaign in difficult and often hostile circumstances. For six of the most critical years in its history, Spain lacked official representation before the government of the United States. Between 1809 and 1815, the administration of President James Madison refused to recognize the appointment of Onís as the minister plenipotentiary and ambassador extraordinary of Fernando VII. While this particular (and not unprecedented) breakdown in diplomatic relations between two states might appear trivial and inconsequential on its surface, the United States had established itself by the beginning of the nineteenth century as the first serious threat to the long domination of the Western Hemisphere by European colonial powers. The rise of the United States was especially problematic for Spain, since the still largely hypothetical dangers to Spanish North America posed by US expansion before 1810 became much more real and immediate as the kingdom's colonies erupted into rebellion in the decade that followed. With Europe convulsed in war at the time, no country was better positioned to take advantage of Spanish weakness than the United States. While Luís de Onís fought stubbornly for three years to deflect French subversion in Spanish America, he also struggled to win the recognition of his American hosts and ultimately failed to parry their interest in Spanish-held territory.

By concentrating on the bureaucratic reaction to the threat of French subversion in Spanish America, I hope to underscore the impact of foreign agency as a primary factor shaping the Latin American independence movements. An essential prerequisite of this goal is the restoration of much deserved attention to the Napoleonic emissary, who consequently plays a central role in the narrative. At the same time, however, this is not a history of espionage, for I do not intend to linger on the motivations, actions, successes, and failures of these agents of French foreign policy. The historiography of Napoleonic diplomacy has long accepted that some form of subversive campaign in Spanish America did in fact occur.[4] This scholarship has identified distinct phases to these operations, reflecting the evolving geopolitical priorities of Napoleon, whose emissaries initially personified the hopes that Spanish America would embrace a new dynasty headed by Joseph Bonaparte but ultimately sought to foment rebellion within the colonies to protect French interests in Europe.[5] Since the activities of many French agents did actually overlap with the outbreak of rebellion in the colonies, historians who have followed this theme have naturally sought to uncover evidence for a causal relationship between the two, with varying degrees of success.[6]

One challenge in establishing a convincing association between foreign agency and independence is perspective. While the historical literature is replete with accounts of French, British, and American intervention in Spanish America, many scholars who have identified a connection between outside actors and the colonial revolutions against Spain only demonstrate the presence of foreign agents in the affected region. An approach that implies that the existence of subversives ipso facto proves causality is problematic, for it can be difficult to link motives, agendas, or even detailed instructions to specific uprisings. One might explore Francisco de Miranda's debt to the transatlantic exchange of ideas in the formation of his personal political ideology and then argue that foreign influence played a contextual role in the outbreak of rebellion in Caracas. Or, one could show that the Argentine general José de San Martín received support from Paris and inspiration from Napoleon, factors that might have provided a framework for his emergence as a revolutionary leader in Buenos Aires. However, while circumstantial evidence exists that the Mexican priest and independence leader Miguel Hidalgo met with a suspected Napoleonic emissary in 1808, would such a fact, if confirmed, be enough for a careful historian to claim that the Hidalgo Revolt was itself the product of French machinations?[7]

An investigation into the efforts of Spanish officials to neutralize French emissaries, spies, and conspirators in the Americas is a complicated endeavor with some ostensibly contradictory characteristics. While this work will bring as many of these suspected agents to the surface as possible, it will only trace them so long as they remained targets for Spanish officials. With some significant exceptions, the history of the emisario francés has yet to be written.[8] In this respect, this account is not so much an exploration of the impact of the emissaries on the inhabitants of Spanish America as an analysis of their impact on the colonial bureaucracy. Their presence in the colonies, real or imagined, isolated the bureaucracy, put it on the defensive, forced it to prioritize security above all else, and caused colonial officials to see signs of unrest in the most benign of activities. Far from reacting to a homegrown threat to Spanish rule, imperial administrators found themselves facing one that appeared to come from across the Atlantic.

While students of Spain's imperial crisis need to consider the impact of the Napoleonic emissary, they will not find a definitive connection between this figure and colonial revolts by tracing his steps or even by proving his existence. What matters above all in this history is the *perception* of the threat. The reaction of the Spanish colonial bureaucracy and its subjects to the potential danger from Napoleon was not based on the confirmed existence of French agents, or their numbers, or their specific motives. It was driven by suspicion and the belief that one could and should act based on reasonable doubt about French designs. This narrative was constructed by Spanish officials, reinforced by the capture of suspected agents and incriminating documents, and then disseminated across the colonies. By far the most important figure in this operation was Luís de Onís. The defensive measures he and others initiated were real, well documented, and probably far out of proportion to the actual threat. By shedding light on the war waged by Spain's colonial officials against Napoleon's shadow army of subversives, the present study confirms the emergence of a bureaucratic paranoia that contributed to the conditions that made internal rebellion possible and, ultimately, successful throughout the empire.

At a time when Napoleonic legions were conquering Europe, a different kind of French force marched across Spanish America with the goal of upsetting the established order. Its officers and soldiers were unquestionably unconventional. They were small in numbers, and they largely remained invisible. Because their Spanish opponents took for granted their existence and mobilized significant military forces in opposition, this French subversive army had an outsized impact on its battlefield, one comparable to a conventional Napoleonic battalion or brigade. This mysterious army of subversives left significant unrest in its wake. Ultimately, its primary victim was the Spanish imperial order itself.

Over the past fifty years, historians have given the interconnected space between Europe, Africa, and the Americas a name: the Atlantic World. The concept first took shape in the second half of the twentieth century in the wake of the rise of the influential French Annales school of history, which resisted the traditional historiography of politics, high diplomacy, great men, and the narrow study of nation-states built around artificial boundaries and time periods.[9] Instead, this movement sought to build a foundation for *histoire événementielle* (history of specific events) by first exploring more lasting and arguably more significant influences on society, such as geography, the environment, and long-term interactions between peoples. Over time, many historians of the Atlantic World have appropriated and modified the Annales perspective to write transatlantic histories of the colonial period (ca. 1500–1825) highlighting the profound human connections across this unique geographic stage.[10]

This study draws upon the multilayered connections of the early nineteenth-century Atlantic World to explore the collapse of the Spanish empire. In particular, it sees some advantage to shifting the main stage of action away from Spanish America to the United States. While this work is built on sources drawn from across the Spanish empire—including colonial capitals such as Havana, Guatemala City, and Buenos Aires as well as frontier outposts such as Totonicapán, St. Augustine, and Nacogdoches—most of the action unfolds within the United States, which served as both a base of operations for Luís de Onís and a staging ground for the shadow army of French subversives. Yet, despite the primary setting, this account is not an investigation of US policy toward Spain and its colonies, a subject that has been the topic of many excellent studies in recent years.[11] In this particular case, it is less important to establish, for example, the motivations of the Madison administration toward Spanish America than to document what Spanish colonial officials believed about the United States. Again, the Spanish perception was that the American president had become another puppet of the French emperor.

True to an Atlantic World framework, this work sees great value in including both France and the United States in the conversation about the precipitating factors behind Latin American independence. Such a perspective must take into consideration the relationship between the United States and Spain and its impact on Spanish decision-making within the empire. It must also acknowledge the most destabilizing force in the Atlantic World at the time: Napoleon. In fact, no investigation of the movements that shook the region during the Age of Revolution can afford to be exclusive or self-contained.[12] No general study of the Spanish imperial crisis and Latin American independence should downplay the complex interactions between the United States, the belligerent European powers, and their surviving colonies in the Western Hemisphere.

On the surface, studies of the years that encompassed the collapse of the Spanish empire and the emergence of independent nations in Latin America have been quintessential *histoire événementielle*, to the extent that they traditionally focus on a specific time period (ca. 1800–1825), discreet episodes, rapid political change, and unpredictable conflicts between individuals and groups. The first century or so of this scholarship, which was dominated by Latin American politicians, historians, and intellectuals, framed the historiographical debate largely within the priorities of nineteenth-century nationalism, local political interest, and great-man biography.[13] By 1900, interest in the topic broadened to include historians from Europe and the United States. These scholars quickly began to add their perspectives to those of their Latin American counterparts and often challenged the predominant local and regional consensus, in which the struggles for independence arose largely from organic causes on the backs of native heroes and popular emancipation movements. By publishing volumes of diplomatic records, these foreign historians increasingly emphasized the significance of external forces on the rise of revolutionary movements and drew as much attention to the causes of imperial collapse as to the birth of new nations.[14]

While the independence-era historiography benefited overall from this broader perspective, much of the scholarship produced in the first half of the twentieth century inadvertently raised the problematic issue of agency by threatening either to erase Latin Americans from their own historical experience or, at a minimum, to make them passive participants in events beyond their control. With Latin American independence effectively subsumed into what came to be known as the Age of Napoleon, academic interest turned to events in London, Paris, and Washington, DC, rather than developments in Lima, Buenos Aires, or Caracas. Now, the protagonists were Napoleon Bonaparte, the British diplomat Lord Castlereagh, and James Madison, rather than Miguel Hidalgo, Simón Bolívar, or José de San Martín. For the first time Latin American independence became a topic of serious investigation beyond the region itself. However, the diplomatic, political, and military historians who took up the subject at times expressed more interest in the larger geopolitical context of the revolutions than in their possible internal causes and idiosyncrasies.[15]

By the 1960s, the history-from-below focus of the Annales school and its adherents enabled a significant reconsideration of well-established approaches to history as a discipline, a development that would also influence the historiography of Latin American independence. Studies that multiplied at an exponential rate in the second half of the twentieth century acknowledged the transatlantic context that included the Napoleonic Wars but increasingly concentrated on the internal forces that paved the way for colonial rebellions against Spain.[16] More recently, a subset of historians drawn to the complex interactions between Spanish America, the United States, Great Britain and its American colonies, and France during the early 1800s have published works demonstrating a perspective that is at once international in scope and local in focus, a trend often associated with the New Diplomatic History.[17] Regardless of the area of focus, though, these studies continue to reflect the long-term influence and durability of the Atlantic World model as well as the inevitability of overlap in current scholarship on the Americas.

Once historians of Latin America turned their attention to the international context of the independence period, the impact of Napoleonic foreign policy on the region became a particularly attractive area of investigation. This scholarship benefited from the fact that general interest in Napoleonic studies had reached epic proportions during the nineteenth century. This public fascination with the emperor and his times led to the publication of hundreds of related biographies and historical narratives. It also created a market for scores of personal memoirs and thousands of pages of correspondence between and among celebrated historical figures of the age. Such easily available primary-source material made it possible for students and scholars of Napoleonic France to conduct significant background work and explore promising areas of inquiry before embarking on intensive on-site archival research.[18]

Among the first scholars who took advantage of this wealth of documentation to publish influential studies on foreign influence in Spanish America were Carlos Villanueva, William Spence Robertson, and John Rydjord, all of whom concentrated on French foreign policy.[19] While interested in their own broader questions, all four began to uncover within the parameters of their individual research the activities of individuals who worked to promote Napoleonic interests in the Americas. The existence of these agents was not a new discovery; in fact, their presence in Spanish America had been documented in published accounts dating back to the 1810s.[20] However, nineteenth-century histories of independence kept them very much on the margins of the broader historical narrative. *Historia patria* (national history) as it developed in Latin America had little use for foreign agitators as instigators of independence; in the absence of focused research on this subject, the motivations and activities of these individuals remained unclear.

As the twentieth century dawned, however, the French emissary emerged as an essential manifestation of Napoleon's foreign policy in the Americas.[21] Once professional historians began to mine government archives for records that illuminated foreign activity in the Spanish colonies during the independence period, they noticed the presence of intelligence agents—including accredited representatives, commissioned but undercover operatives, and sympathetic but self-motivated actors.[22] Notably, by the middle of the century research had shed light on numerous mysterious figures who appeared in Spanish records and elsewhere as potential or likely subversives due to their suspected connections to Napoleon.[23] Even when the agents were not readily identified or doubts persisted about their real motives, the scholarship suggested that their rumored or actual presence did have an impact on the colonies; as a result, many historians were willing to assert that Napoleonic intrigue could be linked in some manner to the subsequent revolutions in Spanish America.[24]

Yet, in spite of this careful accounting by specialists in Napoleon's foreign policy, the broader historiography on independence has not fully embraced the argument that Napoleonic agency was a factor in the Spanish American movement toward independence. In 1959 the historian Jacques Houdaille, who made the influence of revolutionary France on Spanish America the focus of three important articles concentrating on the activities and impact of Napoleonic emissaries, despaired that his colleagues had failed to give sufficient consideration to what he considered a promising line of inquiry.[25] In subsequent decades, as historiographical trends began to de-emphasize diplomatic and political themes in favor of social and cultural topics, the question of the French emissaries all but disappeared from investigations into Latin American independence.

More recently, however, a new wave of historians who share an interest in Atlantic studies has begun to put the spotlight back on the impact of foreign agency on Spanish American emancipation in ways that creatively rethink the traditional national, diplomatic, and political approaches to the subject. Late Bourbon Spain has been reimagined as a more dynamic metropolis in the works of François-Xavier Guerra, Scott Eastman, Natalia Sobrevilla Perea, René Silva, Victor Uribe, Jaime E. Rodríguez O., and Barbara and Stanley Stein. Karen Racine has raised the profile of Great Britain as an intellectual and cultural center for Spanish American revolutionists. Borderlands studies from J. C. A. Stagg, James G. Cusick, Andrew McMichael, and James E. Lewis have provided insight into the relationship between the United States and neighboring Spanish territories. Robert Laughlin, Rafe Blaufarb, Christophe Belaubre, Jordana Dym, John Savage, and Matt D. Childs have offered creative approaches to reconsidering Napoleon's influence over the region. And Claudia Rosas Lauro, David Geggus, Lyman Johnson, Jeremy Adelman, Laurent Dubois, Marixa Lasso, Wim Klooster, Caitlin Fitz, Ada Ferrer, Cristina Soriano, and Janet Polasky have emerged at the forefront of important new scholarship devoted to the diffusion of revolutionary ideology across the Americas. During this exciting and creative time in Atlantic World historiography, Luís de Onís and the emisario francés should now return to the stage and assume their appropriate place in the ongoing debates about the causes and context of Spanish American independence.

The first chapter of *A Great Fear*, titled "Francophobia and Spanish America," begins by reviewing the conditions within the Spanish empire after 1789 responsible for incubating a growing anxiety about the threat posed by revolutionary France. It then outlines the initial efforts of colonial officials to maintain order in the wake of Napoleon's overthrow of the Spanish monarchy. Chapter 2, "On the Edge of the Abyss: The Spanish Legation to the United States, 1807–1809," summarizes the developments that brought the transatlantic interests of Spain, France, and the United States together circa 1808. The chapter also explores the initial challenges facing the Spanish mission to the United States after the Bayonne coup by focusing on the travails of its then chargé d'affairs, Valentín de Foronda. Chapter 3, "Luís de Onís: From Cantalapiedra to Philadelphia," introduces the Spanish ambassador at the center of this study, summarizes his life and career up to and including his presence at Bayonne, and provides the context for his subsequent counterespionage operations against Napoleon. Chapter 4, "The Spanish Diplomat versus the French Emissary, 1809–1810," highlights the obstacles confronting Onís during his first year in office, including his negative reception by the Madison administration, and details his first entanglements with suspected French agents. Chapter 5, "Onís on the Offensive, 1811," explores the evolution of the Spanish counterespionage campaign in the Americas as Onís sought to engage the imperial bureaucracy in his crusade against French subversion. A change of perspective and scene comes with chapter 6, "Fighting Napoleon in Totonicapán," which moves the narrative deep into the Guatemalan highlands in order to assess the repercussions of the new security measures on colonial officials and their subjects. Finally, the concluding chapter considers the impact Luís de Onís and his obsession with the emisario francés had on the Spanish empire at the time of its greatest existential crisis.

To assist the reader in understanding the mindset and motivations that drove Onís during this period, the appendix consists of English translations of three documents prepared by the Spanish ambassador in early March 1810. In the first, Onís notifies his superiors that he had managed to acquire critical intelligence about French plans for subversion from the home of Napoleon's agent in Baltimore. The second document is the purported Instructions to this agent, Joseph Desmolard. In the third, Onís identifies the names of the French emissaries destined for the colonies and singles out their intended targets. More than any other report, this dispatch proved fundamental in the transformation of the Great Fear from what had been a largely nebulous threat posed by France to Spanish America into a clear and convincing danger to the colonies.

I

Francophobia and Spanish America

Why, Sovereign King of Kings,
Have you placed loyal Spain,
So long favored but now humbled,
At the feet of a vile Tyrant?
Oh, Great Lord, Enough! Give your hand
To the young and illustrious Bourbon,
And ensure that he triumphs over the Monster that seeks
To subjugate the Spanish empire.
Unleash the thunderbolt of your strong arm
On the cruel Napoleon, erase his glory,
Bury his power beneath a sad fate.
And, by crowning him with happy victory,
Restore Fernando so that even Death
Cannot extinguish his memory.

—*Redactor Americano del Nuevo Reyno de Granada*,
Santa Fe de Bogotá, September 19, 1808

While the specific events that led to the collapse of the Bourbon monarchy in May 1808 could not have been foreseen by even the most perceptive observer of the Hispanic world, rarely if ever in the previous three centuries of its existence had the Spanish empire entered a new year in such a profound state of insecurity. Spain had had more than its share of crises in the past, but the traumatic impact of its economic collapse in the late sixteenth century, military defeats in the mid-seventeenth century, and a controversial dynastic transfer from Habsburgs to Bourbons at the start of the eighteenth century were largely confined to the Iberian Peninsula. Throughout, the wider empire remained insulated from the rapidly shifting nature of European power politics. Isolated from its metropolis by time and space, Spanish America rarely prospered in this environment, but it cultivated a high degree of political, economic, and social stability based on its very remoteness. Even when Spain was at its weakest, its enemies found the distant empire nearly impossible to attack directly. However tempting the resources of the kingdom's portion of the New World might be, powers inimical to Spain invariably fell back on indirect commercial maneuvers to access its wealth. Beyond the loss to its rivals of a few marginal territories in the Caribbean Basin, Spain retained a powerful grip on its overseas colonies through the end of the eighteenth century.

By this time, however, the integration of Spanish America into the Atlantic World was effectively complete.[1] As a result, cultural, economic, and political transformations in Europe resonated in the Americas more profoundly than ever before. Spain itself contributed to this process with the eighteenth-century Bourbon Reforms, a series of administrative, commercial, military, and political policies designed to stimulate economic activity and centralize the empire under a more activist monarchy.[2] While these measures to reassert the authority of the metropolis proved controversial in the colonies and were perhaps counterproductive in the long term, during the enlightened reign of Carlos III (1759–1788) the Spanish monarchy achieved a level of international influence and prestige not seen since the 1500s. The short-term impact on the American colonies was profound. By midcentury, drawing upon the energy of a revived Spanish empire, the Caribbean had become the center of Atlantic trade, catering to the needs of English, French, Dutch, Portuguese, and Spanish merchants whose commercial interests spanned the globe. Fresh metropolitan interest in historically unproductive colonies in Central and South America resulted in valuable new export crops such as indigo and cacao, as well as the rise of strategic ports such as Buenos Aires and Caracas; simultaneously, renewed investments in traditional industries such as mining breathed life into the economy of New Spain. Many Spanish Americans profited from the expanding Atlantic economy. As they did, their cultural and intellectual ties to Europe strengthened as well. Enlightenment ideas, transmitted via books and pamphlets carried by foreign travelers and immigrants, found passage alongside commercial goods on the ships crossing from Europe to the Americas.

Inevitably, economic and political competition between the European powers resulted in war. During the frequent international conflicts of the 1700s, dynastic interests held Spain and France together in the so-called Family Compact against Great Britain and its allies. Most such confrontations—for example, the War of Jenkins's Ear (1739–1748)—resulted in military reversals for Spain. However, the colonial wars never interrupted the empire's economic development. Occasionally, they brought benefits: in the wake of Spain's defeat during the Seven Year's War (1756–1763), which resulted in the loss of Florida to England, France compensated its ally with the Louisiana Territory. Shortly thereafter, the revolt of the English colonies in 1775 gave Spain the opportunity to recover its Florida territories and deal a sharp strategic blow to its British imperial rival. As a result, by 1788 the Spanish empire was larger than it had ever been before.

One year later, however, the French Revolution threatened to undermine all of the foundations of the early modern Atlantic World. Over the next two decades Spain, and by extension its empire, became a principal casualty of the destructive forces unleashed by the fall of Louis XVI. By turns an enemy and an ally of the French Republic, the country suffered devastating and repeated military defeats. Ruled by an incompetent new king, Carlos IV, the government lurched from one political crisis to another. To make matters worse, with Atlantic commerce in a state of disarray because all its principal participants were now belligerents in the European-wide war, the Spanish economy collapsed. More so than ever before, these metropolitan misfortunes affected the Spanish American colonies, which now faced frequent loss of contact with Spain, economic stagnation, and increasingly vocal political discontent with Spanish rule.

This growing imperial instability coincided with the rise to power of Napoleon in 1799. With evidence of his global ambitions on display in the wake of the French invasion of Haiti in 1802, it seemed only a matter of time before the entire Western Hemisphere would become another battlefield in the already decade-long European conflict. Having secured the return of Louisiana from Spain in 1800, Napoleon had taken a significant step toward re-establishing a dominant French presence in the Americas by the time the collapse of the Peace of Amiens forced him to turn his attention back to Europe in 1803. Bound by its "destructive alliance" with France, Spain followed Napoleon into this latest war in 1804.[3] Within a matter of months, the combined Franco-Spanish navy was decimated at the Battle of Trafalgar. Seizing upon Great Britain's military advantage at sea to the misfortune of Spain, in 1806 British forces launched their first assault on the Río de la Plata and briefly held Buenos Aires, a campaign that continued into the subsequent year. By the end of 1807, the Spanish government was in chaos. Public opinion had completely turned against the *valido* (royal favorite) Manuel Godoy, whose power rested on his intimate relationship with the king and queen and who also promoted the interests of Napoleon. In October, the heir to the throne, Fernando, was briefly imprisoned on suspicion of plotting against his father. As the year came to a close, thousands of French troops began to garrison strategic positions in Spain in the wake of Napoleon's invasion of Portugal.

It is this historical context that must be considered when discussing the widespread fear that Spanish Americans expressed about the French after 1808.[4] Napoleon's decision at Bayonne to remove the Bourbons from the

Spanish throne that year (discussed in detail in chapter 3) exacerbated this condition but did not create it. Instead, beginning with the fall of the Bastille, Francophobia had already become a ubiquitous and enduring phenomenon across the region, a prejudice that increased in intensity as Spanish subjects found multiple reasons to blame France for the precipitously declining fortunes of their empire. In many ways, anti-foreign sentiment in Spain had important historical precedents. The Crown had used it to great effect in the late fifteenth and early sixteenth century to exclude Jews and Moors from the embryonic Spanish national identity. And during the late sixteenth and early seventeenth centuries, the period when Catholic Spain found itself in conflict with Protestant England, Anglophobia was common across the empire. Whereas both of these earlier examples of xenophobia had a religious foundation, the version that emerged after 1789 was somewhat more complex. Many Spaniards certainly recoiled from the Enlightenment-driven deism and atheism that the Revolution's advocates and leaders appeared to promote. However, some also held a visceral belief that the French had become carriers of an unprecedented disease—exemplified by the revolutionary motto *liberté, egalité, fraternité*—holding fatal consequences for all aspects of the established order. From this perspective, any contact with the cultural mindset associated with the events of the Revolution could only bring ruin to the Hispanic world.

Unfortunately for Spanish traditionalists, keeping the empire free of the revolutionary contagion after 1789 was fraught with significant obstacles. History, geography, and culture all conspired to give France an oversized influence in both Iberia and the American colonies during the eighteenth century. From the arrival in 1701 of the first French-born Bourbon king, Phillipe d'Anjou—who assumed the throne as Felipe V—to the death in 1788 of Carlos III, Spanish politics included a powerful pro-French faction. For much of the century, innovative statesmen such as the marqués de la Ensenada, the conde de Campomanes, the conde de Floridablanca, and the conde de Aranda dominated the senior ministries of the Crown, introduced French-inspired reforms, and appointed like-minded followers to positions in the colonial bureaucracy and military.[5] Until the French Revolution, in fact, an understanding of and support for progressive French philosophy was critical among the *ilustrados* (enlightened ones), those advocates of a Spanish Enlightenment who sought to draw the Hispanic world into the European cultural mainstream.[6] Furthermore, by the end of the century, economic, social, and demographic forces far beyond the control of any individual or group drew thousands of French migrants into the lands ruled by the Spanish king.[7]

Still, the Spanish Crown did not remain passive in the face of its neighbor's turmoil. Beginning in 1789 José Moñino y Redondo, the conde de Floridablanca, who served then as chief minister in his role as *secretario de estado* (secretary of state), undertook to establish a cordon sanitaire around Spain that would prevent French revolutionary sentiment from infecting the Iberian Peninsula. The measures enacted included the suppression of the press, in particular newspapers and periodicals from France. And, in a related act, the Holy Office of the Inquisition was charged with overseeing the removal of all suspected propaganda vehicles. Spain's overland border with France was closed to foreigners, with troops stationed there to enforce the order. Meanwhile, royal officials began to register foreigners residing in Spain, distinguishing between residents (who were compelled to become Spanish subjects) and travelers (who now required special permission to remain in the country). These measures, among many others, have been described as a product of Floridablanca's "great fear" of revolutionary contagion. However, they reflected the prevailing views of the governing elite and were seen as essential to the preservation of order and stability in the Hispanic world.[8]

Despite the pervasive French presence across the Spanish empire, or perhaps because of it, reaction against the Revolution was popular, widespread, and intense. Warnings about potential French subversion, in fact, started only a few months after the fall of the Bastille. In September 1789, Crown officials released reports that members of the French National Assembly, including a Monsieur Cotein, intended to send to the colonies a seditious document encouraging the local population "to throw off the yoke of Spanish domination, following the example provided by France."[9] During the 1790s, public sentiment in the Hispanic world drove suspicion not only against those who espoused controversial political or social ideas linked to the Revolution but also against those who merely had cultural affinity or ancestral ties to France. Indeed, the preoccupation with French-inspired subversion that arose in Spanish America during the five-year period between 1793 and 1798 provided an important precedent for its revival after 1808. In the meantime, colonial authorities gradually awakened to the increasingly radicalized Revolution and began to focus on the dangers posed by the potential transmission of revolutionary ideology across the Atlantic. At the top of the proscribed list were documents such as the *Declaration of the Rights of Man and Citizen* and the French Constitution. French newspapers as well as books and pamphlets supporting the Revolution were also considered dangerous. It was also feared that radicalized Spanish subjects might make use of their private correspondence to spread the contagion into areas where revolutionary propaganda normally would not be encountered.[10]

By 1793, civil, military, and ecclesiastical officials began investigating what might be considered the fruits of this invasion of the printed word: subversive activity directly linked to French revolutionary ideas, including anonymous pasquinades promoting liberty and freedom, conspiracies to introduce French law, and even rebellion against Spanish rule. This de facto state of emergency continued to the end of the century. By 1800, with Spain firmly under the control of revolutionary France, the official colonial preoccupation with French-inspired subversion declined but never quite disappeared. In 1808, with Napoleon now unquestionably the enemy, the French menace quickly reestablished itself in the minds of Spanish officials and now assumed monstrous and diabolical proportions, far more frightening and threatening than anything seen before. While much of this new imagery was fantastic in its depiction of the actual threat facing the colonies, by this time Spanish authorities could point to enough recent examples of French-related subversive activity to convince themselves that there might be some substance to the nightmare scenarios. Neighboring Haiti provided proof enough that the wide Atlantic Ocean could not prevent the revolutionary contagion from infecting the Americas.

Considering the significant French presence in the West Indies, the shockwaves from the French Revolution were felt first and most intensely across the Spanish Caribbean.[11] The disintegration of the French colony of Saint-Domingue after 1791 bore witness across the hemisphere to the destructive power of revolutionary sentiment. Due to their island's proximity to Haiti, Cuban officials were forced to anticipate the possibility of internal unrest shortly after the outbreak of rebellion in the French colony. It was not until November 1794, however, that tensions rose significantly in Havana, following the discovery of an incendiary pasquinade and reports of seditious talk among some slaves.[12] In 1795, as one consequence of its military defeat by the French Republic, Spain ceded its oldest colony—Santo Domingo—to its new ally, though in short order the revolutionary armies of Toussaint L'Ouverture swept east from the Haitian side of the island and assumed control over all of Hispaniola.

Blocking the spread of revolutionary ideas was hard enough for colonial officials. Potentially even more destabilizing was the demographic dislocation that followed in the wake of the Haitian Revolution. In little more than a decade, Cuba found itself absorbing nearly twenty thousand French Caribbean émigrés.[13] Other colonies also saw an increase in the number of migrants from French possessions. In one case, Puerto Rican officials refused to grant asylum to nine French colonists and fifty slaves fleeing Saint-Domingue because the slaves had been educated "among these same Frenchmen and in the midst of an insurrection."[14] Spanish authorities and their subjects had reason to worry that the French arrivals threatened to undermine the colonial order. In particular, the temptation to ascribe guilt by association confronted the Spanish governor of Louisiana. In 1793 the barón de Carondolet wrote to Manuel Godoy, the new secretario de estado, that he would work diligently to block revolutionary sentiment from entering the province, since it was reasonable to expect that the majority French population would find such ideas attractive.[15]

In New Spain, concerns about French intrigues began within a year of the fall of the Bastille. Fearing the negative impact of revolutionary propaganda, the Mexican Holy Office issued an edict on March 13, 1790, prohibiting the importation of "seditious books and papers which might excite the people to rebellion against the legitimate powers."[16] Between 1791 and 1792 the Crown sent multiple warnings about French agents to the viceroy, the conde de Revillagigedo, who took steps to reinforce the colony's military defenses, though otherwise he remained tolerant of the diverse French community in Mexico City.[17] His successor, the marqués de Branciforte, however, had cause to investigate this population more intensively shortly after his arrival in the summer of 1794. In August of that year, a pro-French satirical pasquinade was discovered that led in turn to the uncovering of an alleged French plot.[18] In the subsequent trial of the Frenchmen Juan Malvert, Esteban Morel, Juan Abadi, and Juan Aroche, colonial officials found evidence that many members of the local French community kept in close contact with France and were at a minimum sympathetic to developments there.[19] This case was quickly followed by the arrest of a Spaniard, Juan Guerrero, who admitted to drawing on revolutionary ideas while planning a revolt.[20] As a consequence, Branciforte decided New Spain could not permit the existence of an unassimilated expatriate population. On September 10, he issued a decree to provincial officials ordering them to make a list of all foreigners in their jurisdictions. In January 1795, the viceroy initiated the long process of detention and deportation. Over the course of this year, more than 180 Frenchmen were taken into custody, and by 1796 many had been exiled.[21] During the subsequent decade, the Mexican Inquisition continued to investigate reports of revolutionary sentiment within the colony.

The Kingdom of Guatemala also began to prepare to defend itself against a suspected threat from French revolutionaries and their allies in 1794. By late October, news of the French conspiracy in New Spain had reached Central America. Captain General José Domás y Valle expressed his concerns about the disturbances in the viceregal capital and declared that they resulted from "the depraved designs by which some Frenchmen and others addicted to their ideas have intended to incite the inhabitants and natives to rebellion by following the example of France." In response, the governor ordered a mounted company of dragoons to patrol the streets of Guatemala City and created a ten-man guard for his residence and the capital's Sala de Armas, "so as to prevent their being surprised" during any uprising.[22] Over the next year, colonial authorities began to target newly established Masonic groups for fear that the secret societies were serving as fronts for the promotion and dissemination of revolutionary ideology.[23]

In Spanish South America, official preoccupation with the French revolutionary contagion can be traced back to the early 1790s. As elsewhere in the Spanish colonies, the earliest concerns reflected frustration over the ready availability of revolutionary literature and the consequences of accommodating refugees from the French Caribbean. In 1793 some members of the intellectual elite in New Granada went so far as to publish and circulate a Spanish translation of the *Declaration of the Rights of Man*. Though all copies were eventually destroyed, within a few months of the declaration's publication seditious pasquinades began appearing in Bogotá and Cartagena. Denunciations, arrests, and public trials followed over the course of 1794, spurred in part by reports that a conspiracy to attack a military barracks had been uncovered. By the end of the following year, the viceregal *audiencia* (high court) had condemned the journalist Antonio Nariño to ten years in prison for publishing the French revolutionary material and leading the proposed conspiracy. More than a dozen others received relatively lighter sentences for the pasquinades and for connections to Nariño.[24] Yet, despite the best efforts of the authorities, seditious material continued to appear. In 1797 Viceroy Pedro Mendinueta wrote to Godoy that French newspapers and government publications had recently been discovered among correspondence arriving from Spain.[25]

On October 21, 1794, the president of the audiencia of Quito awoke to discover that seditious writings, some of which sought to "entice the masses into a state of rebellion," had been placed on the walls of the city.[26] Within a month, other pasquinades appeared that made reference to the recent conspiracies in Bogotá. In January 1795 the authorities arrested Francisco Javier Eugenio de Santa Cruz y Espejo (the director of the Library of Quito and a well-known *ilustrado*, scientist, satirist, and journalist) on charges that included conspiracy against public order. The prosecution's case was supported by evidence that Espejo had visited with Antonio Nariño on a recent trip to Bogotá and claims that he had made past statements in support of the French revolutionaries.[27]

Still, in the south it was the Captaincy General of Venezuela that faced the brunt of the demographic displacement caused by the Haitian Revolution, on par with the pressures felt by Cuba and Louisiana. By 1795 the colony had received hundreds of immigrants from Santo Domingo and Martinique, a development that caused Captain General Pedro Carbonell to complain that "keeping the French in these lands is never good."[28] Officials were concerned above all that the new arrivals would bring with them revolutionary sentiments and materials. Furthermore, it was feared that subversives would sneak into the colony by hiding among the mass of exiles. In the spring of 1795 such concerns were borne out with reports of a rebellion in the region around Coro that appeared to be sparked by hundreds of enslaved and free Afro-Caribbeans motivated by the success of the French and Haitian Revolutions.[29] Two years later, inspired by the so-called *ley de los franceses* (French Law) that had been transmitted by revolutionary sympathizers along the northern coast of South America, Manuel Gual and José María España led a creole-dominated conspiracy that shook the port of La Guaira. Reporting on the hunt for the leaders of this rebellion, Venezuelan authorities noted that among the subversive papers taken from the rebels was a small, roughly bound book, of the kind commonly found in Guadeloupe, titled *The Rights of Man and of the Citizen*.[30]

As far as the Viceroyalty of Peru was concerned, with the horror of the 1780–1783 indigenous uprising known as the Great Andean Rebellion fresh in the minds of their subjects, officials in that colony had particular cause to fear the spread of revolutionary sentiment. As elsewhere, the Inquisition assumed the responsibility for tracking French propaganda across the region.[31] A common response, undertaken separately by the Holy Office and the Crown in 1792 and then repeated often during the subsequent decade, was the prohibition of books and other literature that were considered subversive. Little revolutionary activity was detected, however, until 1794, when seditious pasquinades were discovered in Lima and Cuzco that declared, among other examples, "Long Live France, and Long Live Liberty." Soon, denunciations began to reach the ears of the civil authorities.[32]

As a result, Viceroy Francisco Gil de Taboada y Lemos decided to launch an investigation of the French immigrant community in Peru. Orders were given to take a census of the French residents of Lima, a list that was expanded to include all European immigrants since 1790.[33] A summary of these reports suggest that those sympathetic to the republican cause, whether French, Spanish, or Peruvian, often gathered in Lima's coffee houses, among other public places, to discuss the news from Europe. Although there were no popular disturbances in Peru against the colonial order, the viceroy decided to order the expulsion of French residents of Lima who lacked naturalization papers, in accordance with Crown decrees from 1793 regulating the expulsion and embargoing of goods of French residents in Spanish lands. In 1794, the watchmaker Juan Trimalle and the dentist Manuel Porre—both of whom reportedly had spoken too openly and positively about liberty—were sent to Spain and imprisoned. One year later, charges were brought against a number of other Frenchmen, including Carlos Fournier, for being "addicted to the seditious maxims of liberty and independence." In a letter to Godoy, the viceroy admitted that these charges were purely preventative and argued that immigrants spoke too freely about the French Revolution: "These conversations, although at the time they did not rise to the level to make a case, could with time become serious and induce dangerous consequences among the masses."[34]

Chilean authorities also demonstrated heightened sensitivity to speech that appeared to question Spanish rule. As was the case in Peru, this frontier outpost did not see any popular unrest before 1808 that could be attributed to French subversion. However, revolutionary propaganda did circulate in the colony, and the ease with which it arrived via correspondence from Buenos Aires caught the attention of Governor Ambrosio O'Higgins in 1795. That year, in a case that echoed proceedings in Lima, Clemente Morán, a cleric from Coquimbo, was denounced for supporting the French in private conversations.[35]

Colonial authorities in the Viceroyalty of the Río de la Plata faced challenges from suspected French subversion as early as 1789. In December of that year, the *Duke of Orleans*, a French corvette under the command of Alexandre Duclos Guyot, docked in Montevideo. The captain was placed under surveillance on suspicion that he had smuggled in documents from France. While nothing could be traced to him, soon the regional press was reporting the most recent news about the Revolution. In March 1790, the viceregal authorities issued decrees designed to block the diffusion of seditious materials and prohibit the importation of slaves from French colonies. By the end of the year, however, a letter from a Potosí merchant to a friend in Buenos Aires suggested that the inhabitants of the interior provinces were well acquainted with the latest developments from Europe. Over the next few years, numerous investigations into subversive activity across the region provided ample evidence that official prohibitions against the dissemination of news from France had failed to have any impact whatsoever.[36]

Whether motivated simply by curiosity or a real adherence to its ideals, the interest shown by inhabitants of the Río de la Plata viceroyalty in the progress of the French Revolution fueled the suspicions of the colonial authorities. Conditioned by the Crown to react with a firm hand against any sign of revolutionary sentiment, officials began to take action against the vaguest suggestion of subversive activity. Some rumors were rather fantastic: authorities in Montevideo apparently took seriously claims that the

French captain Duclos, who remained imprisoned there in the wake of the Spanish declaration of war against France, had written to the National Convention to request that a naval expedition be sent to conquer the Río de la Plata.[37] At the same time, customs officials in the city also discovered multiple copies of banned books in the hold of a French privateer that had been seized following the declaration of war.[38] In this environment, the fear of a slave insurrection that spread through Buenos Aires at the end of 1794 makes more sense, especially considering recent events in Saint-Domingue. By now a thriving commercial center, the La Plata estuary remained in close contact with the north Atlantic, in particular the Caribbean. Thus, it was only a matter of time before the same anxiety gripping the Spanish colonies that neighbored Hispaniola reached Buenos Aires.

In a sequence of events already familiar in other colonial capitals, viceregal officials came to believe that the rebellion would occur sometime during the early part of 1795.[39] Precautionary investigations were launched and soon seditious pasquinades were discovered that appeared to confirm the threat. Many individuals came under suspicion, but official scrutiny quickly fell upon scores of mostly "foreign-born artisans and shopkeepers."[40] Not surprisingly, many of those imprisoned and interrogated for inciting rebellion were French. By March the list of prisoners had risen above thirty and included the name of one individual, Santiago Antonini, who would later become a nemesis of Onís. Many in this group of arrestees had met regularly at the home of Juan Luís Dumont. Other gatherings had taken place on the estate of the comte de Liniers, a French-born nobleman whose brother, Santiago, was implicated in the conspiracy but never charged. In the end, while the viceregal audiencia ordered all the suspects to be deported, the unreliable testimony that condemned them, combined with a campaign by the French ambassador to Spain to question the conduct of the prosecution, appears to have prevented the execution of the sentences. The men remained in Buenos Aires and gradually reintegrated themselves into the life of the colony.[41]

On July 22, 1795, Spain signed the treaty of Basle, which brought the war against the French Republic to an ignominious end. One consequence of this peace was a parallel, if more gradual end to the colonial campaign against French subversion. Once the two countries agreed to the treaty of San Ildefonso in August 1796, Spain became an ally of its revolutionary neighbor, an awkward embrace that undermined anti-French sentiment, at least on the surface. In the Americas, colonial officials remained suspicious of foreigners, including the French, and the Inquisition continued to investigate banned literature and subversive activity. But the imminent *threat* from France and its expatriates now disappeared and remained dormant until revived by the events of April 1808. The Napoleonic invasion of Spain and its attendant dynastic complications forced imperial officials to confront the distinct possibility that French armies, Napoleonic agents and their afrancesado Spanish allies might pose a greater danger to the colonies than ever before imagined. With the 1790s serving as an important precedent for the colonial bureaucracy, this revived and more sinister French menace evolved into a convenient excuse for the militarization of colonial administration well ahead of the outbreak of internal rebellions. A comprehensive overview of the diverse colonial responses to the Bayonne coup is beyond the scope of this study. Nevertheless, an examination of developments in Cuba, New Spain, and New Granada suggests that a second wave of anti-French sentiment, one built firmly upon the experience of the 1790s, had emerged again among the officials and inhabitants of Spanish America (see map 1).

The Captaincy General of Cuba

In the first months following the overthrow of the Spanish Bourbons, the most dramatic repercussions of the political chaos were felt in the Captaincy General of Cuba, a colony that included both the main island and the Spanish possessions of East and West Florida. While the small Floridian outpost of St. Augustine was forced to wait impatiently for confirmation of the political crisis in Spain, Havana had more direct contact with Europe. As a result, its newspapers published accounts of the Iberian conflict throughout the summer of 1808, reports that generated a great deal of popular unrest. The colonial administration responded with a series of official pronouncements designed to maintain public order, demonstrate the continuity of the legitimate authority, and channel patriotic fervor into productive channels.[42]

The first of these came on July 17, when Captain General Salvador de Muro, the marqués de Someruelos, announced the arrival that day of a number of publications from the newly installed Junta Suprema of Seville, which had declared itself the legitimate government of Spain during the exile of Fernando VII. This material confirmed the details of the fall of the monarchy, the usurpation of the throne by a "hateful foreigner," the consolidation of a loyalist opposition on the peninsula, and the new alliance with England. Beyond simply relating this news, however, Someruelos took the opportunity to frame the events to suit his priorities: He excoriated the "horrifying conduct of the French" and celebrated the heroism of the Spanish resistance; he recognized the "ardent desire" of many Cubans to go to the assistance of their besieged Spanish brothers and captive king; at the same time, he pressed his subjects to suppress this urge and, instead, contribute to the cause in a more sober, restrained manner. Rather than giving in to their emotions, Someruelos encouraged Cubans to reduce their expenses, "establish a Spartan economy," and "renounce all superfluities." He agreed that this was the time for Spanish America to demonstrate its "greatness of heart and achieve as much glory as the heroic inhabitants of Buenos Aires recently attained" but argued that Spain required American funds more than American men. In this charged environment the preservation of order was fundamental, and the captain general encouraged Cubans to remain calm and even extend a hand of fraternal hospitality to the "peaceful, hard-working, and helpful Frenchmen, our comrades and friends" who sought asylum on the island.[43]

Through such appeals, Someruelos sought to contain the overwhelming popular reaction to the news from Spain, which was a massive patriotic outburst in favor of the deposed king. On a symbolic level this meant both organized and informal gatherings to support Spanish resistance, some of which were used by the authorities to conduct newly mandated oaths of loyalty to the Bourbon monarch. One such ceremony took place in St. Augustine on September 3, when Fernando VII was formally proclaimed king by the local civil and military officials amid repeated shouts of "*Viva el rey*" by the assembled population.[44] On a more practical level, the patriotic surge facilitated plans to raise funds for the loyalist cause, with a fundraiser formally launched by Someruelos in October and subsequently directed by local officials.[45] Meanwhile, the captain general began to mobilize his colony's defenses to prepare for a potential attack from France.

As it happened, security issues soon moved to center stage, and reservations about the large French émigré population in Cuba and the Floridas began to grow. This occurred despite the earlier pleas by Someruelos to treat this community with moderation. On September 10, Governor Enrique White of East Florida completed a tentative census of the French residents of St. Augustine, a list that included fourteen soldiers in the Cuban infantry battalion then stationed at the settlement.[46] Less than a week later, White provided the names of nineteen Frenchmen who swore the oath of loyalty to Fernando, as well as of a handful who refused and therefore were subject to expulsion from the colony on orders from Someruelos.[47]

By the end of the year justifiable concerns about the true allegiance of the French immigrants devolved into hysteria among both the Cuban public and the colonial bureaucracy. Some of this shift in attitude and policy was a product of increased communication with Spanish officials in the homeland. At the end of February, Someruelos distributed copies of a *real orden* (royal order) dated November 1, 1808, which commanded him to block "the introduction into the districts under your command of anyone addicted to the French government, along with seditious papers."[48] In the cover letter he wrote to the governors of the two Floridas, Someruelos emphasized the importance of the preservation of "public tranquility" and the promotion of "the patriotic zeal and charity of the inhabitants [of Florida] so that they may continue to assist the Mother Country with donations."[49] However, the captain general did not need to look to Spain to justify policies that targeted the French. On February 21, Vicente Folch, the governor of West Florida, wrote from Pensacola that he had sent Esteban Olivier Dalcour to New Orleans on the basis of an August order from Someruelos requiring him to exile suspicious individuals. Dalcour, a French refugee from Havana, had left Cuba four months earlier fleeing what he described as persecution "for being a Frenchman."[50]

Among those who received this information were the councilmen on the Havana *ayuntamiento* (city council). On March 2 these local leaders declared their support for the expulsion of the French community, members of which they considered "vipers . . . in our bosom," citing among other faults their "bad conduct, immorality, depraved customs [and] their inveterate hatred for Spaniards, our habits, customs, and religion."[51] By this time, the captain general had already established *juntas de vigilancia* (surveillance committees) to oversee the French immigrants.[52] On March 12, in his latest effort to calm the rising tide of anti-French passions, Someruelos responded to the Havana council's recommendations by issuing orders to his provincial governors to "keep a prudent watch over the conduct of the French population."[53] By paraphrasing the November real orden, this same decree also appeared to confirm growing suspicions that Napoleonic emissaries were targeting Cuba: "Finally, once again I charge you, the commanders of the ports, and any good Spaniard to contribute to the public tranquility, and to take care that no French emissaries or addicts to their cause find their way into this province through their respective districts; and if any unknown person from any nation, including Spaniards, is introduced, be sure to notify immediately the respective authorities so that all necessary action can be taken, and we can proceed according to the situation."[54]

However, even these steps proved insufficient to calm popular pressures. Bowing to this new reality and seeking, perhaps, to burnish his own loyalist credentials, Someruelos decided that the time had come to order the expulsion of Cuba's French community, a process that he left largely in the hands of the juntas de vigilancia.[55] Not surprisingly, the merging of popular and official fears proved combustible. Between March 21 and 23, Havana was rocked by riots sparked by mobs screaming for French blood; the public commotion devolved into the sacking and looting of French-owned properties. While the unrest quickly burned itself out, the anti-French sentiment was now both visible and palpable, a climate that facilitated the exile process. By August, officials recorded the departure of 8,870 people from Santiago de Cuba alone, out of an estimated émigré population of 15,000. By the end of the year, the vast majority of French refugees in Cuba had left the island for the United States. Concentrating in New Orleans, they reinforced the Franco-Caribbean nature of that city and continued to excite the suspicions of Spanish authorities.[56]

The Viceroyalty of New Spain

While the fear of French intervention profoundly upset the social order in Cuba during the eighteen months following Napoleon's decision to replace the Spanish Bourbons, the political implications of the overthrow of Fernando VII were perhaps greatest in Mexico City. Here, in the capital of the sprawling Viceroyalty of New Spain, the colonial authorities struggled and failed to establish a consensus during the summer of 1808 between members of a fragmented elite with competing visions of a post-Bayonne colonial order. News that Carlos IV had stepped down in March in favor of his son arrived in Mexico City on June 9. The colony had little more than a month to adjust to this development before the French brig *Centinelle* arrived at Veracruz bringing the latest news from Bayonne. Finally, on July 29 the capital received confirmation that Spain was in a state of rebellion against the French occupation.[57]

The immediate reaction in Mexico was confusion, particularly between and within the three poles of the colonial bureaucracy: the viceregal audiencia, the ayuntamiento of Mexico City, and the viceroy. In July, two city councilmen floated a plan for an autonomous governing junta that would rule the colony during Spain's political crisis. Such a move, however, was strongly opposed by more conservative members of the audiencia, who preferred to make no changes to the established order. When the colony learned that Spanish loyalists had convened governing juntas, other elites argued that the Mexican authorities should recognize one of these bodies, preferably the Junta of Seville. Unfortunately, the unpopular viceroy, José de Iturrigaray, whose connections to Manuel Godoy constrained his authority at this critical juncture, failed to move decisively in any of these directions. In the eyes of traditionalists, the viceroy compromised himself with unnecessary delays in confirming the ascension of Fernando VII and his willingness to entertain creole desires for autonomy. Over the course of August and into September, Iturrigaray invited members of the governing institutions of the colony to debate the viability of a Mexican junta. After six weeks of partisan conflict, the peninsular elite in Mexico City began to plan a coup. On September 16, with support from the Consulado de Comercio (Merchants' Guild), the audiencia, and the archbishop, Iturrigaray was overthrown and replaced by Field Marshal Pedro de Garibay. This action ensured that New Spain would remain not only loyal to Spain but also a decidedly royalist bastion for the immediate future.[58]

In this environment, the authorities and inhabitants of New Spain proved particularly susceptible to fears of French intervention. As early as July, anticipating the likelihood that the American colonies would become a new front in the Napoleonic Wars, Iturrigaray had authorized the purchase of arms from the United States to counter a possible French invasion.[59] Then, on the morning of August 10 the French warship *Vaillant* sailed into the harbor at Veracruz under suspicious circumstances. Port officials fired on the schooner before receiving a signal that it wished to communicate. After allowing it to anchor, they learned that it had sailed from Guadeloupe with orders to deliver dispatches to the government of New Spain, including documents from Bayonne. At this point, Captain Ciriaco de Cevallos, the commander of the port, placed the ship in quarantine until further notice. Not surprisingly, rumors began to fly among the residents of the city, and a mob soon formed convinced that the *Vaillant* was carrying a French-appointed viceroy along with other afrancesado officials charged with bringing New Spain under French control.[60]

Fearing an attack upon the schooner, Cevallos was forced to place the *Vaillant*, its contents, and crew under heavy guard both to ensure their safety and to prevent French propaganda from entering the colony. Such precautions had limited effect, however. By the afternoon, an agitated crowd yelling "Death to the traitors!" had control of the streets and demanded an emergency meeting of the city council. Much of the agitators' wrath was directed against Cevallos, who was now regarded as a French puppet and was forced to flee the city for the safety of a Spanish warship. During their meeting, the leaders of the insurrection and the ayuntamiento agreed that all incriminating material should be removed from the French ship and brought to shore, a task which was quickly accomplished by two councilmen. The crowd then seized the suspicious documents, which included proclamations from Napoleon's brother, the *rey intruso* (intruder king) Joseph Bonaparte, and "burned them in the center of the plaza, while giving voice to the most execrable denunciations of the Emperor of the

French." An impromptu ceremony in which the assembled audience swore its allegiance to Fernando VII followed. But the unrest continued for a second day and included the ransacking of Cevallos's house and a second public burning of correspondence from the *Vaillant*. In the end, while the popular commotion subsided within a matter of days, the viceroy decided to deploy dragoon regiments to the city to maintain order, fearing that the French might take advantage of the disturbances to launch an invasion.[61]

As the August turmoil in Veracruz demonstrates, the population of New Spain had no need to await an accumulation of evidence regarding French intentions toward the colony to assume the worst—and to act upon its fears in the absence of a forceful official response to any perceived threat. To his ultimate misfortune, Captain Cevallos serves as an example of a colonial official who had not fully assimilated the popular sentiment against the French. However, the arrest of Gaetan Souchet d'Alvimart in Nacogdoches only five days before the arrival of the *Vaillant* suggests that the Veracruz commander was something of an exception within a colonial bureaucracy that had already become sensitized to the dangers of foreign intervention. A remarkable individual whose life has been examined in depth elsewhere, d'Alvimart found himself in the custody of colonial officials as he sought to cross the border from Louisiana into New Spain after spending the summer of 1808 in West Florida.[62]

The arrest was significant in part because d'Alvimart's residence in Baton Rouge had been strikingly uncontroversial, at least to the governor of the city, Carlos de Granpré, who befriended the foreigner following his arrival on July 4 and promised to hold his trunk while he continued his travels through the Interior Provinces to Mexico City.[63] D'Alvimart's presence in Louisiana, however, had already caught the attention of its governor, William Claiborne, who notified the Spanish consul in New Orleans. A report was duly sent to Mexico City, and officials at the border were put on alert. When d'Alvimart presented himself in Nacogdoches on August 5, he lacked the required passport to enter the Spanish colony and was detained. Under interrogation, he claimed to be an envoy from Napoleon, though he carried no evidence of such an assignment. According to the summary of the case written by Governor Folch to Captain General Someruelos, however, the inhabitants of Nacogdoches were prepared to tear d'Alvimart "to pieces" since "nothing can equal the fury of the People toward the French."[64] When his trunk was opened, it was found to hold some incriminating material, most notably a number of French military uniforms. While no conclusive proof emerged to link the French general to any subsequent uprisings in the area, the circumstances following his capture proved as controversial as his apprehension. D'Alvimart was transported overland to Veracruz after a brief imprisonment in the Coahuilan town of Monclova, from which he tried to escape. His subsequent journey through much of central Mexico proved remarkably leisurely, and evidence suggests that he met with Miguel Hidalgo, Ignacio de Allende, and Juan Aldana while on the road.[65] Finally, in January 1809, d'Alvimart arrived in Veracruz and remained imprisoned there for another eight months before being exiled to Europe.

As 1808 came to an end, the colonial authorities in Mexico City had begun to recover their balance following six months of wild political gyrations precipitated by the Bayonne coup. Throughout the turmoil, the loyalty of the colony to Fernando VII was never truly in doubt, though conservative groups in the capital were more than willing to sacrifice a viceroy to ensure this outcome. Even the Veracruz riots provided convincing evidence of popular sentiment, though they also demonstrated how easily mass movements could spin out of control. From an official perspective, much more productive were the efforts of the president of the audiencia of Guadalajara, who claimed to have mobilized more than fifty thousand recruits from the western part of the viceroyalty to serve as an ad hoc militia against a potential French invasion.[66] For the colonial bureaucracy, the d'Alvimart case provided a timely warning about the dangers of French conspiracies.

Over the course of 1809, these earlier lessons solidified into a more concerted campaign to defend New Spain. Newly sensitized officials saw potential threats all over the colony, and they brought cases of subversion against a variety of individuals.[67] Perhaps to a greater degree than anywhere else in the empire, Mexican society struggled during the imperial crisis to diffuse deeply rooted tensions between the *gachupines* (European-born Spaniards) and the *criollos* (American-born Spaniards). This wound became inflamed with the coup against Iturrigaray, for many Mexicans interpreted it as a preemptive strike by the peninsular elite to block moves toward creole autonomy. At the same time, as French forces advanced across Spain, others presumed that all European Spaniards were in effect to blame for the loss of Fernando VII and, at least indirectly, in league with Napoleon, an opinion which, if made public, was considered subversive.[68] By September, in a significant case of institutional reform, the new viceroy, Francisco Javier Lizana y Beaumont—who assumed office in July while remaining the archbishop of Mexico City—created the Junta de Seguridad y Buen Orden (Committee of Security and Public Order). This unprecedented tribunal, which took precedence over the criminal courts and survived until 1813, existed specifically to uncover and prosecute cases of *infidencia* and related political crimes against the public order, particularly conspiracies that could be linked to the French.[69] Thus, by the time that the Hidalgo Revolt exploded across New Spain in September 1810, the viceregal authorities had institutionalized a system of counterintelligence and counterespionage that would evolve easily into a counterinsurgency campaign.

The Viceroyalty of New Granada

Geography afforded the residents of the Spanish possessions in northern South America relatively easy communications with Europe. As a result, Venezuelans were among the first Spanish subjects to receive, digest, and react to the political turmoil that convulsed Spain in 1808. Responding to reports of the first abdication of Carlos IV at Aranjuez, the ayuntamiento of Caracas proclaimed Fernando VII as king on May 9.[70] However, by the beginning of July colonial officials and their subjects were sorting through often conflicting information regarding events in Bayonne that poured in from a variety of sources, including the French and British colonies in the Caribbean. Any lingering doubts about the veracity of such reports were laid to rest on July 15, when Lieutenant Paul de Lamanon, the commander of the French brig *Serpent*, arrived in Caracas carrying dispatches for Captain General Juan de Casas and the colonial bureaucracy. This material included official accounts of the Bayonne abdications and the transfer of the Spanish crown to Joseph Bonaparte, decrees from the Council of the Indies, and correspondence from both the new minister of the Indies and Napoleon's foreign minister. After presenting the documents, Lamanon asked Casas to recognize the new king and the new political order.[71]

Either unprepared or unwilling to make such a significant decision on his own, Casas dismissed the French officer and held an emergency meeting with leading civil and military authorities. In the meantime, however, the residents of the capital gathered in the thousands and demonstrated their unequivocal support for Fernando, with many crying "Death to Napoleon!" Under this popular pressure, which included a formal plea from the city council, the captain general decided to embrace the loyalist cause and made a public proclamation in favor of Fernando VII by the end of the day. With his mission a failure, Lamanon returned under guard to La Guaira, where he encountered the English frigate *Acasta* at anchor in the harbor. Seizing the opportunity, its captain, Philip Beaver, raced to Caracas to inform the authorities there that Spain had revolted against the French and that England supported the uprising. He then returned to La Guaira to discover that his lieutenant had seized the *Serpent* and imprisoned Lamanon.[72]

Within a week, the governor of Maracaibo learned about the new alliance between England and loyalist Spain: "From that moment I redoubled my vigilance in the province under my command in order not to be surprised by French emissaries entrusted with the task of wresting these dominions of the Indies from the legitimate authority of our beloved sovereign Fernando VII by means of dispatches where were at the same time both absurd and null."[73] By August, the local authorities in cities such as Valencia and Mérida had also proclaimed their support for the Bourbon king. As in Mexico, however, the broad public opposition to the French masked growing divisions among the Venezuelan elite over the best means to manage the political crisis in Spain. The creole aristocracy, known as the *mantuanos*, dominated the Venezuelan economy and held a political power base in the Caracas ayuntamiento. Many in this group favored the establishment of a local governing junta. Other elites, particularly the pillars of the peninsular governing class, sought to preserve the established order. Nevertheless, by the end of July a shaky consensus had emerged between the captain general and the ayuntamiento in favor of a junta. This plan collapsed, however, with the arrival in the colony of an emissary from the Junta Suprema of Seville. Seeking to consolidate its authority in the Americas, the ruling Spanish junta reconfirmed the Venezuelan colonial officials in their positions and, in return, sought confirmation of its legitimacy. Captain General Casas responded by dropping plans for home rule and submitting to the Spanish loyalist government, an act that seemed at the time to satisfy most Venezuelans.[74]

Autonomist sentiment did not disappear, however. By October the destabilizing shadow of Francisco de Miranda had once more spread across the colony, as the Venezuelan revolutionary sought from his exile in London to use the imperial crisis to reawaken anti-Spanish sentiment in his homeland.[75] In the short term, leading creoles with diverse motivations—some believed that colonial officials had no right to recognize the Spanish Junta Central; others thought Spain was doomed; still others were afrancesados, and, certainly some were in favor of independence—decided to present the captain general with a petition requesting the establishment of a Junta Suprema in the capital. While the *mantuanos* gathered an impressive number of signatures, they did not have the support of the lower classes, nor could they count on another important power base: the *pardo* (mixed-race) militias. As a result, following the delivery of the petition on November 24, the colonial authorities began to arrest the movement's leaders, a preemptive move which allowed the loyalist cause to monopolize the public stage for the next fifteen months. On January 12, 1809, Captain General Casas launched a ten-day celebration to mark the formal ceremony recognizing Fernando VII. His successor, Vicente de Emparán, arrived in Caracas in May to assume command of a colony that appeared to be firmly loyal to Spain.[76]

The heart of New Granada, which was ruled from Santa Fé de Bogotá, learned about the Aranjuez abdication during the second week of June 1808. Over the next six weeks the principal cities of the viceroyalty proceeded with ceremonies to recognize the ascension of Fernando VII.[77] By this time, rumors of more traumatic events had reached the colony, largely via English newspapers that circulated along the Caribbean coast, causing many people to revise their opinion of Napoleon. In one illustrative case, the Bogotá curate Antonio de León was forced to recant earlier, more enthusiastic comments about the French emperor with a blistering attack on Spain's new enemy. He wrote, "We already know all about the vile character of the villain Napoleon, that monster who has a soul blacker than the smoke of Babylon, about the sacrilege and perjury which has violated all laws divine and human, about the libertine Apostle, who has sold his soul with shame, about that bloodthirsty traitor who is Tantalus with the blood of his fellows, about that cruel and malicious creature, who is a thousand times worse than the damned Leviathan."[78]

Formal notification of the Bayonne abdications came on August 9 when commissioners from Seville disembarked at Cartagena. These men, Juan José Sanllorente and Antonio Vacaro, slowly proceeded to the capital, arriving on September 3 and meeting with Viceroy Antonio Amar y Borbón. The representatives confirmed the events at Bayonne and the subsequent imprisonment of the king. They also described the consolidation of a Spanish loyalist movement and, while underscoring the need to swear loyalty to Fernando VII, encouraged the viceregal authorities to submit to the authority of the Seville Junta. Finally, Sanllorente and Vacaro requested aid for the war against the French and warned their hosts to beware of Napoleon's efforts to undermine the colonies.[79]

As in other parts of Spanish America, the response from New Granada was overwhelmingly loyalist. Cities across the region began swearing their allegiance to the Bourbon king, offering donations to the war effort, and scheduling masses for the cause.[80] But the mission of the Spanish commissioners was also controversial. Ayuntamiento members from Cartagena to Bogotá began to complain that decisions about the security of the viceroyalty were now being made without their input, that the Spaniards preferred to work with military officials instead of civil authorities, and that the pressure to swear loyalty to the Junta of Seville raised troubling issues of legitimacy. In fact, news of the formation of the Junta Central, which unified the loyalist resistance in Spain, did not reach Cartagena until November 22 and was not publicized in Bogotá until the end of December. The formal ceremony recognizing the legitimacy of the Spanish loyalist government did not take place until January 19, 1809. In the interim, uncertainty festered.[81]

In such an environment, the Spanish colonial authorities also began to express concern that the loyalty of their subjects remained tentative and easily manipulated. In October, Manuel Mariano de Blaya, a *fiscal* (Crown attorney) on the audiencia of Santa Fe de Bogotá, encouraged Viceroy Amar to take specific steps to ensure the allegiance of New Granada to Spain. He recommended first that the government collect and publish all available documentation that demonstrated the tyranny of Napoleon. These measures would be combined with efforts to block the introduction into the colony of all "seductive and deceptive papers." To administer this program, Blaya suggested the appointment of a special judge. He also believed it would be necessary to create new positions for secret commissioners for each of the provinces in order to ensure that the entire viceroyalty received sufficient oversight. Meanwhile, Blas de Soria, the governor of Cartagena, made a similar request, arguing in November that the superior authorities needed to take effective measures to eliminate seditious materials. He noted in particular that the Bayonne Constitution, as well as proclamations from Napoleon and Joseph Bonaparte, were in circulation on the streets of Cartagena.[82]

Concerns about the impact of French-inspired subversion precipitated an official crackdown on news in New Granada, a move that would have far-reaching implications. In a colony that demonstrated nothing but profound loyalty to Fernando VII at the time of his overthrow, viceregal officials adopted a siege mentality that failed to embrace the allegiance of the local population. Near the end of 1809, shaken by a rebellion in neighboring Quito and recognizing the debilitating and growing distance between colonial authorities and their subjects, the Bogotá councilman Camilo Torres expressed his personal frustration in his famous *Representación* on behalf of the ayuntamiento of Bogotá to the Junta Central. Here it is possible to see how a desire for equal treatment, later made manifest in movements for autonomy, began to divide Americans and Spaniards and eventually led to independence. Torres wrote:

> On the same principles of equality, provincial juntas composed of representatives of the town councils should have been formed and should be formed in these lands, just like those that have been established and exist in Spain. This is a point of the gravest significance, and the *cabildo* does not want to and cannot omit it. If this

> important step had been taken in this capital on the 5th of September of 1808, when the deputy from Seville came so that the so-called supreme junta could be recognized, today we would not be experiencing the sad consequences of the unrest in Quito. This is the result of a lack of confidence in that kingdom for the authorities that govern it. The people fear that they will be turned over to the French, and they complain about the mysterious hesitation of the government in communicating news, of its inaction in preparing defenses, and of the various unjust actions taken by those who govern towards the American Spaniards. All this would be forestalled if the people saw that there was an intermediate authority composed of its representatives charged with overseeing their security.[83]

Despite fifteen years of political, military, and economic crisis, the inhabitants of Spain and its empire were caught off guard by the unprecedented events of the spring/summer of 1808. The collapse of the Bourbon monarchy, which culminated with Napoleon's intervention at Bayonne, had to all intents and purposes begun in late 1807, so even the remotest regions of the Americas were able to absorb with some equanimity the first abdication of Carlos IV in March 1808. In fact, news of the ascension of the young prince Fernando was broadly (if briefly) celebrated as the beginning of a new era. The French-led coup, however, was an existential threat to a widely shared vision of empire that had survived for three centuries, a disaster mitigated only by the fact that it presented Spanish subjects with a clear enemy and, thereby, a comforting sense of unity. Spanish Americans, like their European counterparts, were overwhelmingly loyalist, a sentiment reflected in the behavior of their colonial officials. As some Spanish subjects discovered to their detriment, it simply did not pay to be pro-French or to be seen as pro-French in the post-Bayonne climate.

By the beginning of 1809, loyalists on both sides of the Atlantic could take some solace that resistance to France did not collapse in the first, precarious months of the crisis. A viable opposition government survived on Spanish soil and claimed some legitimacy, however tenuous it might be. By this point, colonial officials had begun to enact measures to preserve order in the face of continuing threats from France and Bonapartist Spain. But now the early unity of purpose forged between these authorities and their subjects began to fracture, as concerns over loyalty came to the fore. In growing numbers, Spanish Americans began to question the efficacy (and sometimes loyalty) of their governors. In return, the colonial administration began to demand explicit proof of loyalty from their subjects. In both cases, the common denominator was France. Officials saw French subversion as the logical precipitator of rebellion in Spanish America. Spanish Americans saw the threat of French intervention as the logical product of the administrative, political, and military failings of the Spanish authorities. As a result, both the autonomist revolts and the counterinsurgency states that emerged in 1810 carried elements of the French contagion in their core.

2

On the Edge of the Abyss

The Spanish Legation to the United States, 1807–1809

> The fact that I have come here is a work of Providence, for surely the Americas would be lost if Foronda had remained or if someone of less energy and skill in these matters had come instead.
>
> —Luís de Onís, Philadelphia, March 29, 1810

In the summer of 1807, Valentín de Foronda received a coveted though arguably double-edged promotion. After serving six years as the Spanish consul general in Philadelphia, this experienced diplomat now found himself in the position of the highest-ranking representative in the United States of His Most Catholic Majesty Carlos IV, an elevation in status that followed the recall of Carlos Martínez de Irujo, who had held the senior appointment as minister plenipotentiary for the previous eleven years and had repeatedly found himself in conflict with the Jefferson administration.[1] In its official capacity, the American State Department recognized Foronda as chargé d'affaires ad interim. According to the still evolving diplomatic language of the period, this title described the temporary head of a permanent mission serving in the absence of a formally accredited, higher ranking diplomat.[2] On July 7, following a cordial reception by President Thomas Jefferson and his secretary of state, James Madison, Foronda undertook his first, rather mundane diplomatic duty: arranging a passport for an American government vessel bound for Gibraltar.[3]

Such a task fell well within the accepted duties of a foreign envoy at the time and in particular fit the somewhat limited authority of a chargé d'affairs. Foronda's primary responsibility while in office was the preservation of the quarter century of peace and good relations between Spain and the United States. Without formal accreditation to the US government, which was a sovereign grant limited to envoys of ambassadorial or ministerial rank, Foronda did not have the power to sign treaties on behalf of Spain, or even the status to negotiate directly with the American head of state. In 1807 no need for such complex diplomacy seemed imminent, however. Meanwhile, Foronda wielded all the other normal tools available to a head of legation to further the interests of his sovereign.

Above all, such diplomats were expected to provide their governments with regular reports about their assigned posts by collecting and analyzing masses of information drawn from official government communications, private contacts, media outlets, rumors, and other sources of public opinion.[4] Matters of national and international concern deserved priority, especially when connected to military developments, though foreign envoys were also expected to follow and interpret local affairs. While he remained in the United States, Foronda assumed the broad responsibility of defending the honor of Spain before the Jefferson administration, the foreign diplomatic corps, and the American public, a duty that required constant correspondence with administration figures and regular ventures into the newspaper arena of Philadelphia and other media hubs. At the same time, he was required to advance the more specific agenda of protecting and promoting Spanish commerce in the region. And, finally, he wielded control over the consular offices that regulated trade, issued passports, and provided protection to subjects of Carlos IV residing in the United States or traveling through the country.[5]

Furthermore, effective diplomacy required that Foronda acquire a clear and unfiltered understanding of the goals, intentions, strengths, and weaknesses of the United States as they might relate to Spain's interests in the Americas. In practice, therefore, the Spanish mission functioned as a base of espionage in accordance with the practice of the time, at least to the extent that diplomats of all countries were expected to use every means at their disposal to gather and distribute information. During this period, Foronda worked out of the legation offices in Philadelphia and traveled to Washington, DC, as circumstances demanded. On his behalf, consular agents and their informants kept track of local developments in the major American cities along the Atlantic seaboard: Boston, Newport, New York, Philadelphia, Baltimore, Alexandria, Norfolk, Charleston, Savannah, and New Orleans. This network of legation staff, official diplomats, and other, unofficial conduits of news, gossip, and rumors—such as Spanish merchants, travelers, and residents—allowed the chargé d'affairs to collect the information necessary to keep his superiors in Madrid appraised of the latest trends and developments in Washington and across the United States.[6]

Despite the rather routine start to his tenure, Foronda assumed his office at a critical turning point in the relationship between two governments whose diplomatic history was as old as the United States itself. While the kingdom's colonial holdings in the Americas were immense and its interests there remained critical to its international standing as a global empire, Spain could no longer be considered the same global power that had intervened to great effect three decades earlier during the ultimately successful uprising of British colonists in North America. As a belligerent in the ensuing international war and a de facto ally of the rebels, Spain achieved a signal triumph during the conflict by recovering West and East Florida from Great Britain, territory that had been lost two decades earlier in the aftermath of the Seven Years' War (1756–1763).[7] As a party to the 1783 Paris Peace Treaties that confirmed its territorial gains and ended the American Revolution, Spain then agreed to recognize the independence of the United States. Arguably, with British influence in North America much reduced and the new American republic still in its infancy, the 1780s marked the high-water point in the long history of the Spanish empire in the New World. This state of affairs proved ephemeral, however. In the two decades after Carlos IV assumed the throne in December 1788, Spain suffered a shocking series of reverses that drastically limited its ability to concentrate resources, project force, and shape events in its favor across the Atlantic. Worse, with the French intervention at Bayonne in 1808 Spain effectively ceased to exist as an autonomous power.[8]

If Valentín de Foronda represented the deeply unpopular king of an aging empire in precipitous decline, his hosts by contrast now governed a youthful and vibrant republic increasingly self-assured, confident of its place in the world, and optimistic about the future (see map 2). The United States had emerged as a result of an unprecedented struggle for independence and weathered multiple postwar existential crises that threatened to undermine all that was won in 1783. Two decades into its constitutional experiment, the American political system had repeatedly proven its viability and flexibility, in the face of multiple occasions when the new nation might have collapsed. Equally important, seizing upon the trading opportunities opened up by its war-weary European rivals and the commercial potential inherent in the rapid settlement of the Ohio River valley and the trans-Appalachian region, the United States made great economic strides during its first three decades of existence. Although deep-rooted regional rivalries and social divisions remained largely unresolved, as Thomas Jefferson approached the end of his second term the American government and its citizens increasingly found common cause (and multiple excuses for distraction) in the vast potential for expansion that beckoned from the interior of North America.

Of course, as American interests turned to territorial expansion in the years after the 1803 Louisiana Purchase secured US sovereignty over much of the continent west of the Mississippi River, the presence of the Spanish empire proved at best an inconvenience to be ignored and at worst an obstacle to be overcome. In the wake of this massive land acquisition, the United States found it difficult to tolerate the status quo along an ill-defined and sparsely settled borderlands region thousands of miles in length. Because of the unforgiving logic of demographic growth, American settler interests continued to press up against the frontier, threatening to force a confrontation over control of this territory. For its part, even when it controlled Louisiana, Spain had repeatedly demonstrated its inability to expand its effective hold on the millions of acres beyond New Orleans. Most of the territory it still retained in the northern Gulf served as little more than a protective buffer for its Mexican possessions.[9]

In the short term, the American government could not ignore three small but sensitive border issues with Spain. First, the vast, undefined frontier that stretched west/northwest from the Spanish settlement at Baton Rouge sheltered a Spanish military and commercial presence along the Mississippi. While the United States controlled the mouth of the river at New Orleans, unrestricted American access to the interior was not secure so long as Spain claimed territory upriver. The second concern was the contested territory known as West Florida, which extended east along the Gulf coast from New Orleans to the Perdido River, a waterway located halfway between Mobile and Pensacola, below the thirty-first parallel. The United States argued that the borders of the original French colony included this strip of land and that it ipso facto fell within the jurisdiction of the Louisiana Purchase.[10] In contrast, Spain claimed that it had not been included in the 1800 Treaty of San Ildefonso that transferred Louisiana back to France and, therefore, that the border between American territory and Spanish Florida remained the Mississippi River. While the diplomats argued, the weakly defended and underpopulated Spanish settlements in the area found themselves under intense pressure from Americans moving east from New Orleans and south from the Mississippi Territory. Meanwhile, Spanish East Florida, in particular the settlements from St. Augustine to the Georgia border, was the third point of contention and served, simply by its continued existence, as a challenge to American commercial and military interests on the Atlantic seaboard. As the United States pushed its borders west and south, these points of contact with the Spanish empire held both promise and peril for the young nation (see map 3).

On the other side, with respect to its American possessions, preservation of the status quo was the priority of the beleaguered Spanish monarchy in 1807. Despite its official and popular claims to neighboring Spanish colonies, the US government had refrained from any overt signs that it would attempt to solve its territorial disputes with Spain by force of arms.

For the most part, both sides remained bound by the 1796 Treaty of Madrid, which fixed the borders between the United States, Spanish Louisiana, and the Florida colonies. However, as has been noted, the transfer of Louisiana muddled the agreement, as the Americans in particular pressed to expand their sphere of influence around the mouth of the Mississippi. Jefferson himself was convinced that a weakened Spain in "her feeble state" would sooner or later cede its rights to the disputed territories he called "the Floridas" to the United States, for the right price.[11] As a result, his administration, with its diplomatic machinery fully engaged in disputes with France and Britain, saw no reason to antagonize Spain with precipitous and provocative actions. A policy of watchful waiting sufficed for the present. Almost by default, the American government saw its advantages on the ground solidify, as events in Europe continued to undermine the ability of Spain to protect its Gulf Coast and Florida settlements.

Despite losing the vast majority of its North American possessions in the treaties that ended the Seven Years' War in 1763, France remained an active participant in the region for the remainder of the century. Its valuable colony of Saint-Domingue on the western end of the island of Hispaniola gave it a significant stake in the Caribbean. During the American Revolution, French military intervention on the side of the rebellious colonists helped secure independence for the United States, a result that was arguably a secondary consideration to the ministers of Louis XVI, who likely relished the opportunity of delivering a devastating blow to their long-standing British rivals. Moreover, despite the multiple transfers of territory between the European powers in this period of colonial wars that caused the British and Spanish empires to absorb a large number of former French subjects into their overseas empires, cultural ties remained strong between the large French Diaspora stretching from Quebec to Buenos Aires and its motherland.

Even on the scale of the French cession of Louisiana to Spain in 1763, the transfer of a colony and its inhabitants from one European power to another in the wake of military defeat was standard practice in the eighteenth century. The French Revolution, however, changed the dynamics of this process and the stakes. The rules that governed the game of power politics being played on a global scale between European monarchies were easily understood and well accepted. Revolutionary politics, however, was something new and dangerous. Already, the existence of an independent

United States in the Western Hemisphere had required some adjustments of traditional practice, but the revolutionary regime and its successor the Napoleonic empire injected new motivations, new threats, and new ideologies. Rather than kings and ministers moving armies and navies across the global chessboard on behalf of dynastic interests, the post-1800 Americas witnessed an unprecedented array of actors, protagonists, motives, and agendas.

As the nineteenth century opened, the French diplomatic position in the United States was as ambiguous as that of the Spanish. While the memory of their military alliance during the American Revolution retained its symbolic power, the unrest produced by France's own revolution only complicated relations between the two nations. In the early 1790s radical elements within the new republican government sought to take advantage of the pro-French inclinations of the Jeffersonians, a political faction that had begun to challenge its Hamiltonian rivals for power within President Washington's cabinet. Instructed to undermine US neutrality in the war between France and Great Britain, the new French ambassador, Edmond Charles Genêt, embroiled himself in domestic politics between 1793 and 1794 to the point where Franco-American relations nearly collapsed. A second crisis between the two republics arose by mid-decade, when French warships began seizing American merchant vessels. John Adams, who sent envoys to Paris in 1797 to negotiate a resolution to the disputes, found these overtures rebuffed by Foreign Minister Talleyrand. The United States and France then entered the Quasi-War, a de facto state of hostilities that ended with the Treaty of Mortefontaine in 1800.[12]

During the Jefferson administration, however, relations quickly improved. Not surprisingly, his new political party, the Democratic Republicans (which held power in Washington until 1826), carried the president's Francophilia into the American political arena. This goodwill was returned in extravagant fashion with Napoleon's decision to sell the Louisiana territory to the United States in 1803. This acquisition, which doubled the size of the country, also gave the young nation a large Francophone constituency of fifty thousand inhabitants. Indeed, between 1793 and 1810 successive waves of immigrants fleeing the revolutions in Saint-Domingue added more than fifteen thousand people to the already existing population of this territory.[13] Despite decades of Spanish rule and now American control, New Orleans remained very much a French outpost on the sensitive southwestern border between the United States and Spain. Ultimately, while the United States avoided an overt alliance with France during the first decade of the nineteenth century, its geopolitical interests remained aligned with its first foreign ally for much of the Napoleonic era.[14]

In this confusing environment, Valentín de Foronda could only hope that President Jefferson and his successors would allow Spain time to restore its interests in the region. From a diplomatic perspective, however, Spain had almost no leverage left in North America by 1807. Foronda might emphasize in his dealings with the State Department the value of a friendly neighbor, the history of friendship between the two states, the growing importance of trade between Spanish America and the United States, and Spain's natural right to its possessions. Under normal circumstances, these arguments might have proven effective. But Spanish-American relations could not be debated in isolation in 1807. Any diplomatic move by Spain or the United States played itself out within the context of the shifting alliances of the Napoleonic Wars and proved as permanent as the voluble events in Europe would allow. Nominally, Spain was allied to France, which at the time worked in its favor in its dealings with the United States, for Jefferson and his party remained inclined toward French interests. In contrast, US relations with Great Britain were far cooler. Despite historic cultural ties, revolutionary antagonisms between the two states had not fully dissipated. More problematically, contemporary wartime pressures compelled the British navy to interfere with neutral American shipping and impress American sailors. Such acts only fed a growing popular movement advocating a declaration of war against Great Britain.

As it turned out, Foronda would have little more than a year to lean upon the vestiges of respect that still clung to the Spanish empire, marshal the resources at his disposal, and direct his operations in the furtherance of Spain's traditional diplomatic interests with the United States. By the spring of 1808, events in Europe would conspire to render his position almost untenable. On August 2, 1808, Spain's representative reported to his superiors that he had given the US government formal notice of the abdication of Carlos IV and the ascension to the throne of his heir, Fernando VII.[15] As ships carried the latest news from Spain across the Atlantic, however, it became clear to royal officials in the Americas that this was simply the first in a rapid and unprecedented sequence of events that began with the March conspiracy against Godoy and ended—for the moment—with the crown in the hands of Joseph Bonaparte and the establishment of a loyalist government determined to protect the rights of the Bourbons (discussed in detail in chapter 3).

For Spanish officials and their subjects in the Americas, not to mention the international community, the primary question now became one of legitimacy.[16] With Spain's fortunes so closely tied to its overseas possessions, representatives from the competing governments sought to confirm the allegiance of the colonies to their respective sides as quickly as possible. As has been mentioned, Napoleon wasted no time upon obtaining the abdications of the Spanish Bourbons to order his ministers to document the legality of the political process that transferred sovereignty to Joseph and ensure the dissemination of this material across the Atlantic. By mid-summer, two leadings Spanish statesmen, Miguel José de Azanza (the duque de Santa Fe) and Manuel de Negrete (the duque de Campo Alange), now serving on behalf of the new Bonapartist regime, repeatedly sought to establish the new, contested, monarch's control over the empire by establishing lines of communication with the colonial authorities in the Americas. At the same time, loyalists countered with their own barrage of letters, decrees, and declarations attesting to the unlawful nature of the French occupation and the fidelity of their movement to the Bourbon cause.

The burden of preserving order while following the correct political path in the midst of this confusion largely fell upon the colonial bureaucracy, and few parts of the empire illustrate the complex reality of post-Bayonne Spanish America than the frontier province of East Florida. On August 27, 1808, the Spanish governor of the territory sent an urgent message to his superior, the captain general of Cuba.[17] Governor Enrique White informed Havana that St. Augustine and its surrounding settlements had been receiving unconfirmed reports for more than a month that Napoleon had overthrown the Spanish monarchy. He hinted that he expected to receive confirmation of this news from Cuban authorities and any necessary orders that might result from such shocking and unprecedented developments. In the meantime, White explained to Captain General Someruelos that St. Augustine was not completely isolated, for a number of newspapers from the United States circulated freely in the colony and provided sufficiently reliable reporting from Europe. Still, he hastened to reassure the captain general that he assumed that official dispatches from Havana had been sent in a timely manner but had either been "lost" or "intercepted" before reaching the province.[18]

From the perspective of Spain's colonial officials, the information that crossed the Atlantic in the summer of 1808 could not have been more traumatic. As the reports of all these events, both confirmed and rumored, reached the Americas, it became the duty of senior officials like Someruelos to ensure that his subordinates receive accurate and timely information, follow the orders and decrees promulgated by the legitimate government of Spain, and coordinate effective regional and local responses as needed. Considering the likely impact of these unprecedented developments on

Spanish America, there is little doubt that colonial bureaucrats made the distribution of this critical information to their colleagues over the summer and fall of 1808 their highest priority. Regardless of the means of transmission, however, the effective dissemination of news from the metropolis to the colonies required many weeks and months. As a result, well into August 1808 East Florida found itself forced to rely on unofficial sources of information in its struggle to keep current with European events.

Governor White's communications with Captain General Someruelos during the second half of 1808 is striking for the fact that it displays the often-ragged efforts of a colonial bureaucracy groping to find an appropriate response to a worst-case scenario no one could have anticipated. More broadly, it also illuminates the complexity of life in Spanish North America at the beginning of the nineteenth century. White's passing comment regarding the presence of US newspapers in his outpost was a not unexpected reference to the proximity of St. Augustine to Georgia. He continued, however, by reminding Someruelos that East Florida was completely dependent upon Cuban food and financial support in the face of US commercial policy—an indirect reference to the Embargo Act of 1807 which closed American ports to European belligerents—and added that Spain would likely lose the colony to the United States without more consistent support.[19]

Simply securing East Florida at the outset of the imperial crisis, then, required the captain general of Cuba to recognize that this otherwise peripheral province on the edge of the Spanish empire had economic, cultural, strategic, and demographic ties that linked it both to France and the United States. Additional reflection on his part would no doubt have also suggested the importance of the region to Great Britain, whose commercial interests often utilized the burgeoning smuggling center at Amelia Island, which was located just south of the international border with Georgia.[20] In the short term, at least, the loyalist campaign appeared unchallenged. Six months following the coup at Bayonne, the response from Spanish America and the colonial bureaucracy was clear and unmistakable: Fernando VII remained king of Spain and the Junta Central served as the legitimate authority for the empire in his absence.

However, Napoleon was the unquestioned master of Europe in 1808. His rise had been meteoric, his victories over such powers as Austria, Prussia, and Russia had been decisive, and his grip on the growing French empire appeared secure. While the local Spanish resistance had been unexpected, there seemed to be little reason at the time to believe that Napoleon would fail in his efforts to subdue Spain and, by extension, gain control of its American empire. This picture complicated matters for the United States as it sought to preserve its neutrality in the Napoleonic Wars. Any decisive move to recognize either one of the Spanish governments carried with it the potential to upset the delicate diplomatic dance that the Jefferson administration was performing and to draw the United States into an untenable position vis à vis one of the belligerent powers. Recognition of Joseph would certainly please Napoleon and strengthen the pro-French party in the United States; however, it would complicate the already fraught relationship with Great Britain, now an ally of the Spanish loyalists, threaten US interests in Spanish America, and perhaps derail efforts to push the frontier deeper into the continent. At the same time, recognition of the Junta Central would be a clear declaration that the United States had turned away from France, a risky move with Napoleon at the peak of his power and influence. Therefore, while the matter remained unresolved, the Jefferson administration preferred to withhold its recognition of any government in Spain. As Foronda discovered to his intense frustration, this decision had a significant impact on his ability to conduct his duties. More important, it turned the United States into a critical stage on which the ensuing conflict between Spain, Spanish America, and France would be fought.

At first, Foronda had reason to believe that events on the Iberian Peninsula would work in his favor. In October 1808 he informed the Junta Central that the Jefferson administration seemed inclined toward the Spanish loyalists and their British allies. The minister reported that Secretary of State Madison had given orders for the removal of US soldiers stationed near or perhaps even inside Spanish territory on the Mississippi. He also suggested that congressional opinion regarding the territory between Baton Rouge and the Perdido River had begun to split, which if true boded well for Spanish interests in the Gulf.[21] This positive report might well have encouraged the Junta to consolidate its diplomatic position in the United States. In the event, over the next six months, the loyalist government proceeded to make a series of new appointments to Spanish consulates there and, most importantly, nominate a high-profile replacement for Foronda as minister plenipotentiary.[22]

If the Spanish legation entertained hopes that it could count on American support in the chaotic weeks that followed the royal abdications at Bayonne, the first few months of 1809 provided Foronda with ample evidence that the United States would not commit itself too quickly to the loyalist cause. Among the factors that complicated relations between the two nations at this time was the impending inauguration of Madison as president. Well versed in European concerns through his service as Jefferson's secretary of state, the new president assumed office on March 4 with a foreign policy designed above all to reaffirm American neutrality in the face of mounting pressure from the belligerent powers and reassert the primacy of the United States over North American affairs.[23]

Within ten days of the inauguration, the new secretary of state, Robert Smith, received a series of blistering letters from Foronda that raised questions about the new administration's commitment to established policy toward Spain. First on the minister's list of concerns was the impact on Spanish commerce of two years of congressional efforts—which began with the Embargo Act of 1807 and culminated with the Non-Intercourse Act of March 1, 1809—to retaliate against British and French interference with US shipping. This legislation included clauses that prohibited direct or indirect trade between the United States and either belligerent. Inevitably, however, Spanish merchant vessels were caught up in the efforts to enforce the restrictions, especially in cases where customs officials feared that the Spanish flag was serving as a cover for contraband imports.[24] The result was that laws designed to hurt France and Britain had a disproportionate effect on Spain. Foronda could not fail to add that the Non-Intercourse Act was passed at a time when the Spanish loyalist government had in contrast relaxed restrictions on foreign access to its American colonies, thereby providing American merchants with multiple opportunities for profit at Spain's expense.[25]

The diplomat expressed his surprise and unease over another troubling development in a letter dated March 14. Enclosed newspaper clippings suggested that Governor Claiborne of Louisiana had decided to block the Spanish right to free navigation of the Mississippi River above New Orleans, as well as of waterways such as the Iberville River (Bayou Manchac), which provided access from the east to the Spanish possessions around Baton Rouge. Foronda declared this a violation of the treaty agreements between Spain and the United States and an insult to his country. He also commented on information that the Madison administration was increasing its troop strength in New Orleans and implied that the United States had decided to take advantage of Spain's misfortune to "achieve its unjust ends with the bayonet."[26]

Over the previous nine months, the Spanish legation in the United States had sought to project an air of continuity. Calling attention to the political turmoil in Spain served no purpose from a diplomatic perspective. Foronda had been welcomed by the Jefferson administration as the acknowledged representative of Carlos IV, and he remained in that position into the spring of 1809 despite the inconvenient fact that the Spanish Bourbons had renounced their claims to the throne. Convincing Madison of the legitimacy of the Junta Central, therefore, remained a critical if elusive goal of Spanish diplomats, especially holdovers like Foronda. In April, still seeking this renewed recognition and hoping to reconfirm a relationship of "peace and harmony" between the two governments, Foronda sent to the State Department a formal decree from the Council of Castile verifying the installation of the Junta Central and validating it as the "repository of the sovereign authority of our beloved Monarch Sr. Don Fernando VII."[27] From a legal standpoint, if nothing else, this declaration gave the loyalist cause reason to feel confident about its claims to legitimacy.

In foreign capitals, however, this debate would be won by events on the ground rather than on its merits. Foronda had been complaining for months that the Madison administration had stopped acknowledging his official letters. In May, the Spanish consul in Baltimore, Juan Bernabeu, now confirmed to his superior a hardening of the administration's position toward Spain. The consul wrote that Secretary of State Smith had notified British ambassador David Erskine that the credentials for the recently appointed Spanish minister plenipotentiary had not come from the king (as they should have, according to protocol) and, therefore, would not be accepted in Washington. In the meantime, the State Department would continue to recognize Foronda in the inferior rank of chargé d'affaires. To soften the blow, Bernabeu added that he was under the impression that the United States would also refuse to admit any formal representative from the Bonapartist government so long as Spain continued to resist Joseph.[28]

Foronda responded to his predicament by attempting to manipulate the Madison administration into a de facto recognition of the Junta. His first course of action was to write to Smith asking for permission to return to Spain. However, he also declared that he could not leave his post until President Madison confirmed José de Viar as his temporary replacement. Viar had only recently arrived at the Philadelphia consulate on an appointment from the Junta Central, a point that was not lost on Foronda. While Smith responded that he could not accept Viar as chargé d'affaires ad interim of the Spanish legation, Foronda argued optimistically to his superiors that their correspondence on the subject served as a tacit recognition of the Junta Central by US officials.[29]

He followed up this rare interaction with Smith by informing the secretary of yet more "proof for this government of [Spain's] noble, generous, and respectful sentiments, along with the most cordial friendship of the Supreme Junta Central, toward this country." In the wake of some disparaging comments linking former president Jefferson to Napoleon that appeared in a Seville newspaper, the Junta Central took extraordinary pains to distance itself from these sentiments by allowing the publication of a formal refutation in the *Gazeta del Gobierno*, the official mouthpiece of the loyalist government. Foronda took pains to contrast this magnanimous gesture with the years of accumulated calumnies leveled in the American press against Spain and its kings that US officials failed to challenge or punish. He concluded by expressing the hope that the administration would now confirm the Junta's representatives in their diplomatic posts.[30]

As the summer of 1809 began, the Spanish legation had in its possession evidence of the possible consequences of delayed American recognition of the Junta Central. On June 10 Secretary Smith received from Foronda a request for a clarification of rumors, which had already reached the loyalist government in Seville, that the French minister in Washington was actively negotiating the sale of Florida to the United States. The ambassador reminded Smith that the French emperor did not hold title to territory in the possession of the Spanish Crown and expressed his dismay that the Madison administration might try to take advantage of the unrest in Spain in such a manner. While it preferred to disregard such reports, the Junta Central now felt obligated to declare that it would consider null and void any transfer of Spanish land by representatives of Napoleon.[31]

By the end of June 1809, Foronda began to shift his attention to a disturbing new threat to Spanish interests in the United States. For both the supporters of Fernando VII and of Joseph Bonaparte, the previous year had witnessed significant missteps and reverses in their respective efforts to consolidate viable governments in Spain. However, as 1808 ended, the position of the Bonapartist regime appeared relatively more secure. Forced to flee Madrid early in August 1808 in the wake of the French defeat at Bailén and less than two weeks after he first arrived to assume the throne, Joseph had had no alternative but to wait for reinforcements from France to regain the offensive. Salvation came in November in the person of Napoleon himself, who took command of the French armies in Spain. Within a month, Madrid had fallen to the emperor, and the loyalist forces retreated further south into Andalusia. Once again in possession of the capital, the government of Joseph Bonaparte now sought to consolidate its gains beyond the borders of Europe, specifically in the Americas where defenders of Fernando remained unchallenged.

Joseph's nascent government and its French allies had wasted little time in reaching out to Spanish diplomats across the Atlantic. Already on August 11, 1808, Campo Alange wrote to Foronda that he had assumed interim control over the Ministry of Foreign Affairs. Two months later the minister requested a list of the employees of the Spanish legation in Philadelphia and an account of their salaries. This was quickly followed by a copy of a decree from Joseph limiting all Spanish overseas embassies to one secretary and one attaché. Felix Beaujour, the French consul general in Washington, approached Foronda on behalf of the Bonapartist court in Madrid early in January 1809, to convince him to accept Joseph as king. However, Foronda immediately rebuffed this advance and printed for public consumption his hostile response to the French-inspired "Spanish Constitution," that is, the Statute of Bayonne, a copy of which Beaujour had presented to him. On January 16, 1809, Campo Alange sent another letter to Foronda ordering all Spanish diplomats in the United States to return to Europe. Of course, having already declared his loyalty to Fernando, the chargé d'affairs refused to respond to this correspondence and instead passed it all to his superiors in the Junta Central.[32]

Having rebuffed these formal overtures from the rey intruso, Foronda learned in 1809 that the Bonapartist court in Madrid had other means of influencing opinion in the Americas at its disposal. On June 28 he wrote to Spain that he would comply with an order that prohibited him from giving formal recognition to any Spanish agents in the United States who lacked credentials from the Junta Central.[33] In another letter he acknowledged the news that the French naval squadron at Brest had left port, with no reports as to its destination, and promised to pass on the information to the American administration.[34] The implications of both sets of warnings would prove to have a profound and lasting impact on Spanish diplomatic operations in the United States over the next two years.

Despite its official neutrality during the wars of the French Revolution, the United States government found itself under pressure to formalize an alliance with Napoleon against Great Britain as 1809 came to an end. Many in Madison's party supported this move, either out of affinity for France or hostility toward Britain. In fact, for most of the year Madison had reason to be concerned that the United States would soon find itself at war with one or other of the belligerent powers, considering the degree to which the commercial interests of the three states remained in conflict as a consequence of Napoleon's Continental System, Britain's Orders in Council, and the American Non-Intercourse Law. As a result, the administration continued to show restraint toward French overtures. Preferring for the time being to remain out of the European conflict, Madison rebuffed all such advances and continued to make formal protests against any belligerent action on the part of both France and Britain that had a negative impact on the United States.[35]

Despite this careful balancing act and regardless of the motivations behind it, Spanish diplomatic opinion in 1809 was largely united in the belief that the United States was a de facto ally of France even if no formal agreement between the two countries had yet been reached. From the loyalist viewpoint, the evidence could not be clearer: Britain, which was now

Spain's ally, was the historic enemy of the United States; Jefferson was both a Francophile and a revolutionary at heart; Napoleon rewarded this allegiance by selling him Louisiana at a bargain rate; the United States sought additional territorial expansion at the expense of the Spanish Crown; and finally, a French alliance could facilitate its designs on the borderland territories, especially if Joseph Bonaparte were to be victorious in Spain. Certainly, Madison's stubborn refusal to recognize Fernando's diplomatic representative suggested that the Americans had no stake in the survival of the Bourbon monarchy.

Of course, the nuances of Napoleonic diplomacy as it pertained to the Western Hemisphere were lost on Spanish diplomats as the first decade of the nineteenth century ended. The Spanish imperial bureaucracy in the Americas, including its diplomatic corps, remained loyal to Fernando VII during this period. Their king was in captivity, their country was occupied by foreign troops, their government was on the run, and thus their own position was in jeopardy. Besieged on all sides, they saw threats everywhere. One of the most dangerous was the possibility that French provocateurs, agents, and spies might turn Spanish America into another front in the Peninsular War. There seemed every reason to believe that Napoleon might achieve the conquest of Spain by encouraging unrest and thoughts of independence among Spanish Americans. It was impossible to ignore France's many advantages on the far side of the Atlantic: a large diaspora, widespread sympathy for revolutionary ideals, a vast stage on which to maneuver, money and resources, plus the all momentum associated with constant success in Europe. Then there was the United States itself. Although it remained a neutral party in the Napoleonic Wars, the Madison administration allowed Napoleonic agents to operate effectively unchallenged within its jurisdiction. Despite occasional flare-ups in the two countries' relations, in many respects American and French interests coincided. As a result, from the perspective of the Spanish diplomats assigned to the United States, fighting the French in the Americas soon became an important part of the defense of Spain.

Valentín de Foronda, however, had little time left on the frontlines of this battle. On September 2, he sent a letter to the secretary of state announcing the imminent arrival of Luís de Onís. He described this high-ranking diplomatic appointment as a marked sign of his government's desire to maintain goodwill between Spain and the United States, noting critically that Washington still remained satisfied with keeping only a chargé d'affairs as its representative before the Junta Central. Foronda then described the admirable qualities of his successor, underscoring his "kindness, intelligence, gentleness, conciliatory nature, and hostility to lies, entanglements, and plots." He took a moment to write his own valedictory, declaring "I have never published a single word against the Congress nor the administration in the Gazettes: I have not sowed lies, or spoken to any representative with the purpose of causing unrest in Congress: I have never been clumsy in my correspondence; while at times it has been emotional, it has always been guided by reason, while never losing the respect owed to this Government: I have breathed frankness and have been led by my logic, but never by a sickly pride."[36]

Ironically, on September 26, in one of his last official acts as Spain's senior diplomat in the United States, Foronda found his patience tested yet again as he asked Secretary Smith for formal clarification of reports published in multiple newspapers that General James Wilkinson, perhaps with the support of troops in New Orleans and the tacit approval of Madison, was preparing an expedition against New Spain or the Floridas.[37] Any response would have to be left for his successor. On November 1, less than one month after the arrival of Onís in the United States, Foronda set sail for Spain.[38]

3

Luís de Onís

From Cantalapiedra to Philadelphia

> I do not know what decision His Majesty will make as a result of this insult to his sovereignty, but as this situation was foreseen in my instructions I remain here in Philadelphia exercising my responsibilities as Minister on behalf of all Spaniards and the constituted authorities of His Majesty in all his Dominions until he judges otherwise.
>
> —Luís de Onís to Enrique White, Philadelphia, October 31, 1809

Few governments in modern European history projected a greater sense of their own imminent dissolution than the Spanish Junta Central in the spring of 1809, exactly one year after Napoleon removed the Bourbon dynasty from the throne of Spain. Despite the best intentions of the French emperor, who expected his intervention to bring peace and stability to the Iberian Peninsula, Spain now found itself torn apart, with rival kings claiming sovereignty over the country and its overseas empire. The government of Joseph Bonaparte, who reigned from Madrid as José I, was supported by a powerful French army and a small cadre of Francophile Spaniards known as *afrancesados* or *josefinos*. Yet, while the Bonapartist regime controlled most of Spain's territory, it failed to impose that dominance on the battlefield of public opinion. Instead, when news of the Bourbon abdications reached Madrid on May 2, 1808, *madrileños* rioted against French forces stationed in the capital. This initial uprising then sparked a generalized rebellion across Spain that forced Napoleon to commit to the military subjugation of the Iberian Peninsula. In the weeks that followed, resistance forces declared war on France and set up a number of competing loyalist governments in major cities to provide a political framework for the opposition to Joseph, now publically dismissed as the rey intruso or, even more disparagingly, as Pepe Botellas (Joe Bottles), due to his rumored fondness for wine. On September 25, 1808, these regional authorities consolidated themselves into the Junta Central Suprema y Gubernativa del Reino, a supreme governing junta that based itself in Seville and claimed the authority to rule in the name of the captive Fernando VII, acknowledged by most Spaniards as their *rey deseado* (desired king).

However, the apparently spontaneous emergence of a massive resistance movement against France proved to be of limited benefit to the government that claimed to represent the loyalist cause. Spaniards could unite against a common enemy: France. They could also unite behind a common cause: the rights of Fernando VII. The role of the Junta Central in this fight, however, proved to be more ambiguous. As the one-year anniversary of the events of Bayonne passed, the Junta Central still struggled to overcome lingering doubts about its legitimacy. Meanwhile, it still had to solve the practical challenges of organizing itself on the run (with few historical precedents), limited resources to wage war against the most powerful army in Europe, and tenuous communications with Spain's overseas territories. Yet, if the definition of effective government includes the recruitment and employment of qualified bureaucrats, officials, and administrators, then the Junta Central could claim at least one great success in June 1809: the appointment of Luís de Onís as its ambassador and minister plenipotentiary to the United States (fig. 1).

Considering the fragile nature and questionable authority of this government, any diplomatic representative appointed by the Junta Central required significant ability and experience, especially if he expected to succeed in such a sensitive post as the United States proved to be at this time. Born in 1762 at Cantalapiedra, a small town in Old Castile located between Salamanca and Medina del Campo, Luís de Onís came from a minor noble family with a history of producing and grooming diplomats for the Spanish Crown.[1] In this particular case, Onís's primary education in Latin and Greek began at home at the age of eight. By 1778 he had moved to the University of Salamanca, where he focused on the study of law, philosophy, and rhetoric. Only two years later, at the age of eighteen, the budding diplomat moved to Dresden to serve as secretary to his uncle, José de Onís, who held the post of minister plenipotentiary at the Saxon court. By 1784 Luís came to occupy the position of interim chargé d'affaires at the Spanish embassy to Saxony. Serving in a post located at the crossroads of European politics gave Onís the opportunity to perfect his French, English, and German language skills. He also found himself a wife. A series of well-received diplomatic missions across central Europe ensued, and, with this intensive apprenticeship successfully realized, the thirty-year-old Onís received an appointment early in 1792 from the Spanish government to serve as ambassador to the United States.

Unfortunately, by this time the political stability that had characterized both Spain and Europe since midcentury had come to an end, and the future diplomatic career of Luís de Onís would be shaped more by the unpredictability of revolution and war than by the entrenched perspectives and

Figure 1. Portrait of Luís de Onís (Wikipedia).

priorities of the Spanish *antiguo régimen* (old regime). The first step away from this old order resulted from the death of the enlightened King Carlos III in December 1788, who passed away after having occupied the throne for thirty years. The loss left the Spanish crown in the hands of his incompetent son and heir Carlos IV. The opening act of an even greater crisis occurred six months later in Paris when the fall of the Bastille in Paris precipitated the French Revolution. On February 28, 1792, as the drama in France unfolded, the conde de Floridablanca, who had served as the chief minister of Spain since 1777, was replaced by the conde de Aranda in a shocking move that nullified Onís's pending nomination as ambassador. As a result, the young diplomat remained in Saxony and watched from the sidelines as Europe descended into conflict. Six years passed before Onís returned home to assume a senior position at the Ministry of State as a specialist in French affairs. The Spain he encountered in 1798 was a far cry from the one he had known as a teenager.

By this time, the Spanish empire had descended into an almost permanent state of crisis. Witnesses to the political and social upheavals that marked the early years of the French Revolution, Carlos IV and his subjects could not avoid becoming combatants in the international wars that it ignited across Europe. In April 1793, three months after the execution of Carlos's cousin Louis XVI, Spanish troops crossed the Pyrenees into the recently proclaimed French Republic on a mission to restore the old order and avenge the Bourbon family. A disastrous three-year war against France ensued. The 1795 treaty that mercifully ended it was negotiated by the king's favorite and new chief minister, Manuel Godoy. One year later, newly graced with the rather pompous title of príncipe de la Paz (Prince of the Peace), Godoy brought Spain into a coalition with revolutionary France.[2]

This shift in alliance made Great Britain the new enemy, and Spanish fortunes took a turn for the worse during the second half of the decade. In 1797 Spain lost much of its navy at the Battle of St. Vincent and was compelled to surrender the Caribbean island of Trinidad to the British. Over the next five years, a continuous blockade of the Iberian coast strangled Spanish overseas commerce and prevented any direct administration of its American possessions, a state of affairs that helped convince Carlos IV to approve the retrocession of Spanish Louisiana to France in 1800. As an experienced and valued diplomat, Onís often found himself at the Paris embassy during this tumultuous period. And in 1802 he served as a member of the Spanish delegation that helped produce the Treaty of Amiens, an agreement between the warring powers of Europe that provided just over fourteen months of peace to a continent that had been at war for a decade.

By the end of 1804, military conflict between Spain and Great Britain had resumed. Over the next three years the enfeebled Spanish monarchy suffered further indignities, most notably the loss of the Franco-Spanish fleet at Trafalgar in 1805 and two successive British invasions of Buenos Aires. In the wake of these reverses, Carlos IV and his government increasingly became a liability to France. At the end of 1807 Napoleon used the invasion of Portugal, which was ostensibly a combined Franco-Spanish campaign, as an excuse to occupy the Iberian Peninsula and gradually seize control of Spain's military posts.

In October 1807 the Spanish court, now hopelessly divided over the French alliance, collapsed into factionalism as enthusiasts of the heir to the throne, Prince Fernando, plotted to overthrow Godoy, who was perceived to be a French puppet. This scheme, known as the conspiracy of El Escorial, failed to remove the king's favorite, but the Crown sustained lasting damage to its prestige. On March 18, 1808, following a series of orchestrated popular disturbances directed against Godoy, Carlos IV decided to abdicate in favor of his son. Though he sought to reclaim the throne four days later by appealing to the commander of French forces in Spain Marshal Joachim Murat, the old king found that events had spiraled out of his control. Fernando arrived in Madrid on March 24 to great popular acclaim, only two days after French forces took up new positions in the capital itself.[3]

It was at this point that Luís de Onís found himself thrust into the middle of one of the strangest events in Spanish history. On April 10, a procession of well-appointed carriages departed Madrid on the first stage of a ten-day journey that would carry a remarkable group of travelers northeast through the heart of Old Castile and the Basque Provinces to the Bidasoa River, which marked the Spanish border with France. In the lead coach sat Fernando VII, king of Spain for all of three weeks. Among his fellow passengers were two Spanish grandees: José Miguel de Carvajal, the duque de San Carlos and Fernando's *mayordomo mayor* (royal high steward), and Valentín Belbis, the conde de Villariezo and captain general of New Castile. Immediately behind the king in an oddly prominent and symbolic position for a foreign military officer rode the French general Anne-Jean-Marie-René Savary. If there was any confusion about his presence among the Spanish entourage, the placement of General Savary was underscored by the unsettling fact that thousands of French troops patrolled the entire length of the road from Madrid to Burgos.

The three men best positioned to appreciate this new reality traveled in the third carriage: Pedro de Alcántara, the duque del Infantado and the newly appointed president of the Council of Castile; Pedro Cevallos, the secretario de estado; and Juan de Escoiquiz, a longtime courtier and tutor to Fernando who had used this connection to become one of the new king's most influential advisors. The fourth carriage held two more Spanish noblemen, Pedro María Jordán de Urríes y Fuenbuena, the marqués de Ayerbe, and Rafael António Alfonso de Sousa, the marqués de Guadalcázar, along with three senior officials from the Spanish *secretaría de estado* (Ministry of State): Pedro Gómez Labrador, Eusebio Bardají Azara, and Luís de Onís. The king's immediate family, his servants, and more junior court officials followed closely behind.[4]

The final destination for Fernando and his entourage was Bayonne, a small French town located approximately twenty-five miles from the Spanish frontier. Here waited Napoleon, a ruler at the height of his power and influence who had negotiated a successful end to his military campaigns against Prussia and Russia one year earlier. With one enemy, Great Britain, left in the field, the French emperor increasingly found his attention turning to southwestern Europe. The conquest of Portugal was designed to prevent Britain from gaining commercial access to the continent through its longtime ally. In the process, French forces assumed de facto control of Spain. Now, in April 1808, Napoleon summoned Fernando, his parents, and other members of the ruling Bourbon dynasty to meet with him in this remote corner of France (fig. 2).

Although the wartime alliance between Spain and France had been in place for more than a decade, the young king and his advisors had good reason to be wary of Napoleon's intentions and objectives for the conference. Many Spaniards, in fact, were willing to entertain rumors that Napoleon sought to dispense with his Bourbon allies altogether and install a regime more dependent on and integrated into his imperial ambitions. Seeking some degree of reassurance regarding his status before crossing the border, Fernando sent four grandees ahead to Bayonne to request a security guarantee from the emperor. The procession paused briefly in Burgos and again in Vitoria,[5] continuing only after receiving letters from Napoleon promising that the emperor would respect "the integrity and independence of Spain" and recognize the ascension of Fernando. With this pledge in hand, the Spanish carriages entered France on April 21.[6]

Within a few hours of Fernando's arrival in Bayonne a perfunctory and superficial encounter took place between the king and the emperor. After this introductory session, Napoleon took Escoiquiz aside and declared his intention to dethrone the Spanish Bourbons.[7] With the worst of the rumors now apparently confirmed, the Spanish entourage spent the next week in a state of turmoil. Meeting in ad hoc councils, Fernando's advisors sought but failed to find a united response to the looming crisis. A minority, led by Escoiquiz, counseled patience and argued that Spanish negotiators should play for time in meetings with their French counterparts in the hopes that Napoleon could be persuaded to accept a less drastic outcome. However, most members of Fernando's entourage preferred to take a hard line, convinced that Napoleon was bluffing and that he was in fact seeking minor territorial concessions from Spain, for instance, Navarre or one of the American colonies. Meeting in an extraordinary council on April 27, the Spanish delegation agreed to present their opinions to Fernando in writing. Following this debate, the duque del Infantado and Escoiquiz were dispatched to tell Napoleon's foreign minister, the comte de Champagny, that Fernando would not relinquish the throne. Champagny, who

Figure 2. "Boney at Bayonne blowing a Spanish bubble." Napoleon convincing the Spanish royalty, who are enclosed in a bubble, of his friendship as he fires a cannonball at Madrid. Published June 12, 1808 (Thos. Tegg, No. 111 Cheapside, London; Library of Congress, http://hdl.loc.gov/loc.pnp/pp.print).

seemed well-informed of the Spanish deliberations, responded that either Fernando must accept the terms set by Napoleon or the emperor would simply bypass him and negotiate exclusively with Carlos IV, who was due to arrive in Bayonne on April 29.[8]

Luís de Onís was one of the members of the king's entourage asked to respond to the French demands. According to the Onís family account, he left no doubt as to his position, declaring "that is my opinion that the king cannot and should not make such a renunciation."[9] The family history then records that when Napoleon learned of this statement, he ordered that the upstart diplomat be imprisoned in Bayonne's citadel. Refusing to allow such a fate to overtake him, Onís joined Bardají and another Foreign Ministry official, Evaristo Pérez de Castro, and fled back into Spain on April 29.[10]

Six days later both Carlos IV and Fernando VII surrendered their rights to the Spanish throne to Napoleon, who then took steps to transfer this authority to his older brother Joseph.[11] Quite unexpectedly, at least from the emperor's perspective, the abrupt removal of the Spanish Bourbons unleashed a massive popular protest movement in favor of the rey deseado, an uprising precipitated by the *dos de mayo* (May 2) revolt against the French troops occupying Madrid.[12] Napoleon had expected a straightforward transfer of power. To that end, he had invited to Bayonne along with the Spanish royal family many leading aristocrats, statesmen, and other members of the traditional political institutions of the *antiguo régimen*. Their presence was critical, for by participating, however reluctantly, in the change of dynasty the Spanish elite might be seen to invest it with a degree of legitimacy. For this purpose, Napoleon assembled a rump version of the Council of Castile in Bayonne and compelled it to give formal approval to the ascension of Joseph to the Spanish throne. The willingness—in some cases enthusiastic, in other cases grudging—of important Bourbon-era statesmen such as Pedro Cevallos to play a role in the establishment of the new regime suggested that Bonapartist Spain was now a fait accompli. The popular reaction, however, indicated that the transition would not be so easy.

In the middle of June, Napoleon selected thirty Spanish dignitaries to participate in a quasi-Cortes charged with writing a new governing charter for Spain. This document, which was signed by Joseph on July 6 and came to be known as the Statute of Bayonne, attempted to blend Bonapartist reforms with traditional Spanish political culture.[13] In combination, the acts of abdication by Carlos and Fernando, the approval of the Council of Castile, and the promulgation of the Statute of Bayonne infused the nascent Bonapartist regime with a veneer of legality that served as something of a counterweight to the heavy-handed reality of the French military occupation. Thus armed, on July 9 Joseph Bonaparte left Bayonne to take up the Spanish throne. He made his entrance into Madrid eleven days later and was proclaimed king in the capital on July 25. In a move that suggested broad support from the Spanish elite, the new king filled the senior positions in his government with such notables as Mariano Luís de Urquijo, who reclaimed the office of secretario de estado that he had held a decade earlier; Campo Alange, who became Joseph's first foreign minister; and the duque de Santa Fe, a former viceroy of New Spain who assumed multiple cabinet-level portfolios at the Bonapartist court.[14]

However, by this time no amount of afrancesado support for Joseph could hide the fact that Spain was engulfed in a national war for liberation. In the weeks after the initial Madrid revolt, the fragmented opposition to the Bonapartist regime coalesced around eighteen separate provincial governing juntas.[15] While these loyalist groups saw their territorial holdings shrink precipitously in the months that followed the May revolts, they managed to hold out against overwhelming French forces. In fact, a surprise victory by Spanish insurgents at Bailén on July 19 forced Joseph to abandon Madrid and much of central Spain to the loyalists until November, when Napoleon himself took command of the French armies on the Peninsula and regained the offensive, along with the capital. In the interim, however, the loyalists took advantage of the breathing space won by such fierce resistance to the occupation to establish the Junta Central. Claiming the allegiance of the majority of Spaniards, this new government proceeded to consolidate power, proclaim its authority over the empire, and sustain an effective guerrilla campaign through the remainder of the year.[16]

Due to his high-ranking positions under Carlos IV and Fernando VII and his patriotic actions at Bayonne, Luís de Onís found himself an important part of the evolving loyalist resistance to Napoleon during the summer of 1808. As a consequence of the political vacuum resulting from the removal of the royal family and so many senior crown officials, Onís and many former members of the Bourbon government soon gravitated toward the conde de Floridablanca, whose status as an elder statesman and vast political experience provided a rallying point during the turbulent weeks after Bayonne. In the wake of the *dos de mayo*, the octogenarian Floridablanca had joined the supreme junta of his native Murcia. As part of the centralization process, he then agreed to serve as the president of the new Junta Central, whose opening session occurred on September 25 at the royal palace at Aranjuez.[17]

By this time, Onís had reunited with his many of his diplomatic colleagues who had served under Pedro Cevallos. Cevallos himself, who had remained in Bayonne with Fernando VII, had accepted the post of minister of foreign affairs under King Joseph in an effort to secure his safe return to Spain and facilitate the transition of power. Upon returning to Madrid at the end of July, however, he denounced the new dynasty as illegitimate and fled for the safety of the loyalist lines. With the help of Onís, he proceeded to write an influential account of the overthrow of the Bourbons that excoriated the actions of Napoleon and served as a powerful counterargument to the official French narrative of Bayonne.[18]

Given these connections, Onís was in line for an important position in the new government. Floridablanca initially suggested making Onís secretary to the Junta Central, but that proposal went nowhere. Instead, the career diplomat found himself placed as *primer secretario* (principal advisor) to Martín de Garay, who had replaced Cevallos as the loyalist secretario de estado despite his lack of diplomatic experience.[19] By the end of 1808, foreign support for the Junta Central became critical, as the embattled loyalist government found itself falling back on Seville in the face of a renewed French offensive across central Spain. In January 1809, Cevallos departed for London with the title of *ministro plenipotentiario y embajador extraordinario* to begin negotiations with the British government. Onís was considered for a similar appointment as the Junta's ambassador to St. Petersburg; however, the nomination collapsed when Russia decided to recognize the government of José I. Perhaps because of his experience in northern Europe, Onís's name was then linked to a possible position in Sweden. Finally, on June 29, 1809, he was confirmed as Spain's representative to Washington, DC.[20]

Luís de Onís left for his new post at the end of August 1809 with—at least in hindsight—a clear understanding of his mission and objectives. Once established in a country that had to that point avoided becoming entangled in Europe's wars, the ambassador was expected "to ensure the peace and friendship" between Spain and the United States. He understood the need "to negotiate sincerely and in good faith" all of the existing differences between the two governments, in particular those that touched on border disputes. Furthermore, Onís recognized that his portfolio also embraced a more significant responsibility: "to keep the Spanish possessions in the New World united to the Motherland," a task that demanded that he "keep watch for adventurers and troublemakers (*incendiarios*)" who might travel from the United States to the colonies in order to cause unrest.[21]

The Junta's representative had no doubt that the campaign against Napoleon then raging across the Iberian Peninsula would also be fought in the Americas. Onís was aware that his new appointment placed him on the front lines of this new theatre of war and assumed his duties with confidence. Thirty years of diplomatic experience had prepared him well for the political gamesmanship to be expected in Washington, DC. More importantly, the ambassador carried with him across the Atlantic the searing memories of Bayonne. There, to the best of his abilities he had faced down Napoleon himself. Fernando VII could have had no more committed defender of his sovereign rights in the Americas than Luís de Onís.

On October 4, 1809, having just reached the port of New York following an Atlantic crossing on the Spanish frigate *Cornelia*, Onís wrote to his superiors announcing his arrival in the United States.[22] Traveling with all the urgency the political crisis in Spain demanded, the new minister plenipotentiary and ambassador extraordinary did not linger long in New York. In fact, his official reception in the city was rather underwhelming, certainly far below the expectations of someone of his ministerial rank.[23] A letter dated October 7, in which the envoy made his presence in the United States known to the secretary of state and mentioned his intention to proceed directly to the capital, suggested that he was impatient to present his credentials to the president and begin his assignment.[24] Onís knew before leaving Cádiz that his diplomatic mission would be controversial and was aware that the possibility existed that the American government would refuse to recognize him. However, he remained optimistic as he turned south. After all, the United States had in Spain a chargé d'affairs, George W. Erving, whom the Junta Central received without condition; the Junta negotiated frequently with this envoy on commercial matters; and it had repeatedly demonstrated its willingness to favor American interests. Besides, while the presence of the Bonapartist regime raised some doubts about the legitimacy of the Junta, Onís could safely argue that the loyalist government was recognized as sovereign by the vast majority of Spaniards on both sides of the Atlantic. Moreover, there was no doubt at all that the colonies answered to it alone. For good measure, the United States surely owed something to a nation that had fought alongside it during the American war for independence and which now sought similar assistance in return.[25]

However, when Onís reached Baltimore, the British minister plenipotentiary, Francis J. Jackson, did not have good news to report to his Spanish counterpart. While no official statement had been issued, it appeared that Madison had decided not to receive the Spanish envoy in any official capacity.[26] Hoping his presence in Washington might yet make a difference, Onís arrived in the capital on October 17 and, after settling himself in Georgetown, immediately notified Smith of his desire for both a face-to-face interview with the secretary and an audience with Madison.[27] The diplomats met two days later. According to Onís's report of the encounter, Smith was sympathetic and even admitted to the legitimacy of the Junta Central. Unfortunately, the American also used this opportunity to make clear the official position of the United States: the administration would not receive any Spanish ambassador, whether from Joseph or Fernando, until the war on the Iberian Peninsula was resolved one way or another. To lighten the blow, Smith avowed that Madison had every desire to preserve good relations with Spain; he further stated that Onís was free to communicate with the American government, particularly on matters affecting commercial relations, either through the Spanish consuls or the British minister.[28]

Despite this rather blunt rejection of his diplomatic mission, Onís declared himself satisfied with his first encounter with the American government. He informed his superiors that Jackson was prepared to tell Secretary Smith that Britain considered the president's decision an insult to its ally and would support Spain in the event of hostilities with the United States. Onís included a copy of a letter he wrote to Smith demanding the administration provide a written explanation of its decision not to recognize him.[29] He also enclosed a recent copy of the *Federal Republican*, highlighting an article that took Madison to task for his Spanish policy. According to the author, the president had put American expansion to the west in danger by opening up the possibility of armed conflict with Spain, a confrontation that might result in the loss of New Orleans and the closure of the Mississippi River to commerce. Clearly, Onís suggested, the American public was not entirely united behind its government regarding relations with Spain.[30]

Not one to retreat in the face of defeat, Onís remained in Washington for the remainder of October, hoping to give the administration an opportunity to reconsider. Many of these days were spent in the company of the British ambassador, who managed to introduce Onís to President Madison at a horserace in Georgetown.[31] On a more practical level, Onís used this time to open communications with all the Spanish consuls in the United States and instructed one in particular, Diego Morphy, who was still serving in Charleston, to take up his duties in New Orleans as soon as possible. The urgency behind this specific order was motivated by reports of a potential French conspiracy against New Spain. According to credible information gathered by Consul Bernabeu, between ten and twelve thousand Frenchmen who had been expelled from Cuba were organizing in New Orleans. With assistance from French Louisianans and the US Army, this force was rumored to have designs on Mexico. Onís responded to the threat by issuing warnings for the viceroy of New Spain, the captain general of Cuba, and the governor of Texas. He also asked his superiors to consider appointing more Spanish agents for New Orleans, as the city had clearly become a hotbed of French machinations against Spanish America. At the same time, Onís learned that the conspiracy surrounding General Wilkinson, which had disturbed Foronda only a month earlier, had evaporated (by this point, the general himself had been recalled). Reports of the new commander of American forces in Louisiana, Major Montgomery Pike, however, failed to reassure the ambassador that US interests in the region were benign.[32]

Onís held one more meeting with Secretary Smith, on October 26. He was comforted by what he considered to be another friendly exchange of views, though Smith refused to amend his stated position regarding US recognition of the Junta Central. As a result, Onís decided to leave the capital and set up his base of operations at the Spanish legation headquarters in Philadelphia (map 4).[33] Two weeks later, in a flurry of communiqués to his superiors, the envoy described the deteriorating situation now confronting him. On November 15, Onís reported on the recent dispute between Ambassador Jackson and Secretary Smith, a diplomatic row that caused the British diplomat to demand his passport so that he could return to England and that the Spanish envoy considered to be evidence of the pro-French sentiment of the administration. That same day Onís received word from Smith that the secretary would only communicate with Spanish representatives in person. He also interpreted this news as a sign that the French ambassador, General Louis Marie Turreau, was manipulating the State Department and argued that the Junta should suspend commerce with the United States until it received formal recognition. Furthermore, the envoy now possessed information that suggested that the wives of President Madison and of James Monroe, another senior member of the governing party, were accepting gifts from Turreau in return for their goodwill. Hoping to buy his own support in Washington, Onís asked for permission to try the same tactic on the two women.[34]

Potentially more serious threats to Spain also emerged in this correspondence. Hinting at some of the more extreme views present in the United States, Onís included a newspaper editorial that supported the administration's refusal to recognize the Spanish representative and declared its desire to see the independence of the Spanish colonies, in particular Cuba and Mexico. He also provided an update on the purported New Orleans conspiracy against New Spain, reporting that his sources had identified a number of Spaniards among the plotters. He also informed the Junta that a thirty-six-gun frigate was being fitted out in New York for a secret voyage. Onís understood that the ship would be manned by Frenchmen expelled from the Spanish colonies and sent out as a privateer to disrupt the

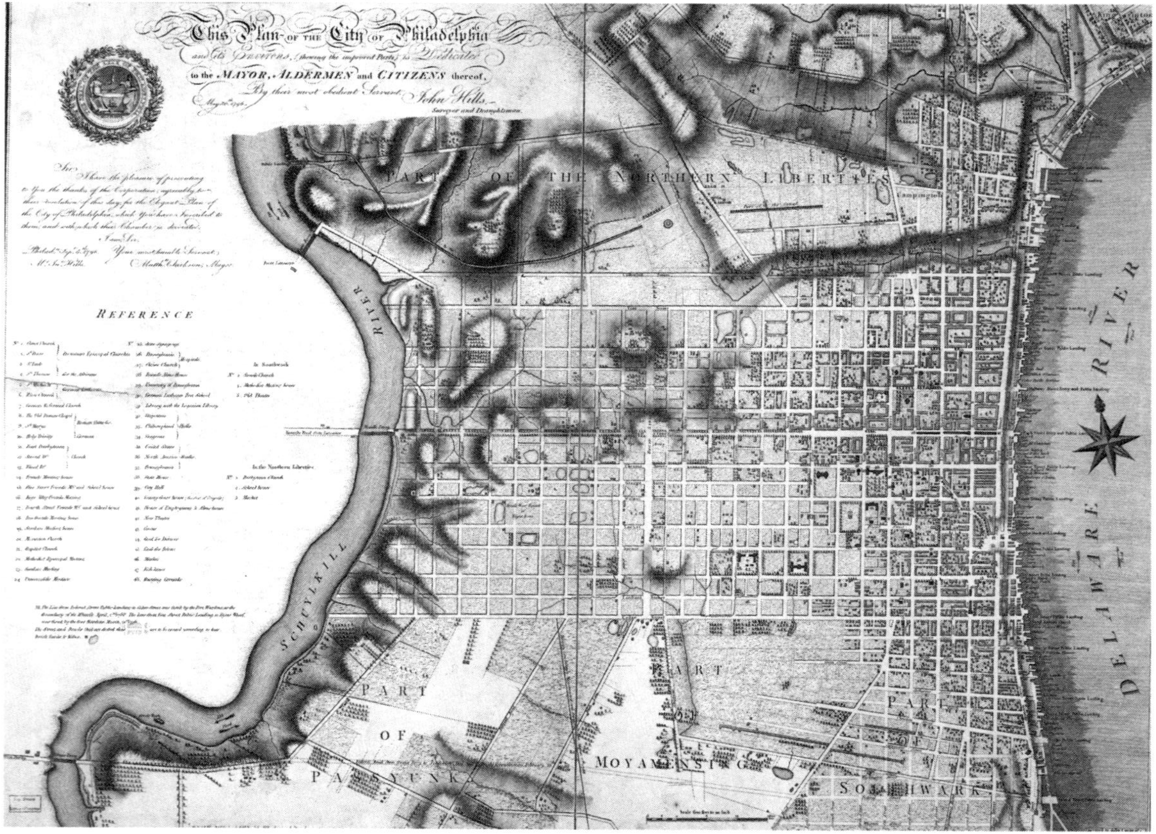

Map 4. Plan of Philadelphia, 1797 (John Hills, Philadelphia, 1797; Library of Congress, http://hdl.loc.gov/loc.gmd /g3824p.ct001369).

commerce of England, Spain, and Spanish America. He noted that he had already posted warnings about the warship to colonial officials and had passed the news on to Ambassador Jackson as well.[35]

Onís elaborated on this disturbing example of Franco-American collaboration in a letter to Enrique White, the governor of East Florida. Repeating his determination to remain in the United States to protect the interests of Spain, he declared that the Madison administration was now fully under the thumb of France ("*sometido de un codo a la Francia*"), having forgotten not only the rights of free nations but also the debt owed to a country that had fought on behalf of American independence. Onís noted that a French agent was in charge of arming the frigate in New York but that it would sail under an American flag in the guise of a commercial vessel. He stated that the crew consisted of three to four hundred Frenchmen who would be well armed with muskets, artillery, and ammunition. While early reports had suggested the ship would serve as a corsair, Onís now had reason to believe the frigate was part of a larger expedition against a Spanish colony. His sources, in fact, had warned him that the owners of some American merchant houses had purchased two additional vessels under suspicious circumstances. These individuals apparently held enough influence in Washington to ignore local port authorities and fit their newly acquired ships out as warships. One, the *Georgiana*, carried twenty guns and was already primed to set sail with a thin crew. The second, the *Camilla*, was another powerful twenty-gun brigantine. Onís presumed that the three ships would proceed to sea together and target the Spanish colonies. Connections between the owner of the *Camilla* and Santo Domingo suggested that their destination might be Hispaniola. However, Onís had no more specific information at present and could only promise White to do everything in his power to impede the departure of the ships by publicizing their hostile nature and demanding that the American government intervene.[36]

By the middle of November 1809, however, any expectation that the Madison administration and the Spanish ambassador to the United States could establish a working relationship had evaporated. Formally and publically unrecognized as a representative of Fernando VII, Onís lingered in Philadelphia determined to remain active despite his lack of diplomatic credentials. In his private capacity, Onís saw no reason not to continue to challenge official US policy toward loyalist Spain in the public arena. As a fully invested minister of the Spanish government, the envoy believed it was still within his purview to oversee the large Spanish consular network within the United States and organize it to serve both as an informal source of contact with American officials and, more importantly, as an information-gathering operation.

Onís also realized that his position as a senior appointee of the Junta Central in the Americas gave him certain status among colonial officials whose authority had geographical limitations. Generally speaking, since the United States appeared to have become an important launching pad for efforts to undermine the integrity of the Spanish empire, he felt obligated to use all the tools available to him to obstruct any conspiracies that came to his notice. In a letter to Martín de Garay dated November 28, Onís explained, "At a time when it is the first duty of the Courts, Officials, and Magistrates to watch and atone for the actions of individuals in order to separate or punish those Spaniards who fail to live up to the name, and who instead of sacrificing themselves for the Just Cause, which loyal Spaniards defend, allow themselves in the most vile and ignominious manner to support the perspective of the current French Government; I have considered it to be my first duty as a representative of the King Our Lord Don Fernando VII, and of the Supreme Junta Central in his name, to embrace this responsibility and investigate the feelings of the Spaniards from either hemisphere who find themselves in this country."[37]

In this capacity, the envoy assumed the right to question the loyalty of his countrymen as part of his official duties. Onís indicated to Garay that he had already found four residents of Philadelphia who deserved more careful scrutiny: Juan Martínez Cardosa, a close friend of Foronda, was a partner in the French commercial house of Juan Francisco Barrie; Luís Francini, a native of San Sebastian, had been seen in the company of Frenchmen; and Manuel and Domingo García, brothers from Caracas, also had French associates. In this environment, even a minor French connection was enough to raise suspicions in the mind of Onís, especially when these men also failed to introduce themselves to their new representative.[38]

As his concerns mounted, Onís decided to keep the pressure on the Madison administration and demand some accountability for American-based intrigues against Spanish possessions. At the end of November, he ordered Bernabeu to visit Washington and seek out members of Congress who might be disposed to favor Spain. He also instructed the consul to deliver a "private and unofficial" letter to Smith and ask the secretary of state for a personal interview.[39] Above all, this meeting was seen as an opportunity for the Spanish envoy to make an official complaint regarding the suspected New Orleans and New York plots. Onís took the possibility of Louisiana serving as a base of operations for those hoping to foment rebellion against Spanish possessions extremely seriously. He had already urged the newly appointed consul, Diego Morphy, to travel from Charleston to New Orleans without delay.[40] In the meantime, he asked Bernabeu to open a line of communication with Leandro Moxó, a Catalan who lived in New

Orleans and was said to know important details about the conspirators. Finally, Onís recommended that the Junta appoint a vice consul for the city due to the "immense frontier" it commanded.[41]

In his letter to Moxó, Bernabeu wrote that an "excellent" Spaniard who had recently traveled from New Orleans to Baltimore had provided the Spanish legation with a disturbing description of the political climate in Louisiana. From these discussions, the consul understood that the region served as refuge for many discontented Frenchmen who had been exiled from Cuba and now "were breathing vengeance against us." In addition, New Orleans swarmed with "infinite partisans of Napoleon . . . who long for a favorable opportunity, which they patiently await, to achieve their projects against the kingdom of New Spain." To counter these threats, Bernabeu asked Moxó to shed as much light as possible on "any attack against any of our colonies from those Franco-Americans, or other malcontents who are found there or who are in league with the traitors or false Spaniards who might hide among our own people." He also had more specific requests: How many expelled Frenchmen from Spanish lands live in New Orleans? What is the attitude of the Louisiana French regarding the war between France and Spain? What do the local US civil and military authorities think about the war? What are the current opinions among the wider Anglo-American community? Where are US forces located? What is their state of readiness? How popular would a war with Spain be in Louisiana? How many Spaniards live there? What are their politics? And, finally, "What is Cevallos, the Escapee from Veracruz, doing there? Is it known whether he has become a conspirator? Are there meetings of malcontents at his home? Does he get money from Mexico or elsewhere? A succinct account of the public and private life of this Cevallos would be greatly appreciated . . . along with a list of all the suspicious people you know."[42]

Broadly speaking, for Onís and Bernabeu the state of affairs in Louisiana was a major source of anxiety, considering the background of its population, their likely pro-French sentiments, the frontier nature of its settlements, and the proximity of the territory to Spanish colonies. In his correspondence with Secretary Smith, the Baltimore consul emphasized that any reunion in New Orleans of insurgents with designs on the Spanish colonies would also call into question the neutrality of the United States. "These revolutionaries have agents all along the border, through whom they have established correspondence with others in Mexico City and Veracruz; but the center of their machinations is New Orleans, where they attempt to win converts from among the American citizens there, as well as the Frenchmen expelled from the Spanish colonies."[43] From this perspective, with the fate of Spanish America and the United States inextricably linked, the failure of the Madison administration to recognize Onís gave free reign to conspiracies against Spanish interests, thereby severely compromising "the peace and tranquility of both countries."[44]

At the same time, the Spanish legation also considered the mysterious outfitting of the ships in New York harbor to be a violation of neutrality. Supplementing earlier reports, Bernabeu provided Smith with more complete details about the vessels in correspondence from the end of November. According to his sources, the thirty-six-gun frigate had originally been English before being captured by the French and then sold to an American merchant in Buenos Aires, who brought it to New York in 1807 under the name the *American Eagle*. Here, ownership was transferred to a Savannah merchant who was "well known as an agent of the French government or of the mulato Petion in Santo Domingo." Bernabeu presumed that the warships were headed to the Caribbean on a mission designed to damage Spanish commercial interests, though he also suggested that they might even link up with the "traitor" Miranda on another assault against the colonies. He asked Smith to bring these matters before President Madison in the hopes that the administration would take appropriate action. Otherwise, Spain would have no choice but to blame the United States for any negative consequences resulting from conspiracies launched on American soil, whether they happened to be undertaken by France or "any particular individual of this or another foreign power."[45]

Smith responded that the United States would not engage in private political negotiations with Onís. If, however, credible evidence were passed to American authorities, the secretary stated that the administration would work to undermine any legitimate threats to Spanish interests.[46] Onís found this reaction insufficient and took out his frustration on Bernabeu for being weak with Smith and for failing to stay in the capital long enough to recruit congressional support for the Spanish cause.[47] In the event, he did not have long to dwell on this particular setback. On December 5, Onís wrote to Spain that he had just received word that a French warship, the *Tilsit*, had recently docked in Norfolk before continuing on to Baltimore. According to his sources, the vessel carried a diplomatic agent from Joseph Napoleon to the United States. For the moment, this individual remained undercover. However, Onís promised to do everything possible to find out more information. As it turned out, this particular hunt would consume him personally and professionally for all of 1810. In the process it evolved into a broader campaign against French intervention in Spanish America that would reverberate across the empire over the next two years.[48]

4

The Spanish Diplomat versus the French Emissary, 1809–1810

> The amount of energy spent by the Emissaries of Napoleon on traveling in secret to our Americas is incalculable. In this city [Philadelphia] and in Baltimore there are swarms of them, among whom may be counted women and a large number of the emigrants from our Possessions who speak Castilian, and they attempt by every possible means to elude the vigilance of the king's officials in those colonies.
>
> —Luís de Onís to Enrique White, Philadelphia, February 16, 1810

By the end of November 1809, it was clear that nearly two months of informal negotiations by Onís and his associates, as well as public and private pressure from the friends and allies of Spain's loyalist government, had failed to convince President Madison to reconsider his decision not to recognize the Junta Central or, by extension, its accredited representative. If the Spanish ambassador was inclined to brood about this diplomatic impasse, events soon provided an effective distraction. During the first week of December, vague concerns regarding the possibility of French subversive activity against Spanish America suddenly came into focus with the arrival in the United States of the *Tilsit*. As Onís's network of informants fanned out across Norfolk and Baltimore seeking more concrete information about this mysterious vessel and its passengers, the nature of the threat became apparent: "Initially it was said that [the ship] had come only to deliver various documents to the minister of France in these States, but later it was learned that an emissary or envoy of the *intruso* Joseph Napoleon had come aboard, that he remained hidden in order to more efficiently carry out the secret commissions entrusted to him, and that his primary objective was directed against the peace and tranquility of the most loyal colonies of His Majesty Fernando VII in this part of the world."[1]

Identifying this shadowy figure was the first challenge. By the end of the month, sources agreed that the French agent in question was in fact the ship's captain, Joseph Desmolard.[2] Their information also suggested the outlines of a major French operation against the Spanish colonies. According to reports, Desmolard carried with him a number of decrees, proclamations, and other seditious papers in the names of both Joseph Bonaparte and Fernando. He was believed to have engaged certain "subaltern agents," some of whom had arrived on the *Tilsit*, who were tasked with the responsibility for distributing this propaganda across Spanish America. Onís warned, "These emissaries will then embark from Norfolk, or some other port in these States, in order to infiltrate our colonies, with the intention of launching their plans for unrest. I have been assured that they will begin in Havana, where it is said that the French have many supporters, and from there they will continue to Veracruz, Caracas, etc., as best suits their plans." Hoping to head off the operation, Onís had already enlisted the Spanish consul in Norfolk in an effort to identify the subalterns. He also declared that he was working diligently with Bernabeu to see if the Baltimore consul could confiscate the publications held by Desmolard, who had set himself up as "Joseph's ambassador" in an ostentatious house in that city after withdrawing significant funds from a Philadelphia bank. Finally, recognizing the importance of these disturbing reports and "despite the poverty in which I find myself for lack of resources," Onís decided to purchase a schooner to deliver the necessary warnings to Havana and Veracruz.[3]

With this looming threat to the Spanish colonies now his top priority, Onís continued his investigations. One week after his first report to Spain regarding Desmolard, he learned that the French emissary had already managed to place three agents into the field, each aspiring to reach Spanish America. Two, it appeared, had traveled toward New England in the hopes of finding passage to the colonies via one of the northern ports, while the third intended to depart from a southern city. Lacking names at this stage, Onís did have some rather specific physical descriptions of two of the men: "One is Basque, approximately forty years old, of normal stature, though a bit more heavy than thin, with a short round face, pockmarked, a large mouth, and blond hair cut like Brutus; the other is Catalan, between twenty-four and twenty-six years old, normal stature, with short black hair, a long, sharp face, and a dark complexion; the first has been seen recently on the streets of Baltimore, while the second has been gone for a few days, and I think it probable that he is one of those who has left to carry out the plan." This information immediately went out to the viceroy of New Spain and the captain general of Cuba. Onís promised to notify the other colonial officials as soon as possible and provide them with instructions on how to combat the threat. "I will also charge the American authorities to take the greatest care with the ships that come into port, checking to see if they have a passport from me or from one of the consuls of their respective districts; I will ensure that the authorities regard as suspicious anyone who presents himself without such papers and that they even take care to examine the papers of the crew so as to avoid the French emissaries who might want to introduce themselves in unfamiliar dress."[4]

Another break in the case came by the third week of January. Now, Onís could report to his superiors that one of the suspected emissaries who had traveled on the *Tilsit* was a resident of Buenos Aires named Santiago Antonini.[5] This man, an Italian native, had called on the Spanish ambassador, "affecting the most profound patriotism, stating that he recently escaped from Madrid and hoped to return to Buenos Aires at the first opportunity." Antonini requested a passport from Consul Bernabeu but was refused due to conduct described by Onís as "very mysterious and suspicious." When asked why he did not bring a passport from Spain, Antonini responded that he was simply returning home, and "that a passport was only necessary for the sea, not for presentation in Buenos Aires where he had his family and where everyone knew him." Other questions "visibly upset him," whereupon he left the consulate. Not surprisingly, Onís made sure that Antonini was carefully watched in the days that followed. According to Spanish informants, Antonini met with Desmolard during his visit to Baltimore. He was overheard speaking "enthusiastically about the *great* Napoleon and abominably about the Bourbon royal family." One of Onís's spies reported that Antonini told him that he was travelling to France on the return voyage of the *Tilsit*. His luggage was in fact loaded on board but then was transferred to an American ship, the *Fly*, headed to Buenos Aires.[6]

Onís could also claim at this point that there were at least fifty subalterns in the United States who intended to travel to different parts of Spanish America with "proclamations and other papers to seduce the patriots and form a pro-Bonaparte party." The Spanish ambassador reported that these agents would pretend to be loyal to Fernando and speak badly of Napoleon and Joseph, but in fact they would provide valuable intelligence to the emperor. Their information would then be used to prepare "two or three expeditions" against the most propitious American targets. In response, Onís noted that he had already dispatched warnings to all colonial officials "so that they remain vigilant." The viceroy in Buenos Aires received a more specific directive to watch for the *Fly* and "take control of the person and papers of Antonini," for this was where "the thread of conspiracy that Bonaparte has laid against the colonies of the king" could be found.[7]

By the end of January 1810, Onís was feeling besieged on all sides. Not surprisingly, he began to draw connections between the policy of the US government toward loyalist Spain and the burgeoning threat to the colonies from French emissaries. In his dispatches to the new loyalist secretario de estado, Francisco de Saavedra, he noted that the French ambassador, General Turreau, was working diligently to buy American support for Napoleon's foreign agenda, arguing that Madison had effectively sold himself to France already. Onís also suggested that the ease with which American merchant ships entered colonial ports severely compromised the security of Spanish America. "I cannot . . . help but repeat that since this country is the point of departure for all the emissaries who seek to spread themselves across our Americas and since their machinations (I have no doubt) are encouraged by this administration, whose chief, Madison, is the worst enemy we have and the most fervent supporter or ally of his oracle Bonaparte . . . there is scarcely a ship that leaves these ports for our possessions that does not carry on board emissaries of Joseph Napoleon."[8]

He elaborated on this theme in a letter to Governor White in East Florida. What Onís found most disturbing about US commercial policy was the fact that American merchants rarely sought permits from Spanish consuls to do business with the Spanish possessions. Passengers on these vessels also neglected to obtain passports from him or Spain's consular representatives in the United States. Onís argued that the only solution was to close ports to uncertified ships and punish undocumented travelers who sought access to the colonies. Of course, agents of Napoleon would be subject to the ultimate punishment, execution, as an example to others. Limited in his own authority, Onís decided to publish notices in newspapers informing Americans that travel to Spanish territory required written authorization from Spain's ambassador.[9]

Two months after the appearance in Norfolk of the *Tilsit*, Onís seemed to have a clearer image of the French conspiracy unfolding around him. Reviewing old information and incorporating new reports from his own agents in the field, the Spanish ambassador painted a picture of an operation funded and directed from Baltimore by Desmolard. In addition to Joseph's principal agent and Santiago Antonini, four other "directors" had also arrived in the United States on the *Tilsit*. According to Onís:

> Two of these emissaries, I am assured, are Spaniards, but they speak and write fluently in French, English, and Italian in order to more easily carry out their duties; one, named Ferrera, has departed from Norfolk on the *Tilsit*, the other, who is called Juan Montero, has left for Saint Barthélemy; the third is Italian, though he speaks French and Spanish, and is known as Formento; the fourth is a Frenchman, but he speaks Castilian extremely well. Formento has recently left from Norfolk, while the Frenchman departed from Baltimore on the schooner *Carolina*, which was bought for the purpose by the supposed ambassador of Mr. Joseph Desmolard, without indicating his destination, without having his papers examined by Customs or undergoing any other formality besides stating that he was taking papers from the minister of France to Guadeloupe.

These emissaries each had orders to proceed to four different parts of Spanish America: the Río de la Plata, Peru or Quito, Venezuela, and Panama or Honduras. Upon arrival, they would link up with their respective associates, distribute materials and coordinate plans for subversion.[10]

There were others. A Monsieur de Pavajot, identified as a creole resident of San Marcos on the island of Hispaniola, was tentatively identified as a subaltern agent. Onís believed this individual had departed for Saint Barthélemy with the intention of continuing on to Jamaica in the guise of a Spanish or American merchant. Once there, he would launch a revolution on the island by sparking a rebellion within the slave population. This Haitian model of subversion was supposedly being followed by other emissaries, many of whom had already left the United States for Havana with the hopes of using Cuba as a springboard for other destinations across Spanish America. Sources suggested that these agents traveled in disguise, as sailors, cooks, boatswains, or merchants, "whatever was most convenient in eluding the vigilance of the authorities." Onís also isolated as a possible emissary a Monsieur de Battelier. This man, who had served as a forest inspector in France, now found himself in Baltimore in the close company of Desmolard. Battelier was suspected of preparing an expedition against Amelia Island, a strategic commercial outpost on the border between Georgia and East Florida. All indications suggested that the attack would be launched from either Guadeloupe or Saint Barthélemy and would threaten Spanish control over Florida. Onís warned Governor White that even his small colony was a part of Napoleon's grand designs, that Charleston was overrun with French agents ready to move on the Floridas, and that the only precaution against the threat was scrupulous surveillance of all travelers in the region.[11]

The day after his letter to White, Onís penned another to Vicente de Emparán, the captain general of Venezuela. While his recent correspondence with Minister Saavedra in Spain and Governor White in Florida expressed a high level of frustration with the US government over its failure to contain the French emissaries on its soil, this latest dispatch focused almost exclusively on the American administration and suggested that the ambassador's sense of impotence in the face of three months of diplomatic isolation had begun to take a toll. Onís saw signs of French manipulation everywhere in Washington. This was not new, as he had long presumed Madison's prostration before "their oracle Bonaparte." What seemed different now was the level of contempt directed at loyalist Spain by American politicians. In one notorious case, Treasury Secretary Albert Gallatin mistook the visiting José González, a former intendant of the Peruvian province of Puno, for a French agent. The secretary then offered to supply the Spaniard with writings from Paine and other advocates of political liberty. González, who had recently traveled through Cuba and Mexico, was asked if he would return to these colonies and "induce them to unite themselves to this Republic." More publically, Virginia representative John Wayles Eppes, the son-in-law of former president Jefferson, had recently introduced a measure in the House encouraging Madison to send an ambassador to Joseph Bonaparte. While the vote failed, the debate provided an opportunity for opponents of Spain to disparage the Junta Central and applaud the administration for refusing to receive Onís.[12]

As a result, Onís argued to Emparán that the American government was so much in the thrall of Napoleon that it could not be dealt with except "by energy, by force, and by chastisement." He hoped that England would be willing to take on this responsibility and suggested that a small military operation directed against Louisiana would result in the fragmentation of the United States into "two or three Republics." In this scenario, the theoretical northern republic would align itself with Spain, while the two southern rump states would find themselves in such conflict with each other that they would be in no position to threaten Spanish interests. If Onís gained some small comfort in hypothesizing the dismemberment of his host nation, the Madison administration was not nearly as pleased. At some point, American agents intercepted this letter. One year later, Madison submitted it to Congress as evidence of the treachery and duplicity of the unrecognized Spanish ambassador.[13]

In the meantime, Onís continued his desperate campaign to hunt down the Napoleonic emissaries. In a follow-up letter to White, the ambassador repeated his concerns about French agents using American ships to penetrate Spanish America and reiterated his belief that the only effective response were the requirements that all foreign vessels carry current documentation, that all travelers carry approved passports, that all passengers and crew receive careful scrutiny from port officials, and that anyone caught breaking the laws receive swift and public justice, including capital punishment. As an example of the extreme measures taken by emissaries to evade Spanish defenses, Onís reported on a case from New York that had recently come to his attention:

> Captain Joseph Fellows of the *Mary*, destined for Havana, has disembarked his passengers, one of whom is a native of the island of Santo Domingo; before legalizing his papers the captain went before a notary public to declare that he no longer had any passengers on board. The cited individual has twice been to the Consulate in New York with a document made in Havana in February 1809, that

> gives his name as Rombeau, age forty-five years. He told the consul that he had traveled without a passport from there to Newport and that he was a carpenter. He wanted to pass for a Spaniard, but although he spoke Castilian quite well he had a bit of a foreign accent. His appearance suggests he has been well educated, and he is travelling with two trunks and a bed. The consul managed to learn what he could, and it turns out that this individual was seen in Bayonne dressed as a soldier the previous July. He carries with him a great deal of money, he lives in a quiet house on a narrow street, and the document he presented to the consul had been obtained from a mulato in Santo Domingo. What remains to be learned is the port he left from in Europe, the ship he traveled on, and his entry point in these States, although by all appearances we can presume he arrived on the *Tilsit*.

Onís considered this a successful outcome since the actions of Captain Fellows prevented Rombeau from continuing on to Havana. The ambassador believed that the warnings he published in American newspapers regarding the new travel requirements for Spanish America struck sufficient "terror" in the captain that the subversive operation collapsed. He hoped that similar "repeated lessons from our colonies will increase the fear of the Americans and the agents, and by this easy method we will see the pretentions of Bonaparte fade away."[14]

Onís added more names to his list of subversives during the first week of February. He informed Saavedra that one of the emissaries was a Monsieur Duclos, a Frenchman who had served in the Spanish navy under Carlos IV and now held the rank of post captain under Joseph. Some sources suggested that this agent might have taken passage for Buenos Aires with Santiago Antonini. Another suspect was a Spanish-born army lieutenant named Alemán. Both "are particularly scheming and skillful, they have nothing to lose, and they are certainly quite capable of undertaking any risky endeavor." There was also additional information about a follower of Viceroy Liniers, one La Croiseé, who, according to rumors, was known in Buenos Aires as St. Croix and who had been an implacable enemy of the British since his daughter ran off with an officer attached to the invading army of General William Beresford in 1806. All these men were carrying false proclamations from Fernando VII in which the king urged Spain and its colonies to submit to Joseph and embrace Napoleon "in spirit and heart" to help ensure world peace.[15]

Onís already viewed the prolific American commerce with Spanish America as a major security risk, noting on multiple occasions in his correspondence with other imperial officials the ease with which a French agent could take passage to the colonies on one of the many ships departing from the Atlantic ports for the Caribbean or the Gulf of Mexico. Until now, he had presumed that the emissaries would simply disguise themselves, either as merchants, simple travelers, or even as crew members, an act of obfuscation that the American authorities appeared unwilling to investigate, much less prosecute. Now, Onís learned of two more tools at the disposal of his enemies. On February 16, the ambassador warned Governor White that the Napoleonic emissaries were seeking to naturalize themselves as Americans to avoid detection. He also learned from a reliable source that they sought to acquire one of his official passports, along with his signature, in order to create passable facsimiles of the new travel authorizations required for passage to Spanish America. In response, Onís warned White to consider as suspect anyone arriving in East Florida who received US citizenship after November 1809, in effect the date of the *Tilsit*'s arrival. As an additional precaution, he also declared that in the future all his passports would be countersigned by the legation secretary, Felipe Fatio. All documents lacking these two signatures "shall be considered fake, and those in possession of them shall be regarded as spies or French agents."[16]

From a legal perspective, the evidence to this date regarding the presence of Napoleonic emissaries in the United States, as well as speculation concerning the nature of their operations and their intentions toward Spanish America, could be considered circumstantial. Since November 1809, Spanish informants had provided Onís with a long list of suspicious characters and questionable activities. There was every reason to believe that the government of Joseph Bonaparte, as it fought to consolidate its position in Spain, also sought to win support and destabilize the loyalist cause in the Americas. Emissaries, whether they were sent by him or his brother, Napoleon, were a time-tested and logical means of gathering intelligence and influencing public opinion. Yet, for Onís, two months of intensive investigations produced a picture of French subversive activity that did not truly come into sharp focus until Francisco Peredo presented himself at the legation offices in Philadelphia during the second week of February 1810.

In an extended dispatch to Saavedra, Onís described how careful undercover work by Peredo had placed the entirety of Napoleon's "Machiavellian" plan in the hands of the Spanish ambassador before the end of February.[17] Onís reported that he had first learned about this young man shortly after arriving in New York City early in October. Seeking relief from his misfortunes, Peredo had written the new ambassador from a nearby debtor's prison. Onís delegated the case to the Spanish consul in New York and then continued on his journey to Washington, DC.

Whether because of consular intervention on his behalf or simply because he had completed his sentence, Peredo appeared in Philadelphia early in February convinced that he owed his freedom to the work of the Spanish legation. By this time, Onís had done some background research on the man. According to his sources, Peredo was either a Spanish or a Portuguese subject and had once served in the role of secretary to the bishop of Charcas, a possible relation. Years earlier, while abroad on a commission from this prelate, he was captured by the English. In the summer of 1808, Peredo found his way to the United States, where with few resources at his disposal he became active in Spanish politics. Apparently on his own initiative, Peredo proceeded to devise a scheme to raise funds to send foreign soldiers to Spain to fight for the loyalist cause. This project, which managed to raise fifteen thousand pesos and attract one hundred fifty men, ultimately collapsed because Peredo could not provide enough security for an advance on the pledged subscriptions. In short order he found himself in the New York prison, where he languished in obscurity for a year.[18]

Having now won his freedom, Peredo asked Onís for a letter of recommendation to the archbishop of Baltimore. It was his intention, he explained, to fulfill his dream of a priestly vocation and take orders there. At this point in their conversation, Onís became concerned that Desmolard would seek to recruit this unattached, adventurous, and impoverished Spanish American. To prevent such an outcome, Onís decided to see if Peredo would agree to work on behalf of the Spanish legation as an undercover agent. The ambassador told the young man that there was a French emissary in Baltimore who would likely attempt to enlist him in his plots against the Spanish colonies. Falling in with Desmolard, Onís warned, would be a fatal mistake, because Spanish authorities were on the lookout for these French subversives. However, someone with Peredo's talent, ingenuity, and patriotism could do a great service for his country by pretending to be one of King Joseph's partisans. If Peredo could gain Desmolard's trust, learn the details of his operations, and report back to the Spanish legation, Onís promised to provide a decent compensation in return. He also made it clear that honors and rewards would come from Spain as well. According to the ambassador's report, Peredo enthusiastically agreed to the plan.[19]

After providing his new agent with some start-up funds, Onís sent Peredo off to Baltimore. Within a short time, the ambassador's wildest dreams had come true. Onís informed Saavedra that Peredo had ingratiated himself with Desmolard to such a degree that the emissary had entrusted him with the plans for subversion and the list of agents.[20] The French envoy was particularly interested in Peredo's firsthand knowledge of the different colonies and asked for his opinion on where to station the emissaries to achieve the desired outcomes. Desmolard then provided his new recruit with a copy of what soon circulated around the Spanish bureaucracy as "The Instructions given by the Usurper Joseph Napoleon to his Commissioner or Principal Agent in Baltimore Mr Desmolard, and to the others who have travelled by his orders to Spanish America with the goal of inciting them to rebellion."[21]

Through Peredo's work, the list of agents and the Desmolard Instructions found their way into the hands of Onís. On February 24, the Spanish ambassador sent the French documents and his report to the Junta Central. Waiting for a response from Spain, however, was dangerous, considering the many obstacles to rapid and effective correspondence with the metropolis. A note, in fact, acknowledged the receipt of this material in Cádiz on June 19. Orders quickly followed mandating that the Instructions and list of emissaries be printed and distributed to all the viceroys and governors in Spanish America, a task Onís had already undertaken. Scarcely twenty-four hours after dispatching the documents to Saavedra, the ambassador sent other copies to Enrique White in St. Augustine.[22] And he did not stop there. As Onís explained to his son, "I have had the pleasure to discover Bonaparte's plan to revolutionize our Americas, the instructions given to his agents and conspirators, the list of their names, and a printed proclamation from Uncle Joseph. I have sent Feliz to bring it to Court; I have dispatched Rafael to Havana and a certain Pereyra to Mexico; the vice-consul of Charleston, Fatio, has gone to Buenos Aires and a pilot of the Royal Navy has gone to Caracas . . . I have sent the same notices to Río de Janeiro, Lima, Guatemala, Santa Fe, Campeche, Quito, Chile, and other important locations."[23] As a result, by May all the Spanish colonial governors as far south as Venezuela were in possession of the Desmolard Instructions.

In his report to Saavedra, the Spanish ambassador made sure to summarize the pertinent details.[24] A careful reading of the documents convinced Onís that Napoleon had concluded that Spanish America would never recognize Joseph as the king of Spain. As a result, France had altered its plans and now sought to induce the colonies to seek independence, dangling before them inducements such as military protection, industrial and agricultural development, and support for the establishment of constitutional government. Of course, what Napoleon wanted above all else was to cut off the flow of American treasure that kept the loyalist cause in Spain alive. Independence under these circumstances would have the added benefit for France of eliminating British influence in the region. To achieve this goal, the emperor had sent more than five hundred agents to Spanish America, all with orders to shift public opinion toward favoring a break with Spain. Particular targets for bribery, if possible, and assassination, if necessary, were provincial governors and intendants. The Instructions also emphasized the importance of winning over military officers and members of the regular clergy. The latter group would be helpful to the French cause in the confessional if they could convince their charges that God had decided to use Napoleon to free them from tyranny and that it would be a mortal sin to resist his divinely inspired plans.[25]

Onís followed this brief summary with a reference to the list of emissaries. He was convinced of its accuracy but admitted that he could not swear to every single word, since Peredo had copied it in great haste. Still, he stated that the information matched reports from other sources. As much as possible, this list confirmed the threats that the ambassador had been collecting in piecemeal fashion over the previous two months. Forty-one French agents were identified by name, not including the already well-known Antonini, Lacroissé, and Duclos, while twenty-eight more remained anonymous. The vast majority of these men were peninsular Spaniards, plus a few creoles and a small number of foreigners. Most were in the Caribbean Basin, with nearly thirty operating across the various islands there, including twelve out of Cuba. New Spain, alone, was the base for fourteen agents, while the Kingdom of Guatemala had four. South America was divided among eleven designated emissaries, including four in Peru, three in New Granada, and one each in Chile, Buenos Aires, and Venezuela. Others worked out of cities in the United States, including Charleston and New Orleans. In all, including Desmolard, Onís could now provide his superiors with reasonable evidence of the identities, location, and activities of more than seventy Napoleonic emissaries.

Onís sent these documents to Spain via a trustworthy courier, that is, someone who was not American. He told Saavedra that he could trust no one from his host country, as Napoleonic agents were spreading gold everywhere to buy informants. He also feared, correctly, as it turned out, that the American government was reading his correspondence. Still, he could take some comfort in the fact that his actions had disrupted Desmolard's plans. Onís noted with pride that his public writings and private conversations had also exposed the administration's dangerous partiality for France. This, he declared, had even reached the point that Madison was looking for a way to demonstrate his fealty to Napoleon by transforming the United States into a monarchy for the son of the king of Westphalia.[26]

Onís also reported that the Federalists had begun publicly protesting against the purported links between the Madison administration and France. He noted that their partisans had even raised a toast to the Spanish patriots at a celebration in honor of George Washington's birthday. According to Onís, the Federalists had seized on one particular rumor that

Napoleon was angling not only to foment rebellion in Spanish America but also to retake Louisiana. The ambassador concluded that a declaration of war against England would cause New York, Massachusetts, Connecticut, Rhode Island, New Jersey, and Delaware to secede from the union, a possibility he believed was the only thing keeping Madison from a formal alliance with France.

With the information acquired from Desmolard's house, Onís seized a rare opportunity to take the offensive in his campaign against the Napoleonic emissaries. Isolated in Philadelphia and prevented from exercising his diplomatic responsibilities by an effectively hostile American administration, the Spanish minister now busied himself with colonial defense. Unable to draw on Spain for funds, Onís learned with relief early in 1810 that the authorities in New Spain had agreed to recognize him as the king's minister. On a practical level, this meant that Mexico City would pay his expenses.[27] With few other means at his disposal, he also turned for support to Francis Jackson, the British minister-plenipotentiary. As the representative of loyalist Spain's only ally, Jackson could be relied to engage the significant resources of Great Britain, in particular the Royal Navy, in the fight against French subversion. An example of a notable success in this common struggle was the capture off Bermuda of the *Fly* by the eighteen-gun sloop HMS *Atalante*. Onís had informed Jackson of the departure of this vessel at the same time he broadcast his warnings to Spanish colonial officials, and he could now exult in the seizure of the emissaries it transported.[28] The ambassador then asked his British counterpart to help track down three suspected agents who were reported to be in the Caribbean: Antonio Bonavita, Juan Tineo, and Ventura Cabrera.[29]

While he remained in Baltimore, Peredo continued to update the Spanish legation. Through his informant, Onís learned that Desmolard was receiving optimistic reports from Antonio Rentería, the rumored head of the French operations in Mexico City. It also appeared that Desmolard had commissioned an account of recent events in Spanish America, which Onís described as a "pastiche of slanders against our Government and Religion promising a happy ending to the campaigns of Joseph," from a Baltimore resident named Luís Rodríguez. A letter from Joseph, dated December 23, 1809, then arrived for Desmolard. Peredo reported that the correspondence informed the French emissary that a new recruit, Ramón Vasco, would be travelling through the United States before embarking for Panama. In addition, it provided optimistic reports regarding Joseph's position in Spain, a spurious decree permitting French emigrants to return to Cuba, and an announcement that one hundred fifty French officers, including a decorated general, were en route to New Orleans. Onís believed that these officers might possibly take over Louisiana and avail themselves of the significant French population there to establish a forward base of operations before marching into Spanish America.[30]

During this tense period, the correspondence flowing from the Spanish legation headquarters in Philadelphia to Spanish colonial officials was dominated by the names of suspected Napoleonic agents. In early March Onís warned Governor White that Juan Tineo had left Charleston in the direction of Savannah and, possibly, Florida, with an ultimate destination of New Orleans or Nassau. He added that there was already a likely emissary in the Bahamas by the name of Ventura Galzevan (aka Cabrera). Furthermore, Onís now placed Antonio Bonavita on the island of St. Thomas. This latter person of interest, reportedly Corsican by birth, had been the parish priest of Yecapixtla in central Mexico before fleeing New Spain in 1808. Onís's sources traced him to the United States and then to Puerto Rico, where he was briefly held by local authorities before finally finding refuge in St. Thomas. His description was clear: "forty years old, thin, olive skinned, with black eyes, and a close beard; he speaks French and Italian and normally dresses in Mexico like a muleskinner."[31]

Onís also informed White that Fermín Esparragosa, the emissary sent to Trujillo, Honduras, had died. Napoleon's chief envoy in Guatemala had apparently found a replacement, but the name of that individual remained unknown. Closer to home, the Spanish ambassador suggested that the Gulf coast faced a new threat from the marqués de Casa Calvo, Sebastián Calvo de la Puerta y O'Farrill. This Cuban-born nobleman had a distinguished career in the Spanish colonial bureaucracy. He had served as the interim governor of Louisiana from 1799 to 1801 and, in the wake of the American acquisition of the territory, as a border commissioner charged with protecting Spanish interests along the new line separating the remaining Spanish possessions from the United States.[32] Following his return to Spain, Casa Calvo threw his support behind Joseph and received from the rey intruso a commission as lieutenant general. Now, Onís expected the marquis to descend upon the Gulf at any moment and use his many contacts there to launch an expedition against Texas. It was even rumored that this operation would be coordinated with an invasion of the Mexican coast somewhere between Tampico and Veracruz led by Vice Admiral José de Mazarredo Salazar, another significant Spanish convert to Joseph's cause.[33]

By March, the outlines of Napoleon's effort to subvert Spanish America had crystalized. As Onís understood it, hundreds of the emperor's agents had deployed across the region since the summer of 1808. The campaign appeared highly decentralized in its earliest manifestations, relying heavily on freelance operatives charged with a vague mission that was effectively limited to winning colonial support for Joseph Bonaparte's regime. At some point in 1809, however, the French imposed a command structure and developed a specific plan of operations for their network of emissaries. Agents now received orders and funding from a designated chief envoy, Joseph Desmolard, who supervised his subordinates from Baltimore in concert with Ambassador Turreau. The new strategy divided the Spanish colonies into four sections, each with a local *diputado en jefe* (chief deputy) who directed a number of subalterns. Their instructions made it clear that their primary goal was to incite rebellion among Spanish subjects. Onís had reason to believe that these internal acts of subversion would be reinforced by French military campaigns against the Spanish possessions in the Americas. Finally, he was convinced that the United States would provide Napoleon with both active and passive support for these schemes.

Drawing a clear distinction between the interests of Emperor Napoleon and those of King Joseph was not a priority for the Spanish ambassador at this time, nor would he have considered it reasonable to separate the two. All French-inspired acts that sought to undermine both the Bourbon right to the Spanish throne and the integrity of the Spanish empire could be seen as part of the same Bonapartist conspiracy that had sprouted in May 1808. As a result, when Onís acquired copies of two new proclamations from Joseph, he interpreted them as simply a public manifestation of the largely undercover subversive activities that had kept him busy for three months. The first, dated October 2, 1809, which was addressed to the "Spaniards of my Possessions in America," appeared to be the latest attempt by the rey intruso to convince Spanish Americans that the Bourbons had voluntarily ceded their rights to Napoleon.[34] Joseph warned that continued resistance to the new dynasty by the loyalist resistance would be both futile and disastrous. "If, against my hopes, you persist in your error, I will punish you like rebellious children; and the exemplary punishments that I will impose on the heads of the rebellion will be so severe that the most intrepid will tremble; but if you submit tranquilly to the cause of justice and reason, I will reward you as you deserve."[35]

The second proclamation, dated only one day after the first, specifically targeted the Spanish American clergy, who were asked to bring "their respective sheep to submission." In Onís's mind, this document was of particular concern, because it viewed the religious faith of the people as a potential point of weakness, asserting that those who failed in their duty to Joseph opposed the will of God and, therefore, placed their souls in mortal danger. Opportunistically, the Bonapartes sought to manipulate the traditional understanding of the divine right of kings for their own purposes.

As the second proclamation declared, God sent Napoleon and Joseph "to regenerate the Spanish nation and ensure its happiness."[36]

According to the Spanish ambassador, this assertion had broad and dangerous implications. Not only did it threaten the ruin of the state "but also the total subversion of our sainted Religion." Ultimately, as Onís explained in a letter to White, both proclamations deserved "serious attention" for they demonstrated the intensive nature of Joseph's propaganda campaign in the Americas and the authenticity of the Desmolard Instructions.[37] Onís subsequently learned that a new agent, Francisco Belmont, had departed Bordeaux with orders to enter New Spain "with the goal of inciting rebellion or seducing the inhabitants to support Joseph."[38] All the evidence at this time suggested to him that the French subversive operations against Spanish America would continue to expand in size and scale.

The curtain descended on this intense first phase in the campaign against Napoleonic emissaries in the spring of 1810. By this point, the top priority for the Spanish legation was tracking the emissaries its sources had identified. At the end of April, Onís noted in a letter to Saavedra that Santiago Antonini had made his way to New York. He did not know how the emissary had escaped British custody, but he was convinced that the Italian would make another attempt to reach Buenos Aires, perhaps through Brazil.[39] More dramatically, within a couple of weeks, Onís reported that Desmolard himself had disappeared from Baltimore. In short order, Joseph's envoy, too, was traced to New York, where he apparently found passage on a ship bound for France.[40] If this development suggested to Onís that the French operations in the United States had been disrupted, the Spanish ambassador did not have much time to gloat. Desmolard might have returned to Europe, but reports of subversive activity continued to arrive in Philadelphia over the summer of 1810. More problematically, other disturbing news from South America at this time indicated that Napoleon's operatives had finally managed to seduce a colony into open rebellion.

Ironically, the April uprising in Caracas was conceived by the local elite as a preventative measure against the threat of French domination. Reports of the fall of the Junta Central in January had recently arrived in the city. Everything suggested that peninsular resistance to Joseph was in its last days, and many in Caracas accused their Spanish governor of hiding pro-French sentiments. Therefore, on April 19, the town council voted to replace Captain General Emparán with a governing junta, the Junta Suprema

Conservadora de los Derechos de Fernando VII, which promised to preserve the colony for the deposed king. In the minds of the upstart rulers of Caracas, the Council of Regency, which Spanish loyalists had recently established in place of the Junta Central, was illegitimate. Thus, the overthrow of the captain general could be justified as a conservative act, fully in line with peninsular precedents.[41]

Of course, Onís was only one of many in Spanish America who did not interpret the news from Venezuela as a display of loyalty to Fernando. Instead, the establishment of an American governing junta was broadly interpreted as the first significant (and successful) sign of rebellion in the colonies since the summer of 1808. Onís was convinced that the uprising was all part of Napoleon's "Machiavellian plan" and that its leaders, who were a small group of "ambitious individuals seduced by France," had managed to deceive the populace with false reports from Europe.[42] Of more immediate concern for him was the reaction from the United States. In July, the Spanish ambassador reported to the new secretario de estado, Eusebio Bardají, that the Madison administration had decided to appoint Robert K. Lowry as its representative in La Guaira, Venezuela's principal port city. Onís believed that this young and fiery Democrat was more than capable of fomenting and leading a revolution there. He added that sources had informed him that Lowry was making copies of revolutionary instruction manuals. Furthermore, Onís considered it probable that the new American consul possessed orders from France. He could see no reason why Lowry might not become a conduit for the subversion of "all of our American possessions," or why the US government would not encourage its representative to serve Napoleon's interests.[43]

Determined to issue a formal complaint about Lowry to the US government, Onís was forced to work through his consul in Baltimore. Thus, Bernabeu wrote to Secretary Smith on July 17 that the appointment of an American "commercial agent" in the colonies was contrary to Spanish law. Moreover, since this province was in a state of insurrection, such a nomination could easily be misinterpreted as a form of diplomatic recognition of the Caracas junta. The consul took the opportunity to underscore the continued unity of the empire in the face of the efforts of Napoleon to subvert it, arguing that every territory within the Spanish monarchy except for "a small part of the province of Caracas" had recognized the legitimacy of the Council of Regency. Unfortunately, having raised the topic, he also was compelled to ask Smith again for an official American response to the establishment of the Regency, news which Bernabeu had sent to the US government more than a month earlier. With diplomatic relations effectively frozen and with Onís persona non grata, the Spanish legation found no satisfaction from the Madison administration on this or any other issue of concern at the time.[44]

In the meantime, Diego Morphy sent word to Onís that a Monsieur Lestique had recently arrived in New Orleans from Philadelphia. Sources indicated that Lestique had travelled to the United States from Bordeaux on the American frigate *Lovely Matilda*. Once established in New Orleans he was overheard stating that he was heading to Mexico on a secret commission from the Junta Central and that he was waiting for a passport to arrive from the viceroy of New Spain. Lestique claimed to know Onís personally, as well as many members of the loyalist Junta and other senior figures in Spain. Morphy found this behavior suspicious, especially when the new arrival spoke out strongly against the French government and praised the Spanish Junta. The consul's sources suggested that one of Lestique's particular talents was to "make one believe the opposite of what he says." Morphy prepared a physical description of the suspect and sent it off to Philadelphia. Confirming that he was not acquainted with the man, Onís declared this to be proof that Lestique was a French emissary. He noted these developments in a letter to Bardají and added that another French ship had recently discharged a number of other suspected agents onto American soil. The list included a "LeRoy, Larve, Lanno, Prere Charle, Luís Dupar, Lafonta, and Geofroy." He expected all to travel to New Orleans, Havana, and Mexico.[45]

By the middle of July, Onís had in his possession another purported proclamation from Joseph, dated March 22, 1810. In his report to Spain, he stated that his agents had intercepted two hundred copies of this document, though he provided no other details about its source. He enclosed some of them in his official dispatch; others he promised to send to colonial authorities with appropriate warnings. While Onís did not doubt its authenticity, four months later the response from the Crown avoided the praise normally heaped on the ambassador for his "burning zeal for the royal service."[46] Unlike the earlier Bonapartist proclamations, which were treated with great concern, the Spanish government regarded this one as apocryphal due to its "context and poor language" and argued that it would have no impact whatsoever on Spanish America.[47]

More substantial evidence of the value of Onís's counterespionage operations came in his August 14 summary of the case of Manuel Rodríguez Alemán de Peña. In this dispatch to Bardají, the Spanish ambassador recounted a letter he wrote in May to the viceroy of New Spain and the captain general of Cuba, warning them to be on the lookout for two new French emissaries. His report was based on news that one of them, Manuel Rodríguez, had presented himself at the consulate in Norfolk in order to request a passport to return to Mexico. The Spanish consul informed Onís, who immediately identified him as a passenger on the *Tilsit*. According to the consular report, Rodríguez presented himself as French when among other Frenchmen; moreover, he "is a staunch supporter of Napoleon, to such a degree that he says with enthusiasm that he is ready to sacrifice his life for his emperor, he speaks of the generosity and philosophy of the *intruso* Joseph, and says he has been an aide-de-camp of Moncey." Onís decided to order the consul to provide Rodríguez with a passport to Veracruz, where the young man would receive a more careful examination by port authorities. Now, however, the ambassador learned that Spanish authorities in Havana had arrested Rodríguez as a spy and that he had in his possession "a number of incendiary papers from Bonaparte." After a short investigation and trial, Captain General Someruelos had ordered his execution.[48]

More good news arrived from the west. Onís received word from Nemesio Salcedo, the commandant of the Internal Provinces, that four emissaries—three Anglo-Americans and one Spaniard named Blanco—had been arrested in Chihuahua following a warning from the viceroy. These men, who had traveled from Baltimore through upper Louisiana and into Spanish territory without the requisite passports, were headed to Santa Fe. They carried with them two slaves, an American newspaper, a letter from a French priest, muskets, ammunition, and hatchets, among other effects. The men said that they only wished to settle in the Spanish territory and that they were sympathetic to Fernando's cause. Yet, Salcedo wondered why they would attempt such a project without permission or papers. As a result, he imprisoned them in the presidio at San Elceario, near El Paso. Clearly relishing this evidence of administrative competence, Onís made sure to publish the news from Cuba and Texas in American gazettes: "The conspiracies of Bonaparte against Spanish possessions in America appear not to have the happy end promised by the usurper, for his tricks fall apart against American loyalty, a faith no less refined and pure than that shown by the inhabitants of the European peninsula to their sovereign Fernando VII."[49]

Ironically, on the same day that the Spanish ambassador trumpeted these victories against Napoleonic subversion, he was obligated to report on a likely new threat to Spanish America arriving from Bordeaux on the French schooner *George Dyer*. According to his sources, this ship carried fifty-four passengers: forty-nine Frenchmen, four Americans, and one "young Spaniard, the son of a rich businessman from Havana, who I am told is poorly behaved." Among the group was a Catholic bishop, reportedly the new archbishop for Kentucky, who traveled with a large entourage, including six theology students on the point of taking orders. The rest were all "suspicious individuals," some of whom already declared their intention to continue on to the Spanish colonies. Onís noted that he had preemptively posted agents to keep track of the travelers and had renewed his orders to the Spanish consuls to deny passports to all but the most respectable applicants, lest the "apostles of Bonaparte" find their way into the Americas.[50]

One month later, Onís forwarded more information about these new arrivals to the captain general of Cuba. He reported to Someruelos that five of the *George Dyer*'s passengers, whom he now regarded as French emissaries, had left Baltimore for Martinique in early September on board the American schooner *Wolf*, while another vessel, the brig *Cirus*, was in the process of being fitted out to carry another group of agents to Guadeloupe. Many of the others had departed overland for Kentucky and lands to the west, though Baltimore remained full of disguised French soldiers, one of whom visited the Spanish ambassador and provided a "detailed account of our Peninsula and of all the French generals he had served under: he explains that he has escaped and wants to travel to our America where he has an uncle, though he isn't sure where, but as soon as he finds out he will request a passport."[51] Another recent arrival from Bordeaux, a young "half-Spaniard" referred to as Ellissondo, hoped to reunite with a brother in the colonies but did not know whether he was in Mexico or Peru. Onís was particularly troubled by the fact that all the French passengers on the *George Dyer* were young men. He presumed that they were soldiers sent undercover by Napoleon with orders to reunite in some secret location to march on Florida or Louisiana, or perhaps to assist the Venezuelan revolutionaries. Whatever they were, their presence served "as proof of the perseverance of Napoleon in his projects against the possessions of His Majesty in America, for he zealously continues to send emissaries and troops to carry out his perfidious intentions."[52]

The Spanish ambassador knew that he needed to rely on more than the vigilance of colonial authorities to undermine French subversive activity in the Americas. During the summer of 1810 he could also take comfort in reports confirming a new British policy that promised to blunt the operations of the Napoleonic emissaries. On September 3, Onís secured the second printing in an American gazette of a letter from a "Spanish gentleman of high respectability, to his friend in Philadelphia" that described the decision by Britain to order its naval commanders to intercept ships bound for the Spanish colonies and search them for "suspicious persons," that is, French agents. The British government also confirmed that it would remain opposed to "the independence of any of the colonies, as long as the fate of the mother country shall remain undecided."[53]

This official declaration of support for the loyalist cause from a powerful ally, which coincidentally served as an indirect confirmation of Onís's worst fears about French intervention, came at a propitious time for the isolated ambassador. While he continued to gather intelligence about Napoleon's plans for the subversion of Spanish America, he also faced growing evidence that the United States had dropped its pretense of restraint concerning Spanish interests along their shared borders. As was the custom, Onís was forced to express his concerns to the Madison administration via his Baltimore consul. On October 1, Bernabeu informed Secretary Smith that reports had reached the Spanish ambassador from the captain general of Cuba that a group of American settlers calling themselves the Confederation of Mobile had infiltrated Spanish West Florida and were seeking the protection of the US government. If true, the consul declared, such acts by American citizens directly contravened Spanish rights, not to mention US law, and deserved the condemnation of American authorities. He then asked that President Madison ease Spanish concerns by ordering American military forces in the region to block any enterprises targeting foreign territory. Unfortunately, the Spanish consul was also forced to ask Smith for clarification regarding rumors that the US army had orders to take Pensacola: "I find it necessary to request you Sir to give me an answer in writing respecting the intention of this Government toward the possessions of the King my master; that I may thereby be enabled to tranquilize the Captain General of the two Floridas, concerning such extraordinary events and prevent that a misunderstanding or a toleration of measures taken by individual citizens (or perhaps by emissaries of Bonaparte) without the interference of this Government, may compromise the peace and union which exists between the two countries."[54]

The Spanish legation found further evidence of American indifference toward Spain's interests in the administration's disruption of Spanish commerce. On behalf of Ramón Navarro, a prominent Havana merchant, Bernabeu complained to Smith about the impounding of the Cuban brig *Isabel* at the port of New Haven until bond could be secured by its owner. In another case, port authorities in Philadelphia detained a Spanish ship on "false charges" that it carried six blacks onboard with the intention of selling them there. Finally, the consul argued that the United States was failing in its duty to patrol its waters against French corsairs. He highlighted two cases of Spanish vessels captured by privateers and brought to the Barataria coast of Louisiana, where their cargos of slaves were then sold. Bernabeu made no direct accusations of prejudice against American officials in these examples; however, he complained that Spanish authorities gave much greater protection to American merchants than Spanish subjects received in return.[55]

Bernabeu also made an indirect reference to the confiscation of a Spanish ship at the port of Philadelphia in early September. Since this vessel, the schooner *Ramona*, carried a cannon, arms, and supplies of ammunition, it was seized, condemned, and put up for auction by American officials on charges that it was in violation of US neutrality laws. Bernabeu complained that it had been purchased in the city *with* the cannon. He blamed a crewman for bringing the munitions aboard and argued that the captain, Francisco Sánchez Crespo, was unaware of this act, being "deaf, partially blind, and unable to understand a word of English." The consul argued that the *Ramona* was not a warship; rather, it was simply charged with delivering official Spanish correspondence to the province of Maracaibo in Venezuela, while the munitions were part of a perfectly legal commercial operation.[56]

What Bernabeu did not mention, however, was the connection between the schooner and Onís. Earlier in the summer, the Spanish ambassador had engaged and outfitted the *Ramona* to provide much-needed military supplies to Maracaibo, which remained loyal to Spain in the wake of the Caracas rebellion. The confiscation of the ship only delayed these plans, for Onís acquired the schooner outright at the public auction and managed to send it off on October 6 with orders to call at Curaçao before continuing on to Venezuela. Unfortunately, the saga of the *Ramona* took another unexpected turn when British officials on the island decided to seize the vessel for carrying military supplies. Ironically, in the end it was the British who prevented Onís from carrying the fight against subversion directly to the front lines.[57]

For these and many other reasons previously described, Onís believed that the tension between Spain and the United States had reached such a combustible point that he was forced to write directly to Smith, proposing that the two engage in direct, confidential correspondence "in order to avoid every possible misunderstanding betwixt the two nations, and with a view to increase the friendship and beneficial commercial relations which thus happily unite them to each other."[58] The timing of this proposal proved inauspicious, however. By the end of October, President Madison had decided to embark upon a policy of territorial expansion that the Spanish legation could only interpret as a blatant act of aggression. On October 27, the president signed a proclamation declaring that the United States would take possession of Spanish West Florida, including Baton Rouge and the coastal strip below the Mississippi Territory between New Orleans and the Pearl River and charged the governor of Louisiana, William Claiborne, with executing the order.[59]

Madison made this act public in his annual message to Congress during the first week of December. By this time, Onís could only express his private dismay, though not his surprise. In a letter to Governor White, the ambassador declared that he had always assumed that Madison intended to take control of West Florida. He interpreted this move as an effort by the United States, provoked by France, to lure Spain and England into a war. For Onís, American perfidy was clearly in evidence now, and he explained this "act of Machiavellian treason" as a consequence of Madison's absolute adherence to Napoleon. As a result, he expected similar campaigns against Spanish territory in East Florida and the Mexican borderlands.[60]

It was Consul Bernabeu who was forced to present the public reaction of the Spanish legation toward "an act of hostility and violence against the territory of the king." In a letter to the American secretary of state, Bernabeu reminded Smith about an October meeting between the two during which the American official, speaking on behalf of the president, had declared that the United States "would not only condemn but also punish with all the force of the law any individual that offers violence or commits an act of hostility against the subjects or territories of Spain." The consul rejected any excuse that the declaration of independence by residents of Baton Rouge in late September provided justification for American intervention, arguing that Spain retained sufficient strength to punish these rebels. He also noted that American citizens only made matters worse by encouraging and fueling the insurrection. The presence in Philadelphia of a Spanish minister plenipotentiary and ambassador extraordinary, who was fully empowered to negotiate a resolution to the differences existing between the two nations, demonstrated Spain's desire to maintain good relations with the United States. The fact that the American administration continued to ignore Onís while embarking upon hostile acts against its neighbor suggested to Bernabeu that the president had compromised himself "in the eyes of the universe."[61]

Despite the protestation of the Spanish legation, the annexation of West Florida was a fait accompli. Onís, however, refused to sit silently in the face of this affront to Spanish sovereignty and instead published a forceful rebuttal to the president's message for the consideration of the American public.[62] This pamphlet, written in the guise of an American citizen under the pseudonym Verus, sought to counter Madison's argument that the territory of West Florida had been contained within the lands sold by France to the United States in 1803. As "Verus" explained, while France ceded Louisiana to Spain in 1764, the French at the time did not possess any territory on the right bank of the Mississippi except for the city of New Orleans. When Spain returned the province and its capital city to Napoleon in 1800, it retained title to all of its historic Florida possessions on the northern Gulf coast. After proving the validity of Spain's claim with numerous references to French and Spanish diplomatic correspondence, Verus then proceeded to challenge the manner in which the United States took possession of the territory by referencing a year of accumulated personal slights and diplomatic grievances:

> Spain has sent us a minister, in whom she placed her confidence, with the most ample powers, not only to settle the limits of Louisiana, but also to exchange, cede, sell, or purchase such part, or parts, of territories which may answer the convenience of either of the two powers. . . . It is a proof of the sincerity of her desires and of the consideration and respect she entertained towards our government. . . . But we are told that the territory was in the possession of the Conventionalists. Flimsy apology indeed! It shall be the task of the writer, at a future day, to consider the machinery by which the agitation in West Florida has been produced, and to examine who it was that sowed the seeds of that disturbance. Sufficient for my present purpose it is to observe, that it was for Spain to punish her own rebels; she, who has been the first to stop the progress of the supposed conqueror of the world, shall we be told by Madison that she is not in a situation to defend herself against a handful of miserable adventurers, who have emigrated from the United States to disturb the tranquility of the honest inhabitants of West Florida?[63]

An implicit critique of Madison's motivations did not satisfy Onís. Having hinted that the president himself had instigated the unrest in Baton Rouge, it took him very little effort to conclude that the French were also somehow entangled in the West Florida controversy: "Let us remember that Bonaparte, from the beginning of his political career, has sought to deceive every nation, and that it is not in his nature to pursue a different conduct towards us. We have an instance in the confiscation of our vessels, in every country under his influence; we have it in his own words, that he does not wish a single republic to exist, as well as in his proposition to England for the dismemberment of this country. The forcible occupation of a part of the territory of West Florida is also a measure of this treacherous friend, replete with incalculable dangers to the United States."[64] Verus argued that the annexation of West Florida effectively placed the United States in a state of war against Spain and its ally, Great Britain. There could be only one solution to this problem. "It is the sincerest wish of *Verus* that our administration do retrace its steps, and return to a friendly negociation [*sic*]. Whatever be the fate of the peninsula, Spanish America never will belong to Napoleon; for he himself now invites them to become independent, and they, in all situations, and under all circumstances, will consider as valid and binding any agreement that may be made with the legitimate government in regard to West Florida."[65] In his mind, the interests of Spain, the Spanish colonies, France, and the United States were inextricably linked. Writing as an American, Onís hoped to persuade his audience that it would be folly to support a foreign policy that drew the United States closer to Napoleon. Instead, in an ironic twist that foreshadowed his future negotiations with John Quincy Adams over East Florida, he argued that the fulfillment of American commercial, political, and even territorial interests in Spanish America could only be achieved by close cooperation with Spain.

One final bit of good news awaited the Spanish ambassador before the close of this annus horribilis.[66] In December, Onís received confirmation of the fate of Juan Gustavo Nording de Witt, who had been detained in Campeche early in September on suspicion of being a Napoleonic agent. Since the propaganda value of this report was significant, he made sure that the case summary from the provincial governor appeared in American newspapers. It described the arrest of Nording de Witt, who arrived in the Yucatan as a crewmember on board an American ship, holding letters of credit worth two million five hundred thousand dollars and credentials from Azanza, the Bonapartist minister of the Indies. Once in custody, the young man produced from a secret compartment in his trunk two dispatches addressed to the viceroy of New Spain, material that included copies of the Bayonne constitution and "the treasonable royal order by which the new government proposed to revolutionize the colonies against our lawful sovereign and lord Fernando VII." After a thorough interrogation and trial, Nording de Witt was convicted of treason and executed by a firing squad on November 12. The seditious material he brought to Campeche received a comparable sentence, being "committed to the flames" at the same time and place.[67]

Onís hoped the dissemination of this report would demonstrate the effectiveness of colonial counterespionage operations, as well as the swift and sure course of Spanish justice. It was also reasonable to believe that knowing the fate of Nording de Witt might dissuade any potential emissaries from following in his footsteps. However, the ambassador had an ulterior motive for publicizing this case. Since the French agent had traveled to the Yucatan on board an American vessel, local authorities had the right under Spanish law to confiscate it. In fact, the American captain and crew, as associates of the suspected emissary, remained in prison during much of the investigation. In the end, however, the Americans, their ship, and its cargo were released. Notably, as the report concluded, "the said vessel, as well as all the others from the United States, that have come here have been received and treated with all the hospitality and attention in our power, with particular regard to the recommendation of the Spanish minister to the United States." Onís made sure to append a brief editorial highlighting "the liberality of conduct practiced by the Spanish government of Campeachy" and then explicitly contrast it with the case of the schooner *Ramona*. Taken to task by critics who accused him of expressing anti-American sentiment in "communications with the Spanish colonial governments," the ambassador hoped that this anecdote would demonstrate the "very reverse, a friendly disposition on his part towards the citizens of the United States."[68]

Luís de Onís arrived in the United States at the end of 1809 confident in his abilities to represent the interests of Spain in a diplomatic posting of critical importance to the loyalist government. His optimism was short-lived, however, as the Madison administration quickly disabused him of any expectation that it would recognize his appointment. While the American government justified this decision on the basis of a stated policy of neutrality concerning the power struggle in Spain, the Spanish ambassador quickly became convinced that American interests were not as impartial in practice as they appeared in theory. Over the course of a year in diplomatic limbo, Onís sought out and obtained significant evidence of American hostility toward the loyalist cause. Some of this related to his personal treatment by the administration. More resulted from an acute sensitivity to French connections within the governing party in Washington and strong suspicions that Madison was yet another of Napoleon's many puppet rulers. By the end of 1810 the seizure of Spanish territory by his dismissive hosts removed any doubt he might have had left about the willingness of the United States to take advantage of Spain's misfortunes. From a diplomatic perspective, Onís found himself as isolated and undermined in December 1810 as he was in December 1809.

In his role as a senior representative of the loyalist government in the Americas, Onís completed a year of service similarly threatened. The ambassador crossed the Atlantic in the fall of 1809 fully aware of the dangers facing the Spanish colonies from France and the broader Bonapartist coalition. He also understood that his position gave him significant influence among colonial officials. In December 1809, vague concerns about Napoleonic subversion coalesced into a sharply defined threat with the arrival in the United States of the *Tilsit*. Over the course of the next year, the Spanish ambassador and his subordinates chased French agents and their shadows all over North America. In the process, they helped set in motion a counterinsurgency campaign that would shape the defense strategies of colonial officials across Spanish America. While Onís could claim credit for the exposure of some conspiracies, any success he had appeared at the time to be the exception rather than the rule. The year 1810 began with the arrival in the Americas of numerous suspected French emissaries; the year ended with yet another wave. On December 27, Onís wrote to Bardají:

> Napoleon does not desist in his efforts to bring revolution to the lands of His Majesty in America and, in accordance with this goal, he continues to ship spies and emissaries to this country, for it is the meeting place for his satellites. Most recently, the following individuals have arrived from Bordeaux: Mr Le Grefe, an officer in Bonaparte's Imperial Guard. He speaks Castilian extremely well, and I have a suspicion that he is a disguised Spanish traitor . . . Carlos Fosso, an Italian, with his wife, and a Turk by the name of Talamar. . . . It appears that the news of the insurrection in one of the provinces of Mexico, and the events from West Florida have been the signal for their departure for New Orleans, where they have gone to carry out the orders of their leader. For this reason I have sent the necessary warnings to Mexico, as well as to Havana, so that the authorities can communicate with their respective frontiers of Texas and Florida to ensure vigilance against the possibility that the emissaries might find entry through those points; and, I will send orders to the Spanish consul in New Orleans to keep track of them there.[69]

As this particular letter indicates, any sense of security enjoyed by the Spanish colonies due to their relative isolation from the European wars had eroded by the end of 1810. Onís continued to struggle against French subversion in Spanish America from his base in a country that increasingly posed its own threat to Spanish interests. However, these external challenges to Spanish rule now had to share the stage with internal rebellions emerging across South America and, following the outbreak of the Hidalgo Revolt in September 1810, within New Spain. In this context, Onís's campaign assumed a new sense of urgency.

5

Onís on the Offensive, 1811

> You cannot imagine the work I am required to do, for it is not only necessary to copy all the governors of America, but, since everything is very secret, I cannot put my trust in anyone. And so I have to run up and down, experiencing bad nights and working without rest for many of them, so that my warnings are not delayed.
>
> —Luís de Onís to Mauricio de Onís, Philadelphia, September 30, 1811

After more than a year serving the interests of Fernando VII from the Spanish legation's offices in Philadelphia, Luís de Onís was a man both frustrated and obsessed. The immediate cause of his disappointment was brutally clear: as long as the United States refused to recognize him as an accredited representative of a legitimate government, his diplomatic obligations would remain unfulfilled. This exasperating fact, which could be interpreted alternatively simply as self-serving prudence on the part of the US government, fed into a larger narrative that had motivated Onís ever since his flight from Bayonne in 1808. While his hosts might indeed deserve some personal blame for their dismissive treatment of Spain and its ambassador, Onís interpreted their stubbornness as confirmation that a far greater malevolency, that is, Napoleon, could shape the course of events across thousands of miles of ocean. From his perspective, little or no doubt remained at this point that the French emperor, who seemed singularly determined to conquer Spain, was also manipulating the Madison administration with a view to undermine the peace and stability of Spanish America.

It would be a mistake to view Onís's obsession with Napoleon as irrational or even delusional. Most inhabitants of the Atlantic World in January 1811 acknowledged the ruler of France as a figure of transcendental stature, a rare historical figure whose accomplishments matched those of Alexander, Caesar, and Charlemagne. By this time, the Napoleonic empire stretched across most of Europe. The last significant clash between the Great Powers had occurred at Wagram in July 1809, in a battle that reconfirmed French dominance over Austria and reinforced France's pride of place over its Prussian and Russian "allies." With the fateful Russian campaign still more than a year in the future, Great Britain was left to carry on the war against

Napoleon alone. However, all signs now pointed to an imminent conflict between that country and the United States, one that had the potential to stretch British military reserves to the breaking point. While Spain had not yet completely fallen, most of the country suffered under French occupation, and Joseph Bonaparte held court in Madrid. Considering this record, Spanish subjects on both sides of the Atlantic had every reason to assume that all the disturbances roiling the Spanish empire by the end of 1810—including the Hidalgo Revolt in New Spain, the establishment of a junta in Caracas, and the successful autonomist movement in Buenos Aires—could be traced back to the machinations of the all-powerful Napoleon.

Onís, of course, had plenty of evidence to support his convictions. Regular reports from Spanish authorities attested to the creation of Bonapartist espionage networks with designs on Spain's empire. The ambassador himself had gathered compelling evidence of French subversive activity in the United States over the course of 1810 and tracked scores of emissaries as they embarked for Spanish America. He then watched helplessly as the territorial integrity of the empire was compromised by US intervention in West Florida. Onís could prove to his own satisfaction that Napoleon was at the heart of every potential and actual affront to Spanish sovereignty in the Americas, a perception that had both professional and personal implications. This fixation on France and its emperor gave Onís a powerful sense of purpose at a time when he could not carry out his diplomatic duties in Washington. It sustained his belief that he nevertheless had a major role to play during Spain's imperial crisis as the leading loyalist representative in the Americas. And it enabled him to concentrate his attention on the French threat to the colonies, helping to sensitize the colonial bureaucracy to the possibility of external subversion and sparking an administrative response to internal revolt.

There were occasions, however, when his diplomatic judgment was compromised by this tendency to see Napoleon's shadow in every corner. As part of his counterespionage operations, Onís opened the legation offices to Spanish subjects who offered provocative information about French activities. On January 10, 1811, the ambassador reported to his superiors that he had met with someone who could prove that Napoleon intended to conquer the United States. The informant claimed he held correspondence from 1807 between Prince Talleyrand, then the French minister of foreign affairs, and Jean Victor Marie Moreau, a French general who had been living in New Jersey since 1805. The letters hinted at a conspiracy to call upon the thousands of Frenchmen in the Louisiana territory to take up arms under Moreau and form a new Franco-American empire. Onís claimed to be unconvinced by the information but used the opportunity to express some long-standing suspicions. The general, he declared, welcomed Frenchmen of "every class and quality" to his home near Trenton. Worse, Moreau had made extensive trips across the country and had even spent "nearly a year travelling the course of the Mississippi" observing the military outposts in Louisiana. Onís argued that it would be prudent to bolster the defenses in Texas and suggested that a transfer of eight to ten thousand men to the region would allow Spain to take back Louisiana from the United States.[1]

What the Spanish ambassador failed to consider was the fact that Moreau was in the United States because of his opposition to Napoleon. The general had become famous during the revolutionary campaigns in the 1790s and even helped the Bonapartes seize power in 1799. Within a couple of years, however, he had begun to ridicule the increasingly ambitious First Consul and draw into his circle of associates a diverse group of people—including both royalists and republicans—who sought an alternative to Napoleon. Due to his status as a potential rival, Moreau was arrested in 1804 and then forced into exile. Over the next five years, the general's home in New Jersey became a center of anti-Napoleonic politics in the United States.[2] Where Frenchmen gathered, however, Onís only saw conspiracy.[3]

Shortly after his report on Moreau, Onís dispatched another analysis of the events in West Florida that suggested his willingness to accept even the most tenuous evidence of French plotting as an explanation for the insurrections at Baton Rouge. The ambassador reported that the Anglo-American insurgents who launched the revolt in September had named Fulwar Skipwith as their governor early in November. Onís fixated on this nomination, for he identified Skipwith as the "nephew of the ex-president Jefferson, whose grateful disciple is the current president." Most suspiciously, Skipwith had spent the previous decade as the American consul general in Paris. Upon his return to the United States in 1809 and "no doubt with the approval and under orders from Bonaparte, the great friend of Jefferson, [Skipwith] immediately traveled to Monticello, the country home and final resting place of the ex-president, his uncle, and then having received instructions from him, and most likely from Mr. Madison, his mentor, he continued on to Florida to develop his plan for revolution."[4] The connections with France seemed straightforward. Skipwith was a Napoleonic agent who had been recruited to the French cause during his time in Paris. Because of his ties to Jefferson, he could serve as a reliable intermediary between the French and American governments. Once in West Florida, operating with instructions from both Madison and Napoleon,

Skipwith would assume command of the insurgency, declare independence from Spain, seek the protection of the US government, and finally ease the province into the American Union.[5]

For a mind sensitized to French conspiracies, this was a plausible interpretation. In truth, the short-term governor of the Republic of West Florida, like Moreau, was a far more complex and enigmatic character than Onís was willing to accept. Fulwar Skipwith certainly benefited from his family connection to Jefferson; however, the former president was a distant relation by marriage and not his uncle, as Onís believed. Independently wealthy and socially prominent, having married Countess Evelina Barlie van den Clooster while in Europe, Skipwith arrived in Baton Rouge as part of a larger wave of Virginia planters who sought economic opportunities along the Mississippi after the Louisiana Purchase.[6] The Anglo-American revolt served his interests well, as did his election as governor.[7] Shortly thereafter, when Madison sent the governor of Louisiana to take possession of West Florida, Skipwith sought to obstruct and delay the transfer in a manner that, according to the American diplomat George Erving, "surprized & disappointed his friends."[8] Such nuances, however, meant little to Onís.

In an environment where the absence of information did not stifle imagination, rumors flew up and down the east coast of the United States about French military intentions. In mid-January, Onís reported on one plan, "which appears probable and we are told is under way" to disembark a large number of French troops at the port of New York.[9] The ambassador also paid an informant for information about a Franco-American naval operation against English forces on the Iberian Peninsula. According to this report, Napoleon intended to disguise fire ships as merchant vessels flying the American flag. Sailing from the United States with merchant crews and trade goods, the ships were expected to attack English convoys and squadrons at the mouth of the Tagus River.[10]

While such a threat proved to be too vague and ephemeral to deserve more than passing reference, the ambassador soon had a more reliable subject to investigate. At the end of January, Onís notified his superiors that a certain Monsieur Brouard, a French naval officer, had recently left Philadelphia for Baltimore in the company of a number of Spaniards. According to his information, Brouard intended to stop in Washington, DC, before continuing on to Mexico. Another Napoleonic emissary named d'Amblimont was also reportedly in the area. Onís had a little more intelligence on this figure. Reportedly carrying a letter of credit worth two hundred thousand British pounds with which to fund his operations, this particular spy had contracted with a local French publisher to run off copies of cipher codes that would enable him "to correspond with the rest of Bonaparte's emissaries in various parts of the Americas." The Spanish ambassador hoped at the time to obtain examples to send to Mexico but, despite receiving assurances from the printer that some would be passed along, soon despaired that they would come.[11]

In much the same way that the shadow of Desmolard cast itself across the previous year, the specter of Jacques Athanase d'Amblimont became a preoccupation for Onís over the course of 1811. On February 6, the ambassador reported the arrival of the Frenchman in Philadelphia and noted that

> his bearing, his connections, and certain reports I have received about his character from the people I hire to follow the steps of all the foreigners who come here have called my attention to this person as someone more important than the others who overwhelm this country. Since then I placed someone in his house to observe him, befriend him, and try to find out whether he is carrying anything from the usurper of the throne of our beloved King or from his brother the Despot of France. This faithful individual, to the extent one can consider him a spy, since he is also French, though someone discontented with and aggrieved by Napoleon, has managed to extract two papers with a false key which, even if they don't give us a complete understanding of the commission given to [d'Amblimont] or all the instructions he has received to carry it out, at least indicates that their objective is the kingdom of Portugal and the New World. I include a copy of both decrees copied by me from the original, which is adorned with the Imperial Seal and all the details that prove its authenticity.

Onís confirmed that he would update Bardají about this "Machiavellian intrigue" as soon possible and promised to alert all the colonial authorities about the presence of the new emissary. At the same time, the ambassador underscored the significant expense he had incurred in acquiring such solid evidence of French conspiracies and implied that he would be grateful if the Council of Regency would reimburse him for his outlays.[12]

The documents acquired by the Spanish legation appeared to have been produced by the French naval ministry in late September 1810.[13] One confirmed d'Amblimont's appointment, while others established the funding for his mission.[14] The most important document, however, which Onís sent to Spain on February 12, laid out the emissary's Instructions in twenty-eight separate articles. Through this latter source, Onís learned that the American decision to attack West Florida had been sanctioned in advance by Paris. Anticipating the success of the uprising at Baton Rouge, Napoleon had ordered d'Amblimont to head immediately for New Orleans to find recruits for French subversive operations in Mexico and Cuba. These agents, ideally in possession of American passports, were expected to insinuate themselves among local elites and paint a picture of the horrors of independence even while fomenting discord between creoles and peninsulars. By invoking the "devastating fury of demagoguery" and the threat to property and personal safety, the emissaries would thus subtly encourage Spanish Americans to emulate the decision of the European nobility to seek the protection of the French emperor.[15]

Shortly after this discovery, Onís informed Bardají that he had acquired, "through a great deal of work," the cipher code used by d'Amblimont in his communications. The key was sent to Spain along with the names of seven additional suspected emissaries. The Spanish ambassador reported that d'Amblimont had dispatched a Monsieur Borel to Río de Janeiro and a Portuguese man named Monteiro to Havana. An existing Napoleonic agent in Lisbon, José Dionisio Monteiro (possibly the same man), was referenced along with a cavalry officer named Lamasliere who was already stationed in the Brazilian capital. Onís identified an emissary called Pedro Mouliat, who was en route to La Guaira carrying instructions for the insurgent government in Caracas, and noted that he had sent warnings to the commanders of Spanish ships blockading the Venezuelan coast. The ambassador claimed that d'Amblimont was corresponding with two Cubans, Felix Sánchez and Juan Caballero, and that their letters were posted with forged seals from the Pennsylvania consulate. Finally, one of Onís's sources, who had attended a closed session of Congress, informed him that funds had been appropriated for the purchase of the Florida territories from Napoleon and his brother. The source claimed that it was common knowledge that Joel Barlow, the newly appointed American ambassador to France, would negotiate the details of the sale.[16]

After receiving Onís's dispatches, the Council of Regency sprang into action. On March 30, Minister Bardají summarized the findings for Henry Wellesley, the British ambassador to Spain, and warned him that naval forces off the coast of Portugal had been targeted by France. He then advised Wellesley to alert London so that the British government could be made aware of the measures being taken by Napoleon to cause unrest in the Americas.[17] Six weeks later, the Regency described d'Amblimont's plans to Viceroy Venegas in New Spain. It informed him that the emissary had orders to seek agents and contacts across Mexico and Cuba and emphasized the need to pay attention to all sources of communication with Havana. Of particular concern to the Spanish government was the suggestion that the French subversives planned to shield themselves by claiming American citizenship.[18]

While senior officials in Cádiz worked out an effective response to the d'Amblimont Instructions, their ambassador in the United States was also tracking four suspicious Portuguese who had arrived from Bordeaux in January. These men, Sebastian Navarro de Andrade, Vicente Navarro de Andrade, Domingo Borgas de Barsos, and Juan Nereira de Sousa, claimed to have fled France with the goal of reaching Brazil; however, Onís had reason to doubt their intentions. He noted in particular that the travelers had made only a perfunctory appearance at the home of the Portuguese consul general in Philadelphia before somehow finding enough money to settle down in style. Convinced that France was the true source of these funds and that the men were most likely French emissaries, Onís forwarded their names to the colonial authorities "so as to impede their introduction in our possessions."[19]

As he chased down suspects, Onís operated within the parameters of a worldview built around the certainty of a vast Napoleonic conspiracy to undermine the Spanish empire. Yet, this did not prevent him at times from recognizing the absurdity of some claims. In late February, the ambassador received a mysterious letter from the Baron de Nierode, whom he identified as a long-established Polish resident of the United States. Nierode claimed that he was in possession of a great secret that could ensure the salvation of Spain and its colonies, one that he was willing to share with the Spanish legation. Onís doubted that the secret amounted to anything more than a vague outline of what was already common knowledge, namely, that France and the United States were conspiring to conquer Spanish America, beginning with Florida, through the use of subversives and other emissaries. He also suspected that Nierode saw an opportunity to trade his information for money. Nevertheless, Onís ordered the nearest Spanish consul to arrange a meeting. According to the ambassador, the story Nierode told was worthless. This "absurd" conspiracy, as he described it, was a "plan"

> to send a governor, an intendant, and a bishop to the island of Cuba, and a viceroy, an intendant, and an archbishop to Mexico. These officials would be Spaniards in the service of Joseph. They would be carrying false dispatches from the Regency, and their goal would be to take control of the armed forces and Royal Treasury before anyone could prove they were imposters. These subjects would be transported in small warships, two of which are under construction in New York, under the direction of Monsieur d'Archambal, the French consul,

> and two more in Charleston. These ships, it is said, will be crewed by Spaniards and Americans and will carry two sets of false papers, thereby allowing them to pass as Spanish warships among the English and English among the Spanish.[20]

Why this particular scheme struck Onís as more ridiculous than some of the plots that he was willing to accept as true is difficult to explain. The results, however, were the same. As in the past, the ambassador decided that the prudent move would be to send the details to the viceroy of New Spain and the captain general of Cuba and let them "take the steps that they consider necessary."[21] In this manner, even the most bizarre rumors received a gloss of official plausibility and helped feed the anxiety of the authorities and subjects of Spanish America.

Still, signs of active social unrest were everywhere to be found, and Onís had to take them seriously. On the same day that he informed Spain about Nierode, the ambassador received letters from his contacts in Louisiana that included news of a massive slave rebellion in the area. This two-day event, known as the German Coast Uprising, began on January 8 on plantations upriver from New Orleans and, at its peak, included more than two hundred slaves.[22] Onís knew by this time that local militias had suppressed the revolt, but he did not consider this to be an isolated or even local incident. Instead, he reported that the French had instigated and funded the uprising and that "it is likely that this revolution was one link in Bonaparte's chain or plan to conquer Mexico, either by making that province [Louisiana] independent or by making himself sovereign over it."[23]

One month later, Onís was forced to pass on even more "disagreeable" news that had just arrived from Diego Morphy, the Spanish consul in New Orleans. As the ambassador had feared, it now appeared that the "vertigo of insurrection has spread through the Internal Provinces." He then summarized the events that began on January 22 at a Spanish military outpost in San Antonio, Texas. A local militia captain, Juan Bautista de las Casas, had conspired with some enlisted members of the fort's garrison to take into custody the provincial governor, Manuel María de Salcedo, and a number of other important Spanish military and civil officials in the region. Las Casas then assumed control of the territory and began to target Spanish loyalists. In short order, most of northern New Spain, including Texas, was in a state of unrest, with royalist forces battling insurgents under the general command of Miguel Hidalgo. Onís argued to Bardají that he had "well-founded evidence that this revolution was incited by Mr. Jefferson and Mr. Madison in agreement with Bonaparte to serve as the second

Florida front. In other words, [they] caused these provinces to rise up as a pretext for the entry of American troops into them, following the justification, which as you know this government promotes, that all are integral parts of the Louisiana that was purchased from France." He promised to keep track of developments and pass further information to Spain with his "accustomed exactitude and punctuality" but added that he now had no doubt that the US and French governments were working hand in hand to achieve Napoleon's ambitions in North America.[24]

At the same time, the news from Texas gave Onís the opportunity to complain bitterly to his own superiors about the way that the colonies had responded to his warnings. The ambassador noted that it was he who had had the great fortune to uncover Napoleon's subversive operations against Spanish America. He emphasized that he had distributed the details to colonial authorities with more than enough advanced notice for sufficient defensive measures to be adopted. Yet, the French appeared to carry out the Texas revolt exactly according to the publicized plan. Onís saw no evidence that precautions had been taken, despite the fact that he had repeatedly explained that the Louisiana frontier (along with Cuba) served Napoleonic emissaries as a principal pathway into Spanish America. To reinforce his point, Onís provided Bardají with an anecdote that reinforced the impression that "despite all my precautions they [the French] can introduce all the emissaries they want." A few weeks earlier, a foreign national, whom Spanish intelligence identified as either French or Swiss, had requested a passport to travel to Havana. Onís refused the permit on the advice of the captain general of Cuba, but he subsequently learned that the man had found passage to the island from Philadelphia disguised either as a purser or sailor and had then established himself as a surgeon on a local hacienda. "In this manner and by similar means," wrote Onís, "all the Napoleonic emissaries we can identify manage to reach our possessions." The ambassador pointedly refused to suggest any failure of "patriotism or zeal" on the part of the Cuban authorities, though he thought that perhaps the governor "lacked the means to work with more energy."[25]

Buoyed by the repeated signals of support from Spain's Council of Regency, Onís continued to express his intense frustration with the foreign policy of the US government in his dispatches home. Unfortunately for him, many different points of contention emerged in the spring of 1811. The extraordinary presence of William Shaler in Havana precipitated one outburst. Though he was not recognized by Cuban authorities in any official diplomatic capacity, Shaler assumed the duties of a de facto American consul on the island. From Onís's perspective, this was provocative behavior, for the Spanish ambassador considered him to be not only "a staunch Jacobin" but also "a spy of Bonaparte." In particular, he feared the consequences of Shaler's declared intention to travel to Mexico and argued that such a man would not be welcome in Spanish possessions during peaceful times, much less in the current climate.[26]

Shaler represented a type of informal diplomacy that Washington had begun to use with increased frequency in Spanish America.[27] The possibility that the United States would send representatives to colonial capitals with the intention of opening direct communication with local authorities was reprehensible to a traditional envoy like Onís and troubling to his superiors across the Atlantic. One rumor that reached Spain in 1810 suggested that Madison had dispatched a personal emissary to Mexico City in the spring with instructions to speak with the viceroy about the possibility of beginning clandestine negotiations on the cession of Spanish Florida. In April 1811, Onís claimed to have confirmed this story and added that the administration had taken this action on the recommendation of notable "standard-bearers of Bonaparte," namely former president Jefferson and former secretary of state Robert Smith.[28]

The Spanish ambassador also complained vigorously about a closely related aspect of Madison's interest in direct engagement with Spanish America. Beginning with the overthrow of the captain general in Caracas in the spring of 1810, newly established autonomous governments across the region sought to establish diplomatic relations with the United States. These rebels, as Onís considered them, sent their own representatives to Washington in the hopes of winning coveted formal recognition. For the most part, the Madison administration held these agents at arm's length, applying to them the same rationale that frustrated Onís's hopes for American recognition of his own government. However, like the Spanish ambassador, the South Americans were tolerated in an unofficial capacity and allowed to promote their interests in private. From the perspective of the Spanish legation, of course, this policy amounted to de facto support for the revolutionary movements, since it did not prevent their agents from achieving some important goals. In August, for example, Onís reported to Spain that Pedro de la Lastra, Nicolas Mauricio de Omaña, and Francisco Armero, who styled themselves "deputies" from the insurgent government in Bogotá charged with "establishing friendly relations and commerce," had completed a significant purchase in New York. The Spanish ambassador was powerless to prevent "fifteen hundred muskets, four hundred pairs of pistols, four hundred sabers, a number of saddles and various agricultural machines and instruments" from being loaded onto the American brig *Sally* for immediate transport to South America.[29]

Despite such reverses to the loyalist cause, President Madison's decision to replace Secretary Smith with James Monroe at the end of March 1811 provided Onís with a glimmer of hope that the administration's established policy toward Spain might be reconsidered. While Monroe was "as much a democrat" as his predecessor, the ambassador recognized his "talent" and suggested that the incoming secretary could be influenced by reasonable arguments. Onís expected Congress to reconvene in the summer and confidently requested "new credentials, new powers, and new instructions" from his superiors at Cádiz to take advantage of any eventualities. It did not take long for such optimism to prove misplaced.[30]

On April 11 Onís sent a private letter to Monroe offering his congratulations, noting "the personal satisfaction I feel in beholding at the head of that department a person who is well acquainted with the character and genius of the Spanish nation." Alluding to his complicated diplomatic status, the ambassador took the opportunity to seek an adjustment to the irregular means of communication between the Spanish legation and the American government. More specifically, since the end of 1810 a worrisome departure from custom had occurred. In December, Onís received a visit from US District Attorney Alexander Dallas, who informed the ambassador that he would now take charge of any legation correspondence with the State Department. With no leverage, Onís agreed to the change and proceeded to forward future letters to Dallas. In the three months that followed, Secretary Smith failed to respond to any attempt at communication. Onís now hoped that Monroe would permit the free flow of correspondence without the need for intermediaries. While Onís continued to rely heavily on the Baltimore consul Juan Bernabeu to communicate with the secretary of state, in this instance he asked Pablo Chacon, who served in the Alexandria consulate, to approach Monroe.[31]

If the ambassador had any lingering questions about the administration's attitude toward him, they were answered during an informal conversation between Secretary Monroe and Consul Bernabeu in early June. Bernabeu had recently provided the State Department with the latest list of Spanish grievances concerning American foreign policy. The occupation of West Florida headed these "acts of hostility," but the consul noted other American incursions into Spanish territory before criticizing the administration's willingness to allow Bonapartist emissaries and French corsairs to use the United States as a refuge.[32] Madison's decision to name a consul in Caracas, a city in revolt, was only the latest sign that the president had dropped any pretense of neutrality and now viewed Spain as an enemy.[33]

Monroe, of course, dismissed these charges in no uncertain terms: the rebellion in West Florida had occurred without official American encouragement, while French corsairs operated entirely without American knowledge. He argued that the United States had been "uniformly friendly" in its conduct toward Spain and that the Madison administration practiced strict neutrality with respect to Spanish affairs. Instead, the secretary suggested that the Spanish government was to blame for any real or perceived breakdown in the relationship between the two states. Monroe then pointedly referenced the "exceptionable" behavior of Ambassador Onís, asserting that the State Department could prove that the diplomat had not only "manifested very hostile views towards the United States" but that he had "even suggested the means by which their union might be dismembered." The fact that Onís had not been expelled from the country despite such undiplomatic conduct, the secretary asserted, should be considered evidence enough of the administration's desire to remain on good terms with Spain.[34]

The Spanish legation wasted little time in attempting to repair the damaged image of its ambassador within the Madison administration. Less than a month after Bernabeu's interview with the secretary of state, the Baltimore consul wrote to Monroe to discredit any "documents existing in the Department of State" that alleged designs by Onís "against the union and tranquility" of the United States.[35] He first suggested that such papers were simply fraudulent, noting that "the Chevalier's passports have been forged and the same has been done with the Seal of Office and signatures of the Spanish consuls in Philadelphia, New York, and Baltimore, and surely you will admit that a letter or any other document can be imitated with equal facility." Then, allowing for the possibility that compromising documents did exist, he then argued that Onís could not be held responsible either for relaying information about possible conspiracies against the United States or for expressing his frustration with American foreign policy through purely speculative revenge scenarios: "At all events, you must be conscious of the difference there is between communicating current reports and giving an opinion thereon, or projecting a plot and acting in any manner therein; or, between projecting similar schemes or merely proposing means of self-defense against an unprovoked, unjust and deliberate aggression." Finally, after a half-hearted attempt to question the existence of documents that the administration would not release, Bernabeu suggested that Spanish foreign policy toward the United States required an envoy like Onís, a refined and cultivated diplomat who would never engage in conspiratorial acts: "For even allowing for a moment what is not the case, namely, that my government had any such intentions, which it is evident from its correct principles, it cannot have, as its first object is evidently to preserve peace and good understanding with the United States; it is not likely it should on such an occasion make use of the Chevalier d'Onis whose established character and truly honorable principles are so well known to permit him to become an instrument of discord to disturb the tranquility of that very nation to which he is sent as a Minister of Peace, with the sole view of consolidating the bonds of friendship, which have hitherto existed between the two countries."[36]

In the end, the unofficial communications between Monroe and Bernabeu served only to give both sides an opportunity to repeat their established positions and reconfirm the status quo. In the meantime, Onís remained in Philadelphia and continued to collect intelligence on the movement of French agents. At the end of December 1810, the ambassador had learned of the arrival in the United States of a Monsieur Le Grefe (or Greffe), who was reportedly en route to New Orleans. In April, this suspicious figure returned to Philadelphia. Onís now informed Spain that this man, whom sources identified as an officer in Napoleon's Imperial Guard, had spent the past four months intriguing against Spanish rule at least as far south as New Spain. According to this report, Greffe had made his way to Louisiana upon hearing of the revolts in West Florida with the goal of "promoting and extending them." He then passed into northern Texas. Onís now declared that he had "little doubt" that Greffe was behind the recent uprisings in the Internal Provinces. He also reported that the Frenchman had been imprisoned in Guatemala where he was almost put to death. However, the cunning spy had in his possession a silver medallion upon which "was represented a column topped by a bust of our adored King Fernando Septimo, a kneeling priest in the act of paying his respects, and an inscription reading 'The Loyalty of the Indians of Guatemala.'" Greffe used it to prove his devotion to the loyalist cause and win his release. In the view of Onís, all the spy's subsequent actions corresponded perfectly with the Instructions that Napoleon had prepared for his emissaries. The episode demonstrated yet again that "these satellites fix their residence in this country and that in spite of all my warnings to our American possessions and unique details that I provide to our governors, [the emissaries] always manage to elude their vigilance and introduce themselves wherever they wish into [our lands]."[37]

In June Onís received word that Greffe had departed for New York, apparently intending to find passage to "Havana, Vera Cruz, and Mexico, no doubt in response to a new commission from his master." The ambassador's source for Greffe's whereabouts appeared to be Diego Correa, a Spanish agent who was living in Philadelphia at the time under the alias of Antonio Gorbalán.[38] At some point, Correa/Gorbalán had befriended the Frenchman, who wrote to him to inquire whether the Spaniard would join him in New York, even though that city "is not much more entertaining than

Philadelphia."[39] Convinced that the French officer intended to "light the fire of revolution" in Spanish America, Onís proceeded to alert the captain general of Cuba and the viceroy of New Spain. Despite Greffe's evident talent for elusiveness, the ambassador still hoped that a timely warning from him would enable the colonial authorities to capture and punish this particular emissary before he could do any further damage.[40]

As Monsieur Greffe found his way across the Mid-Atlantic states, a new antagonist for Onís made his first appearance in Washington, DC. In early May, Louis Charles Serurier arrived to assume the position of ambassador of France to the United States. Within a matter of weeks, a "very respectable source," identified only as a "Spanish Patriot," provided the *Boston Sentinel* with a translation of a state paper titled "Additional Instructions to Mr. Serurier" that had been captured by Spanish loyalists on the road connecting France with the Basque port of San Sebastian. Signed by the French foreign minister Champagny, this document described a tangled web of intrigues resulting from Napoleon's foreign policy toward both Spain and the United States. Deeply implicated in these plots, according to this source, was former president Jefferson:

> With Mr. Jefferson you must have no secrets—He has too much exposed himself, and is too great a fanatic in his hatred towards England, not to be trusted—Tell him the Emperor regrets not having already been able to proclaim him Prince Regent of Columbia from London. England is, however, now in her last agony. . . . Tell him not to suspend, even in case of a war, his usual communications by the usual channels. One campaign will be sufficient to convince his countrymen of the necessity of an union with France, and of a submission to the political and commercial code of the emperor. . . . Confide in none of the Spanish subjects employed in the United States by the cabinet of his Spanish majesty, king Joseph; and employ no more any American democrats in missions to the Spanish colonies, if none of their above mentioned countrymen will be responsible both for their fidelity and their capacity. None of those trusted by your predecessor ought to have been sent, because those, who were capable, turned rogues, and those who remained faithful, were also such indiscreet fools, as to cause themselves to be apprehended or executed, in consequence of their own blunders before their deeds deserved either a gaol or a gibbet.[41]

Whether or not the Spanish legation was responsible for leaking this document to the newspaper is an interesting but open question. Onís had used the American press on multiple occasions, both publicly and anonymously, as a platform to advance the loyalist cause. The opportunity to raise questions about the reputation and motivation of the new French ambassador must have been tempting. And, Onís already suspected Jefferson of having sold himself to Napoleon. A "respectable" source such as the ambassador would have been able to produce and pass on a newsworthy forgery such as this one to a New England paper like the *Sentinel* with little trouble. What is more, if the document were authentic, Onís would have every motive to bring it to the attention of the American media.

However the story originated, it had no appreciable impact on the Madison administration's reception of the new French ambassador. As Onís informed Bardají on August 8, Serurier quickly inserted himself into the ongoing talks between Monroe and the British ambassador, Augustus Foster, in an effort to derail them. According to the Spanish ambassador, Serurier utilized all his influence to provoke war between England and the United States: He shamelessly manipulated the prevailing pro-French sentiment within the cabinet; he "never left the president's side"; he worked with Secretary Monroe to coordinate the American position in the negotiations; and, once the talks were suspended, he helped convince the administration to leave the trade restrictions against Britain in place for an additional four months.[42] In effect, Onís described an American government that had become a client state of France.

If this viewpoint were valid, the Spanish ambassador knew there would be consequences for the Spanish empire. In the same extended dispatch, Onís reported that the Americans were raising forces in New Orleans and Baton Rouge for an attack on Mobile and that troop transports were already in place at the mouth of Mobile Bay. He presumed that the American commanders were simply waiting for the collapse of the British-American negotiations and the inevitable declaration of war to begin their operations. Confirmation came with the arrival of a French warship in the port of Philadelphia. While its captain declared that he was headed for Batavia but sought refuge in North America after being chased by a British ship, Onís noted that fourteen French officers were onboard, along with a number of engineers and artillerymen. He was convinced that their true destination was New Orleans and that these soldiers were part of a planned Franco-American campaign against Spanish Florida or, perhaps, Caracas.[43]

Yet again, Onís chafed in his dispatch to Spain at the multiple examples of French impunity that were reported to him. Despite the lack of a passport or any other sign of approval from the Spanish legation, American officials allowed a certain Monsieur Roux to travel to Havana. This individual was one of many in the French community in Cuba who had been forced to immigrate to the United States following the crisis of 1808. He now sought to return in a ship owned by another Frenchman named Ducomb. Onís was dumbfounded that these men, who by travelling without authorization to a Spanish possession were subject to arrest as spies, would take such a public risk. Concluding that Roux's motivations were too "mysterious" to ignore, the ambassador relayed the appropriate warnings to the Cuban authorities.[44]

Two additional names of suspected emissaries appeared in the August 8 dispatch to Spain. The first, "the famous d'Amblimont," had been known to Onís since the beginning of the year. Describing this man now as one of the "principal revolutionary agents" in the region, the ambassador reported that he had in fact gone to Mexico. Another known only as Ledrezenech seemed to be preparing to do the same. Returning to a favorite theme, Onís bemoaned the fact that these agents would likely succeed in reaching New Spain, since he could not rely on the local authorities to adequately scrutinize travelers arriving either by land or sea. Without effective communication between the United States, Spain, and Mexico, he added, "all of my efforts, sleepless nights, and determination to counteract the conspiracies of Napoleon will be for naught."[45]

After receiving this report and in response to Onís's complaints, the Council of Regency commanded the viceroys and governors of Spain's overseas territories to obey "rigorously all the orders regarding those individuals who wish to enter them without the necessary documentation and to redouble their vigilance in order to uncover any French and American emissaries."[46] Such support from Cádiz likely meant a great deal to Onís, who remained relatively isolated in Philadelphia and embraced any opportunity to contribute to the loyalist campaign. In practice, however, colonial authorities could do little to seal off their borders from any real or imaginary threats coming from the outside world.

In the meantime, Onís carried on with his counterespionage operations. At the end of August, he reported a major development to his superiors, one with the potential to rival his discovery of the Desmolard Instructions some eighteen months earlier or, more recently, the d'Amblimont Instructions from the previous February. Unable to put to rest his suspicions about the French schooner that had found its way to the United States despite claiming to be en route to Batavia, the ambassador charged a team of confidants with uncovering the true story of the ship. Because of this fieldwork, Onís came to possess a trove of astonishing documents, which he summarized for Bardají as follows: "Your Excellency will find attached to this dispatch the name of another new agent [Louis Jean Marie Ledrezenech] sent to foment revolution in our American possessions. You will find a copy of the original instructions provided to him to accomplish his commission, as well as a letter to him from Minister Serurier, both of which I transcribed by hand from the originals and which are authorized by imperial seals and valid signatures that I recognize, having seen them before in our Ministry." After two years of hunting down shadowy conspiracies, the Spanish ambassador now held evidence that appeared to link Paris directly to a vast espionage network targeting the American colonies.[47]

These Ledrezenech Instructions, as transcribed by Onís, carried the signature of the duc de Bassano, the French foreign minister, and were dated April 12, 1811, at the Tuilleries Palace. They included nineteen articles, the first of which ordered Ledrezenech to make immediate contact with Serurier after arriving in the United States. The French ambassador would provide the spy with further instructions and a key for coded communications. Ledrezenech was first told to seek out d'Amblimont in Baltimore, Philadelphia, New York, or Boston and support his departure for a new mission to Tangiers. If d'Amblimont were unavailable, Ledrezenech and Serurier were expected to find a suitable replacement. With this task completed, Ledrezenech received orders to concentrate on promoting the insurrection of the Spanish colonies with assistance from d'Amblimont, Pio Azara, Pierre d'Alcantara, and Jacques Pereira.[48]

From a diplomatic (rather than an operational) perspective, articles eleven to fifteen of the document are the most dramatic. Article eleven directed the emissary to gain assurances from President Madison that the United States would facilitate indirectly "the political independence of the Spanish states in the New World." Ledrezenech was then charged with helping the administration draw new borders. Article twelve required him to organize a lobbying group with the goal of pressuring the US to declare war on Spain. Article thirteen encouraged him to promote the return of French emigres to Cuba to promote the island's independence. Article fourteen ordered d'Amblimont to take charge of the independence operations in Mexico and its neighboring colonies, while article fifteen required Ledrezenech to oversee the operations in South America. For all of this, the emissary was given access to more than one million francs in credit from the Bank of France.[49]

A July 14 letter from Serurier to Ledrezenech focused on two specific issues raised by the Instructions. Having failed to find d'Amblimont in time, the French ambassador recommended one Monsieur Achard (or Achart) for the mission to Tangiers, noting this officer's ability to speak Spanish, Portuguese, and Arabic. Serurier then turned his attention to the Spanish American agenda and suggested that Ledrezenech reconsider his intention to send an envoy to Caracas. The popular support for independence in that city was so great, Serurier argued, that it would be better to focus on Cartagena.[50]

Taken together, the Ledrezenech Instructions and the Serurier letter provided powerful evidence for Onís's long-standing contentions. They confirmed a vast French conspiracy to undermine Spanish authority in the Americas through the use of a network of agents provocateurs. Perhaps even worse, they implicated the American government in these operations. One might reasonably question the manner in which this material reached the Spanish legation. However, regardless of the actual provenance of the documents, the Spanish ambassador never doubted their authenticity, and this certitude shaped his recommendations to his superiors. Onís used this opportunity to stress the importance of authorized travel between the United States and the American colonies. Taking the Caribbean as his example, he argued that the local authorities in Cuba never complained about anyone holding one of his passports. Yet, it was well known that Puerto Rican officials commonly admitted ships without consular documents, a practice which "facilitates the entry of emissaries and the passage of malcontents from the interior of our possessions to this country [the United States] and to France." Apparently, Onís's insistence on this point had made him enemies among some colonial governors who thought that he was protecting the financial interests of his consuls. Unlike their English counterparts, Spanish consuls charged a fee for travel permits, compensation that supplemented a rather meagre salary. Onís, of course, claimed that his motives were purely patriotic.[51]

Despite this rare (but perhaps unsurprising) example of discontent with Spain's ambassador to the United States from members of the colonial bureaucracy, the Council of Regency took Onís at his word and acted accordingly. The Cádiz government acknowledged the report in late November and announced a major show of force as an initial response. It informed Onís that three ships of the line, a number of frigates, and transports containing more than three thousand soldiers had already embarked for Veracruz. A second expedition was also being planned for New Spain, one that would be strong enough to eliminate the rebellion there *and* defend Spanish sovereignty all the way to the US border. Finally, Spain seemed to be in a position to assert itself in the Americas, news that must have been quite welcome in its legation offices in Philadelphia.[52]

The counterespionage coup represented by the capture of the Ledrezenech papers was incomplete, however. The whereabouts of d'Amblimont were cause for concern, as were the potential implications of the Tangiers mission mentioned in the Instructions. Fortunately, during the first week of September Onís informed Bardají that a second letter from Serurier had come into the possession of the Spanish legation. As with the earlier documents, this communication, which occurred between the French ambassador and Ledrezenech on August 19, provided some explosive intelligence. D'Amblimont, Onís learned and then immediately reported to Viceroy Venegas in New Spain, was shifting his attention from Mexico, where he had been fomenting revolution under the name Antonio Xavier Ramírez.[53] The spy, who was moving north toward Santa Fe, had contacted Serurier to ask that funds be deposited for him in New Orleans. As Ledrezenech now controlled these resources, the French ambassador forwarded the request. He also suggested that the new emissary write directly to d'Amblimont and provide all the details corresponding to their respective missions "so that in case of accident the thread of things is not lost."[54]

There was more. Onís included in this dispatch a copy of the code that Ledrezenech and Serurier were using to disguise their communications. He said that few people could read what the French were calling "Arabic." However, he believed he had the correct alphabetic translation. From now on, he declared confidently, it will be "incredibly easy . . . to decipher the correspondence of these Agents."[55] The Spanish ambassador also speculated on the nature of the Tangiers mission and suggested that it might have something to do with a conspiracy in Cádiz. He assured Bardají that he intended to uncover more details as soon as possible. Finally, Onís warned his superiors about a Portuguese man named Lucas Scabra da Silva, whom he identified as the leader of "all the French intrigues in Lisbon."[56]

The evidence that Onís sought with such determination arrived in his hands within a week. Now the Spanish ambassador forwarded to Bardají transcriptions of three letters ostensibly written by the duc de Bassano on April 14. The first was addressed to Scabra da Silva in Lisbon.[57] After referencing a certain "project" that the Portuguese had suggested to Napoleon, the foreign minister confirmed da Silva's appointment as the emperor's "plenipotentiary and minister" in Lisbon and informed him that an agent had been sent to Tangiers with instructions to assist in his operations.[58]

The second was intended for d'Amblimont. Here, Bassano informed the emissary that Napoleon was particularly satisfied "with the success of your operations in the Kingdom of Santa Fe and the arrangements you have made with respect to Mexico." He encouraged d'Amblimont to accelerate his plans for revolution in New Spain and then move on to Cuba. The duke added that special agent (*agent particulier*) Ledrezenech would put two hundred thousand francs at his disposal to support these operations. He then informed the spy that he had been made a grand officer of the Legion of Honor and member of the Privy Council for his services to the emperor.[59]

In his communication with d'Amblimont, Bassano made reference to the archbishop of Mexico, Francisco Lizana y Beaumont, and implied a preexisting connection between the two men. The third letter acquired by Onís was, in fact, directed to this prelate. Having learned from d'Amblimont of the archbishop's antagonism towards England, the foreign minister took this opportunity to flatter him while, at the same time, blaming the British for the prolonged war with Spain and confirming Napoleon's desire for peace and respect for the Church.[60] As soon as these letters reached Spain, the Council of Regency ordered Minister Bardají to update his British and Portuguese counterparts, taking care to thank Onís again for his ceaseless zeal in "uncovering the infernal intrigues of Bonaparte" and for warning "all of our American governors so they can take the necessary precautions."[61]

As it happened, the Spanish ambassador was not the only source of evidence testifying to Napoleonic machinations directed against Spanish America at this time. In August, Juan José de Estrada, the interim governor of East Florida, learned that a French brig carrying diplomatic correspondence had been captured by a British warship. Included in the cache of letters was one from the French consul in Charleston to Bassano recommending a naval expedition against Amelia Island. As a frontier outpost near the border with Georgia, the island had long held significant strategic value for Spain. In the months since the Non-Intercourse Act had closed the US market to British trade, it had also become a critical repository for British commercial goods. Amelia, however, was poorly defended, a fact which compelled Estrada to request support from Onís. Hoping to defuse the threat through quick action, the Spanish ambassador turned to his British counterpart in Washington and asked that warships, cannons, muskets, and ammunition be sent to defend the port of Fernandina and the rest of Spanish East Florida against a French invasion. In his response to Estrada, Onís took the opportunity to update the governor on the documents that he had recently uncovered which confirmed Napoleon's continuing efforts "to create revolution in our possessions on this continent so as to better sacrifice and conquer them."[62]

Reports that the insurgent government in Caracas had taken the uncompromising step of declaring its full independence from Spain reached Onís a few days after he addressed the Amelia Island controversy. The disturbing news from South America provided a rather different challenge for the ambassador. Now, he informed Bardají, the American brig *Minerva* was about to depart New York for La Guaira with twenty-six French, four

Irish, and an uncertain number of American revolutionaries, all of whom had decided to answer the Venezuelans' call for support. Onís was particularly concerned about the French emigrants, for they appeared to confirm once again the shadow of Napoleon behind the unrest in the Spanish colonies. Following the receipt of this dispatch from Philadelphia, the Council of Regency determined that its ambassador in London needed to prod the British cabinet to be more engaged in what they recognized as another front in the war against France.[63]

What began on October 7 as the departure for Venezuela of one ship with a score of French subversives became a small fleet and "upwards of one hundred Frenchmen" only forty-eight hours later. Onís now reported that Maracaibo was their destination and that they intended to introduce themselves as "enemies of Bonaparte and loyal to the cause of Spain and Fernando VII." In fact, he explained that these emissaries sought to "sow discord among those loyal subjects of the king, while secretly scheming with the Caraqueños, so as to begin preparations for a second group that is being organized in this country for the same purpose." According to the ambassador's sources, two brigadier generals, Petit and Roncarty, were part of this invading force and planned to arrive looking like "men who had lost everything defending the cause of Our King, displaying the wounds they had received in the service of the Tyrant as if they were the result of fighting against France in the Legion of the marqués de San Simón."[64]

While these false loyalists were undermining Spanish authority in Venezuela, Onís reported that a smaller expedition was also being outfitted for Cuba. Instead of assuming the role of Spanish veterans, however, these subversives intended to make their way to the island disguised as American merchants. In what can only be described as an audacious and original scheme, at least as described by Onís, the French intended to ingratiate themselves with Cuban women by offering them luxury goods at moderate prices. How this would facilitate Napoleon's designs was left unsaid; however, the ambassador's sources indicated that the emissaries also planned to promote uprisings among the enslaved population by distributing money, weapons, and falsified government proclamations offering the Afro-Cubans their freedom. As with the Venezuelan expedition, Onís named four French officers who were already on the island: La Batiste, Sicart, Po'o, and La Farrie. Finally, he indicated that a Captain Mitchell would transport the rest of the conspirators on an American ship, the *Eagle*, sometime in the middle of October. Onís confirmed that he had already sent warnings to the governors in Havana, Puerto Rico, and Maracaibo in the hopes of disrupting Napoleon's plans. Of course, this outcome was contingent on the Spanish authorities following his advice and examining "with the most scrupulous circumspection" any Frenchman or American arriving without an official passport.[65]

Cuban concerns preoccupied the Spanish legation for the next month. Early in November Onís reported the arrival in the United States of a number of travelers from Havana. A few of them called on the ambassador in Philadelphia, as was expected. However, he noted that many preferred to keep their distance, failing even to check in with the consuls. Onís was suspicious because it appeared that these Cubans were gravitating toward the notorious former deputy to Cádiz, José Álvarez de Toledo, who had fled to the United States earlier that summer after arguing in favor of Spanish American independence. Toledo was keeping company with Frenchmen and Americans who shared his views, and the ambassador was convinced that they were plotting "ways to bring revolution to the island of Cuba." To make matters worse, Onís learned that Secretary Monroe had written to the ex-deputy and invited him to Washington where, no doubt, the two planned to conspire together against Spain.[66]

From the ambassador's perspective as he approached the end of two full years serving the loyalist cause from Philadelphia, the threats to the Spanish empire had become unrelenting. In yet another sign of the shifting diplomatic grounds, Onís reported in late November that two agents from the rebel government in Buenos Aires had arrived in the United States. He also noted that the Caracas representative, Telesforo de Orea, had managed to procure an order for twenty-five thousand muskets from the American government.[67] Meanwhile, his sources in Louisiana informed him that a group of Frenchmen in New Orleans were plotting to seize the port of Baracoa by outfitting a gunship and transporting one hundred fifty men to Cuba. Again, it fell to the Spanish ambassador to alert the island's authorities of the danger so that they might take the necessary precautions to frustrate the expedition. While Onís made sure to ask the American government to arrest the subversives, he expected little relief from that quarter and, therefore, ordered Consul Morphy to track the Frenchmen and report on their movements.[68]

Suspected emissaries continued to make appearances in the ambassador's dispatches to Spain. For example, December brought five Spaniards and an Italian who came "to direct new machinations against His Majesty's possessions in America." At the time, their names were unknown. But Onís was tracking them and hoped to have more detailed intelligence, perhaps confirming their connection to Toledo, in short order. In the meantime, the ambassador enlisted the help of a somewhat controversial figure, Miguel Cabral de Noroña, who had made his name as a newspaper editor in Spain before settling in Philadelphia in September 1811. Onís believed that Cabral, a talented but freethinking writer, would be effective in rebutting the "sentiments expressed by Toledo and others" in the American press. As he explained to Bardají, commissioning pro-Spanish editorials for publication in American newspapers seemed to "be the best way to assure ourselves of a man whose pen would have been dangerous to us had he taken the side of the other dissidents in this country."[69]

As January approached Luís de Onís more and more found his attention drawn to Washington, DC, since the latest reports from Capitol Hill suggested that the United States had begun to mobilize for war with Great Britain. The outbreak of hostilities between the two countries would have significant hemispheric consequences for Spain, regardless of the outcome. Not surprisingly, given his personal preoccupations over the past two years, the Spanish ambassador chose to interpret the American preparations for war within the context of the Franco-American plot against Spanish America. In a letter to Governor Estrada, Onís noted that Congress was debating a bill to raise twenty-five thousand regular troops and fifty thousand militiamen for a campaign "to conquer Canada." Still, Onís doubted whether the United States truly was in a position to wage war on a Great Power at that time. It seemed to him much more plausible that the Madison administration intended to use these troops to advance the revolutionary movements in New Spain and the Floridas, "as the favorite project of this government is to unite the Viceroyalty of Mexico and Florida to this Confederacy."[70]

From this perspective, Onís had no reason to think that 1812 would bring any significant change to his personal or professional situation, much less the wider geopolitical currents that had governed the Atlantic World for the past three years. Spain would remain a battlefield. Spanish America would continue to fragment. His personal war with Napoleon would endure, as would his purgatory in the United States. And, yet, the New Year in fact unleashed a series of events that sent the history of Europe, the Spanish empire, and the United States spinning in new directions. While the Atlantic World adjusted to these new realities, the emisario francés would increasingly become a secondary concern to both Onís and the Spanish imperial bureaucracy more generally.

6

Fighting Napoleon in Totonicapán

> Now I have received exact warnings that the Maquiavellian French government has dispatched a number of emissaries to different parts of our Americas with proclamations and letters supposedly or forcibly drawn from our king Fernando VII. Some of these vile messengers have arrived in the United States of America where they seek transportation to different points in our most loyal possessions. Among these are the Gulf of Honduras, where they are crazy enough to believe that they will be able to spread their venom and find allies among the faithful inhabitants of the most loyal, religious, and peaceful kingdom on earth.
>
> —Antonio González Saravia, Guatemala City, April 22, 1810

Following the collapse of the Spanish monarchy in 1808, the Kingdom of Guatemala faced a political challenge without precedent in its history. On the surface, despite the unprecedented nature and consequences of Napoleon's intervention into Spanish politics, the colonial bureaucracy survived the shock of the Bayonne coup that brought down the Bourbons. On the far side of the Atlantic, a captain general and audiencia remained in place to sustain the sovereignty of the deposed Fernando VII across the length of the Central American isthmus. At the provincial level, a secondary tier of Crown-appointed governors personified Spanish authority over fifteen distinct and largely autonomous jurisdictions. Finally, at the local level a diverse group of authorities administered the colonial population within both municipal and district boundaries as they had done for the past three centuries.

Nevertheless, after 1808 this traditional political framework had to adapt quickly to a new threat. In short order some of the most minor figures in the colonial bureaucracy found themselves on the front line of defenses designed to protect the Spanish possessions from Napoleon. By 1810 a rational fear of the threat posed by the French emperor had combined with rumor, gossip, propaganda, and genuine intelligence to convince senior Spanish officials that the danger of a French invasion of the colonies was both legitimate and imminent. Ultimately, local officials there became critical links in what would become a long, rapidly evolving, and occasionally awkward administrative chain stretching from Spain to the Americas, as these bureaucrats were expected to block an anticipated first-wave assault on the Spanish colonies by French emissaries, spies, and provocateurs. Direct communication between loyalist Spain and the Americas fanned some of these concerns. However, as the preceding chapters have shown, by 1810 the person most responsible for defining and shaping the colonial response to Napoleon was the Spanish ambassador to the United States, Luís de Onís. By using the Guatemalan *alcaldía mayor* administrative unit of Totonicapán as a case study, this final chapter evaluates the impact of the Onís warnings on Spanish America by tracing them through the layers of the Spanish colonial bureaucracy and deep into the most isolated corners of the empire.

As the nineteenth century dawned, the one million inhabitants of the Kingdom of Guatemala found themselves living in the backwaters of the Spanish empire.[1] While it was not blessed with significant natural resources, Guatemala's strategic location kept the colony geopolitically relevant, especially in a region that had witnessed multiple conflicts between colonial powers during the previous century. Most notably, the colony served as a land bridge between the Spanish possessions in North and South America. Its western frontier, which then incorporated the province of Chiapas, extended deep into the southern part of modern Mexico and almost reached the Tabasco coastline on the Gulf of Mexico. At its southeastern end, the colony bordered the Viceroyalty of New Granada (modern Colombia) in the province of Panama. To the east, a vast coastline offered access to the frenzied commerce of the Caribbean and the Atlantic Ocean beyond. At the same time, the narrowness of the Central American isthmus kept the Pacific Ocean tantalizingly close and hinted at the kingdom's potential as a global crossroads of empire.

The economic promise of the kingdom, however, was never fully realized despite three centuries of Spanish rule. In Central America, geography proved to be a double-edged sword. Due to volcanic activity, much of the isthmus proved too mountainous for easy communication and transportation by land. Despite a long Pacific coastline, this geologic process also inhibited the formation of bays and harbors necessary for ports. While access to the Caribbean was not blocked by rugged terrain, the intense tropical climate along the coast proved an even greater obstacle to settlement and commercial development. Instead, the vast majority of the colonial population clustered at higher elevations in the temperate mountain valleys that dotted the interior. With the exception of a small mining economy in western Honduras and a late eighteenth-century boom in indigo and cochineal production along the northern Pacific coast, most of the population survived through subsistence farming and small-scale commerce.

Because of its strategic location, the Kingdom of Guatemala, while technically subordinate to the viceregal authorities in Mexico City, remained largely self-governing during the colonial period. However, geography also diluted the effectiveness of those appointed to lead the isthmian bureaucracy from Guatemala City. Most of the kingdom's settlements evolved in relative isolation from each other, and these "sovereign villages" tended to concentrate power at the local level.[2] Even the imperial drive toward political centralization that dominated the Bourbon Reforms of the late eighteenth century produced more political fragmentation—or at least confusion—than had heretofore existed in the colony. As a result, the term *reino* (kingdom) of Guatemala implies a degree of political uniformity that did not exist at the time.

Such as it was, kingdom-wide authority was vested in two supreme institutions: the captaincy general and the audiencia.[3] At an administrative level, the colony was subdivided into multiple provincial-level jurisdictions. The political, economic, and demographic heartland, which included the territory that later coalesced into the nation of Guatemala, embraced eight *alcaldías mayores* and two *corregimientos*. Four *intendencias* (Ciudad Real, Comayagua, Nicaragua, and San Salvador) and one *gobierno militar* (Costa Rica) made up the rest of the kingdom. Each of these administrative units preserved significant regional autonomy from Guatemala City and retained its own network of provincial and local authorities.[4]

The broad geographic, socioeconomic, and political features of late-colonial Central America were all represented to an extreme degree within the alcaldía mayor of Totonicapán.[5] By 1800 this large province commanded the highlands of western Guatemala, a spectacular region dominated by the Cuchumatán Mountains (map 5). From the perspective of altitude, few corners of the kingdom were more remote than the villages that clung to the sides of these peaks, some of which exceed three thousand meters in elevation. Yet, despite the challenging terrain, the province was also one of the most densely populated on the isthmus. Contemporary accounts estimated some sixty thousand inhabitants by the end of the 1700s, the vast majority of whom were Mam or K'iché-speaking Maya Indians. According to a 1778 census, this population was divided into nearly fifty indigenous towns and villages (*pueblos*) and a couple of Ladino settlements (*aldeas*). The largest municipality was the provincial capital, San Miguel Totonicapán, with ap-

Map 5. The Alcaldía Mayor of Totonicapán, circa 1810 (Timothy Hawkins).

proximately sixty-five hundred residents. A number of other urban areas, including Santiago Momostenango, Santa María Chiquimula, San Francisco El Alto, and San Sebastian Huehuetenango, exceeded three thousand inhabitants, while Jacaltenango, Nebaj, and Sacapulas approached two thousand. Many more were about half that size, for example, San Sebastian Coatán, Chiantla, San Andres Cuilco, and Todos Santos Cuchumatán. A handful of villages on the western edge of the province, including San Andrés Huista, San Antonio Huista, San Miguel Acatán, and San Pedro Solomá, were even smaller. With most of these communities established at more than fifteen hundred meters above sea level, the majority of Totonicapán's population survived as subsistence farmers, growing corn, wheat, and beans in lower elevations and raising livestock, particularly sheep, at higher altitudes.[6]

In this environment, what kept the province of Totonicapán from complete isolation was the *camino real*, the royal highway that served as the principal overland route within the Kingdom of Guatemala and provided its outlet to the wider world. Travelers heading west from Guatemala City toward the town of Comitán in Chiapas, for example, reached San Miguel Totonicapán after about three days in transit. From there, the road ascended into the Cuchumatán highlands in the direction of Huehuetenango, neatly bisecting the province in the process. It continued northwest toward Jacaltenango, before a sharp descent brought travelers out of the mountains near Comitán, a journey of approximately two hundred fifty miles that could easily take an additional four days. Those continuing on to Ciudad Real, the capital of Chiapas, remained on the road for another day from that point. Once there, travelers could continue into New Spain toward Mexico City or veer north in the direction of the Gulf ports.[7]

Following his appointment in 1839 as the US representative to Central America, John Lloyd Stephens provided a vivid description of the landscape of the western highlands in his memoir *Incidents of Travel in Central America, Chiapas, & Yucatan*. After a stay in Quezaltenango, Stephens and his companion, Frederick Catherwood, "emerged from the woods and very soon saw Totonicapán, at a great distance and far below us, on a magnificent plain with a high table of land behind it; a range of mountains sprung from the table." Their journey continued: "At dusk we reached the top of a high mountain, and by one of those long, steep, and difficult descents of which it is impossible to give the reader any idea, we entered the village of Agua Caliente." Stephens described multiple obstacles to their progress: "The road was broken and stony, and the track scarcely perceptible." In the end, though, it was worth the struggle, for "on the top there broke upon us one of those grand and magnificent views which, when we had wiped off perspiration and recovered breath, always indemnified us for our toil. It was the highest ground on which we had yet stood. Around us was a sea of mountains, and peeping above them, but so little as to give full effect to our own great height, were the conical tops of two new volcanoes." That particular day's journey was twenty-seven miles, but it was "harder for man and beast than any sixty since we left Guatemala."[8]

While the general course of the camino real between the provincial capitals of Ciudad Real and San Miguel Totonicapán had been established for decades, if not centuries, the exact route varied over time and often reflected shifting local priorities. For example, before 1800 a visitor to Guatemala arriving from Chiapas would likely stop first at Santa Ana Huista before continuing on to Jacaltenango.[9] With the new century, however, economic priorities encouraged local officials to develop a more northerly alternative intended to draw travelers through Yalixján and San Sebastian Coatán.[10] Either way, the camino real prioritized certain stopovers as it traced its way through the rugged landscape of the western highlands. The major urban centers of Huehuetenango and San Miguel Totonicapán were obvious destinations for visitors to the province. On the way to those points, however, many smaller pueblos, including Jacaltenango, Santiago Chimaltenango, Todos Santos Cuchumatán, Rosario, Chiantla, Aguacatán and Sacapulas, became important way stations and rest stops.

From the perspective of colonial governance, the term Totonicapán can be misleading, for it had three distinct applications at the time.[11] In its broadest political sense, the province of this name functioned as an alcaldía mayor, a traditional descriptor for a particular kind of regional administrative organization that in practice became interchangeable with two related terms, the corregimiento and the intendencia, by the end of the eighteenth century.[12] As such, it was ruled by a governor who, notably, received a direct appointment from the Spanish Crown. This senior administrator, or *alcalde mayor*, governed his jurisdiction from the *cabecera* (provincial capital), namely Totonicapán, or San Miguel Totonicapán to be exact. Finally, the alcaldía mayor of Totonicapán was in fact a binary province that comprised two separate *partidos* (districts): Totonicapán and Huehuetenango.[13]

Both in real and symbolic terms, the powers held by the alcalde mayor over his province were significant.[14] An effective alcalde mayor funneled local concerns up and out of the province of Totonicapán to his superiors in Guatemala City and Madrid. In much the same way, the office served as the principal means by which mandates and directives from the captain general and the Crown were disseminated and implemented at the provincial, district, and local levels.[15] For the most part, however, this bureaucrat's traditional responsibilities were largely supervisory. Much of the actual governance of the province took place at the local level through the institution of the *cabildo indígena*, a model of municipal government that the Spanish established in indigenous communities following the Conquest.[16] The Quiché and Mam pueblos of Totonicapán selected their own *alcaldes* (magistrates) and *regidores* (councilmen) who held limited authority over matters of commerce, justice, labor, infrastructure, and tribute. It was the alcalde mayor who ensured that such local actions conformed to Spanish priorities and expectations. Furthermore, in his judicial capacity the provincial governor served in an appellate role for cases initially brought before local magistrates.[17]

Oversight of indigenous communities from a variety of Spanish authorities was expected. In an indirect form, the Catholic Church made its own administrative contributions to provincial governance. The alcaldía mayor of Totonicapán was divided into eleven parish districts, four of which were administered by the regular orders as *doctrinas*. While priests were not appointed to each parish, the clerical presence in the province was impossible to ignore. To take two examples, at the end of the 1700s seven churches and twenty-nine *cofradías* (religious brotherhoods) served the pueblo of Huehuetenango, while the Dominicans operated three churches and thirteen cofradías in the village of Nebaj.[18] As with the municipal organization, each *cabecera de doctrina* (parish seat) oversaw multiple *pueblos anexos* (subject towns) within its jurisdiction. Jacaltenango, for example, was the cabecera de doctrina for the pueblos of San Marcos, San Andrés, Santa Ana Huista, San Antonio Huista, Petatán, and Concepción.[19]

However, in Totonicapán (and elsewhere) the colonial administrative model imposed another layer of intermediaries between municipal government and the alcalde mayor. This was a class of minor royal officials who held the position of *juez comisionado* or *alcalde pedáneo*.[20] Appointed to their positions by the captain general upon recommendation of the provincial governor, these local justices utilized existing parish boundaries as their jurisdictions. In fact, the parallels with the clerical model go even further, for these secular officials operated from a cabecera de doctrina and exercised authority over its subordinate villages as well. In theory, there was a difference between the title of juez comisionado and that of alcalde pedáneo, one that reflected the growing demographic diversity of rural districts. In provinces such as Totonicapán, which was overwhelmingly indigenous, the alcalde pedáneo was normally charged with administering to the interests of the small numbers of mixed-race *castas* (ladinos). The juez comisionado, on the other hand, had primary authority over the Mayan communities.[21]

Regardless of the title they held, these officials had multiple supervisory responsibilities at the parish level that touched on all aspects of daily life, including tribute collection, labor draft, and economic infrastructure.[22] For the purposes of this case study, however, the juez comisionado (the term that will be used exclusively from this point forward) played two critical roles during Spain's imperial crisis. First, this official functioned in a manner similar to that of the justice of the peace in early modern England. He had the authority to police communities and make arrests in order to prevent breaches of social order, and he could punish minor infractions by operating as a local magistrate with the power to apply summary justice. Second, the juez comisionado was the lowest-ranking colonial bureaucrat in the province. As such, he was expected to gather information at the local level and transmit it up the administrative chain to more senior officials while ensuring that their orders were carried out in return. While the province of Totonicapán had only one alcalde mayor, it had nearly twenty *jueces comisionados*.[23] After 1808 their strategic deployment into the most remote corners of the province made this lowly official an unanticipated but critical link in the defense of the Kingdom of Guatemala. In effect, these local justices became frontline soldiers in the Napoleonic wars.

In the event of an actual military threat, the colonial officials in the Kingdom of Guatemala expected to rely heavily on local militia forces supplemented by small contingents of professional Spanish soldiers.[24] However, these troops were not dependable as a proactive force in times of crisis. Enlistments at the end of the eighteenth century, which approached thirty thousand men in uniform according to contemporary reports, appear impressive on the surface. However, such numbers are deceptive. Overall, the units were poorly trained and equipped, and most were stationed in strategic garrisons along the Caribbean coast, in large population centers such as Guatemala City and at the kingdom's borders with New Spain. Despite its size, as the nineteenth century dawned, the alcaldía mayor of Totonicapán could only rely upon three militia companies: one based in San Miguel Totonicapán, one in Huehuetenango, and one in nearby Chiantla. This left the total number of men in arms in the province at fewer than two hundred.[25]

As a result, the captain general leaned heavily on the colonial bureaucracy to preserve order within the kingdom.[26] Because the Spanish model of governance encouraged its colonial officials to blend multiple portfolios, provincial governors such as the alcalde mayor of Totonicapán could expect to prioritize their military roles in the wake of the imperial crisis far beyond their traditional oversight of the provincial militia. In the same fashion, the responsibilities of the local juez comisionado shifted to address the new reality. Decisions made one hundred miles away in Guatemala City meant little if they could not be implemented among local communities.[27] Much as the captain general maintained a tenuous connection to the Spanish subjects in the western highlands via his alcalde mayor in San Miguel Totonicapán, this provincial governor relied on his own network of deputies, the jueces comisionados, to enable effective governance at the town and village level. How, then, did this system respond to the extreme pressures produced by the collapse of the Bourbon monarchy in distant Spain?

The imperial crisis effectively began in the Kingdom of Guatemala on August 13, 1808, when Captain General Antonio González Saravia received confirmation of the May abdications of Carlos IV and Fernando VII. In the short term, the colony could do little except make symbolic demonstrations of its support for the burgeoning Spanish resistance movement. The possibility that Central America might be a direct target for Napoleon only crystalized in the summer of 1809 when senior colonial officials received a decree from the Junta Central regarding the need to construct security measures to address those whose loyalty might be in doubt. This did not yet include the possibility of external subversion, though Spanish authorities now revived an underenforced regulation in the Laws of the Indies (a collection of imperial ordinances) prohibiting any interaction with foreigners. At the same time, the Crown ordered colonial officials to expel anyone who fell under suspicion. On August 2, Gonzalez ordered the distribution of the decree among his provincial and military governors. Within a few days, a copy and enforcement instructions ended up in the hands of Prudencio de Cózar, the alcalde mayor of Totonicapán.[28]

Over the next ten months, the kingdom began to experience signs of political panic as concerns about loyalty opened up fissures in the colonial order. In May 1809, authorities in Guatemala City convicted a barber named Agustín Vilches on charges of infidencia, fearing that the man's rumormongering about French superiority and diatribes against Spaniards might spark unrest among the lower classes. In the summer charges of disloyalty were also brought against José Antonio Bustos, a town councilman from Rivas, Nicaragua. And, in a more dangerous precedent, the municipal council of Ciudad Real unilaterally removed the intendant of Chiapas, José Mariano Valero, from office in September, justifying its actions on the grounds that the provincial governor was an acolyte of Napoleon.[29]

In the wake of these developments, the authorities took stock of the kingdom's defenses. As reports from Spain suggested the imminent defeat of the loyalist resistance to Napoleon, the possibility that France might shift its military attention to the Spanish colonies did not seem so farfetched any more. This provoked a growing level of anxiety that caused municipal councils across Central America to demand that the colonial authorities in Guatemala City take action to improve regional security. Among the demands were the immediate purchase of military supplies from England or the United States to address widespread scarcities among existing forces; the expansion of urban militias; the development of local armories; the deployment of armed forces across the countryside; and the suspension of transfers of regular forces from established garrisons. A series of councils of war in March and April 1810 confirmed the dire reality: the Guatemalan kingdom lacked the financial means, the military resources, and the sufficient men-in-arms for effective self-defense.[30]

By the end of April, the colonial authorities in Guatemala City had received credible intelligence from Ambassador Onís that Napoleonic subversives were positioning themselves around the perimeter of Spanish America in preparation for widespread intervention. With few weapons at his disposal to repel the expected invasion, Captain General González sent new orders to his provincial governors. Echoing the language in the travel prohibitions advocated by Onís, the first three regulations precluded the disembarkation of foreigners in Central American ports and established a process for the careful examination of all papers brought to shore. The final four recruited local magistrates into operations that now called for near-continuous oversight of Spanish subjects who found their way to the colony from the outside:

> 5th In the case of national boats coming from Spain or other points in our America, a careful examination of the certification, the ship's roll, and the passports must take place. There will be no disembarkation without a careful inspection and permission from the Port commander. Any captain suspected of carrying spies or of disloyalty should be arrested. . . .
>
> 6th Since the emissaries can travel in the guise of sailors, servants, naval officers, or any other disguise, the greatest care must be taken with all strangers without distinction. The actions, conversations, friendships, and connections of all who disembark, stay over, or continue inland must be observed. Anyone who receives strangers in their homes is obligated to provide daily reports to the Commander and Magistrates about what is noted concerning conduct regarding public matters. Those who hide anything from the Government will be punished as traitors.
>
> 7th All strangers must report to the local magistrate and provide, whenever asked, not just a passport but also all papers and letters and must justify themselves and their reason for coming; unless someone else is in a position to vouch for them—with same penalties as above.
>
> 8th Finally, reiterate the need for caution when engaging without motive with good subjects; however, we are imposing the heavy responsibility on the Commanders, Magistrates, Officials, and other employees of the ports and provinces, if because of omission or carelessness any of the malignant enemies are introduced into the king-

> dom and, proven in their horrible crime, are not quickly reduced to prison.[31]

The list of emissaries that Onís surreptitiously acquired from Desmolard reached Guatemala City in early May via a private letter sent from Oaxaca.[32] As these warnings began to pile up, a coherent bureaucratic response started to emerge. On May 10, González directed his attention to the province of Chiapas and provided its officials with the names of the four principal emissaries destined for Central America, per Onís.[33]

A copy of these directives was also routed to Cózar in Totonicapán with the admonition that provincial authorities undertake "a scrupulous examination of passports, papers, and conduct of all strangers." González also ordered the publication of an edict "requiring prompt reports of all those arriving at inns or homes, so that magistrates could immediately investigate [the travelers] and proceed as necessary." The captain general required his governors to ensure that their subordinate officials and local magistrates remained vigilant for the arrival of all strangers, of all classes and gender. They were expected to arrest anyone who looked suspicious and report immediately up the command chain: "In the event of the discovery of an emissary or spy, be he a foreigner or a Spaniard, he should be held securely in the most highly guarded prison in the district and his testimony and his papers should be forwarded to me without delay." González noted that the vile emissaries would not travel under their own names but rather appear in a wide variety of disguises, including as traveling merchants, contrabandists, and servants. Local authorities should even expect to see Spanish women among the subversives.[34]

Moving quickly now, on May 15 the captain general published a kingdom-wide edict with updated orders for the colonial bureaucracy:

> 1st All outsiders, whose residence does not extend beyond two years in this kingdom, even if they presented their passports upon arrival, must now repeat the process before the nearest Chief or Judge within two days of this publication. In addition, their papers must confirm their occupation or the reason for their arrival. And if this is not sufficient, they must provide verbal testimony of witnesses until the Judge is satisfied of their loyalty.
>
> 2nd The outsider who does not comply with this will be considered suspect, their conduct will be investigated, and even if nothing comes of it, they will receive an appropriate punishment for disobedience.
>
> 3rd Those who receive guests or travelers in their homes or in public inns will report to the magistrate, within two hours of any arrival or check-in; and they must then present themselves to the same mag-

> istrate within four to six hours, with their papers, subjecting themselves to whatever careful examination the Judge wishes, until he be satisfied.
>
> 4th Since the emissaries and spies can travel in the guise of mule drivers, it is an obligation of the Justices to check up on everyone of this class, especially those who come from outside the kingdom, without detaining or extorting those who are known by locals and natives of these provinces and who carry current papers.
>
> 5th For all the outsiders who have resided here for fewer than two years and for those who come from this point on, a list must be made, taking down all their affiliations with as many details as possible. This list must be sent to me regularly so that I can compare it with the warnings I receive.
>
> 6th Anyone who denounces a spy or emissary or shines light on acts or conversations that would lead to them, will receive a reward of no less than five hundred pesos.
>
> 7th On the other hand, anyone with such knowledge and who does not come forward and denounce these people will be treated and punished as complicit in the most infamous and horrible crime that can be committed and for which there is no indulgence.[35]

In addition to such dramatic measures, González also sought to reassure the public that the kingdom was relatively well positioned to withstand Napoleon. He argued that: Guatemala had powerful natural allies; the Caribbean coast was notoriously unhealthy; the population of the Pacific coast could rely on the buffer of an enormous ocean; and, the interior was so mountainous that a single, well-placed "cannon could contain a large army." Should an invading army breach these defenses, the captain general declared that it would have trouble maneuvering along paths that "scarcely merit the name of roads." And, to remove any lingering doubt, he asserted for public consumption that "the garrisons in the northern ports are fully outfitted with good artillery; the local militias are like veteran troops and have been getting regular training; and, the regular forces will come under my direct command."[36]

Five days later, however, a decree ordering the creation of a Tribunal of Loyalty was published.[37] This direct administrative response to the French threat provided an institutional framework whereby the regulations of May 15 could be codified and adjudicated. Informed by these actions, Cózar prepared a similar declaration for the officials and inhabitants of his alcaldía mayor.[38] Explaining that he had received various orders and warnings from the captain general regarding foreign subversion, the alcalde mayor proclaimed the following:

> 1st No outsider (*forastero*), whether from this kingdom or from Europe, will be allowed to settle in any community while remaining unknown. There will be no exceptions, even to someone dressed as a priest. This rule includes women, too—white and of color.
>
> 2nd When a stranger arrives, you must find out his name, where he comes from, what his occupation is, and whether he carries a passport or documentation that serves as accreditation. You must inform me as soon as possible. Magistrates must pay close attention to what he does, with whom he deals, and if he says anything that "demonstrates his passion for the French."
>
> 3rd If he manifests any inclination to them and suggests anything contrary to our Government, he must be apprehended and secured. He must be sent to this Cabecera by the same magistrates who captured him, and all his goods must be embargoed and gathered up and sent to me, with special concern for any papers.

The fourth order repeated the promise of a five-hundred-peso reward for those who turned in a spy, while the fifth underscored the punishment for those who assisted the emissaries. Finally, Cózar commanded that the edict be copied, distributed, and fixed to all the cabildos of the towns in the province.

With these preventative orders in place, Totonicapán witnessed no disturbances over the subsequent year. In fact, only one potential threat emerged during this period. At the end of October 1810, Cózar received word from the Tribunal of Loyalty that a man named Andrés was reported heading for San Miguel Totonicapán with an ultimate destination of Ciudad Real. It included a description: the suspect, who claimed to be Andalusian, was about fifteen years old and medium in size. He was also pockmarked and poorly dressed with a cloth hat and a ring on one finger. If Andrés appeared in the province, the Tribunal asked Cózar to interrogate him about his travels and examine his passport for signs of forgery. The governor was told to detain the young man until further notice in the event that anything seemed suspicious.[39]

By the spring of 1811, the political situation in the province had changed dramatically. Totonicapán now confronted more detailed warnings about Napoleonic subversion with a new alcalde mayor, Narciso Mallol, and a new captain general, José de Bustamante, in office.[40] On April 13 the captain general introduced himself to his new subjects via a kingdom-wide proclamation. In response, Mallol promised that he and his subordinates would carry out their responsibilities "with the greatest precision" while helping Bustamante carry out his duties.[41] It was not long before the captain general provided Mallol with an opportunity to demonstrate his administrative effectiveness. On June 18, he wrote that he had new and credible "warnings that the abominable French government is now trying to introduce emissaries through Campeche, Tabasco, Laguna de Terminos, and other areas." Bustamante wanted this information distributed to all of the magistrates in the province to ensure that these officials would increase their vigilance. The captain general expected, in particular, that local authorities would scrupulously review the travel documents and identifying material of travelers and notify their superiors in the event of suspicious activity.[42]

Mallol responded two weeks later, writing that his magistrates were now in possession of the latest reports about Napoleonic subversion. He emphasized to his subordinates that the emissaries should be easy to uncover because, as representatives of the "abominable French government," they do not follow the rules of normal society. The alcalde mayor agreed with Bustamante that the French would target Totonicapán because of its proximity to the coast of Campeche and Villahermosa and its easy communication with Laguna de Terminos through the Lacandón forests. He also offered some administrative advice, arguing that Bustamante should separate the parish of Chiantla from the supervision of Huehuetenango and appoint a local Spaniard, Joaquín Mont, as its own juez comisionado. To support this position, Mallol emphasized that anyone entering the kingdom from the areas under watch would pass through Chiantla, thereby ensuring that it be the focus of those interested in public tranquility.[43] The captain general accepted the recommendation but included specific orders that Mont "watch out for and monitor the introduction of strangers and contrabandists" in his new jurisdiction.[44]

In a new warning, dated August 3, Bustamante included descriptions of two suspected agents and directed Mallol to look out for them among visitors to the province. He ordered the alcalde mayor to notify all inns, boarding houses, and other such establishments that they must report the arrival of any unknown guests or direct their boarders to present their passports to the local authorities. Anyone who refused would be held responsible for those who "through their nature, luggage, conversation, or otherwise cause just suspicion." Bustamante expected immediate compliance from Mallol and his officials, as well as prompt notification following the apprehension of a suspect who fit the descriptions or otherwise made himself suspicious. Mallol made copies of the orders for his subordinates.[45]

One month later the captain general had more warnings for his alcalde mayor. This particular report referenced the notorious Monsieur Greffe, who had been identified as a threat by Onís earlier in the year. Bustamante declared that good intelligence suggested that the Frenchman "intends to introduce himself into our possessions, as an emissary and spy" of Napoleon. Including a description of the suspected subversive, Bustamante called particular attention to Greffe's habit of camouflaging distinctive head wounds. He therefore ordered Mallol to pay careful attention to strangers with wigs. The captain general ordered his alcalde mayor to redouble his vigilance in the midst of "such a grave affair" and ensure that all the local magistrates and faithful inhabitants of the province redouble theirs as well.[46]

Less than a week after the Greffe warnings, Mallol's superiors provided him with a new counterespionage policy requiring province-wide distribution. Bustamante now confirmed that travelers from Guatemala City would require an authorized passport or signed papers from the captain general. Unless they were well known or high in rank, all visitors to the capital now required comparable authorization from a provincial governor or senior magistrate. Even the clergy was not immune, for Bustamante explained that the French emissaries were known to use all kinds of disguises to carry out their perverse designs, even abusing "the sacred habit of the regular orders."[47]

At this point, Mallol began to receive reports from his subordinates regarding local implementation of the Bustamante orders. On September 21, Hermenegildo López, the juez comisionado of Nebaj, wrote that he had received Mallol's most recent inquiry asking whether anyone resembling a French emissary had passed through the jurisdiction. The magistrate responded that he had not come across such a figure but would be sure to investigate all strangers to the area. He then implied that the political insecurity was beginning to disrupt the social order. According to López, "without a doubt some kind of devil or demon is lose in the province, for I can no longer tolerate the insolence of the Indians, for as their rights increase they no longer obey orders or follow my commands, leaving me with no alternative but to put this complaint in the hands of my alcalde mayor."[48]

Three days later, the juez comisionado of Jacaltenango and San Antonio Huista, whose jurisdiction served as the gateway to Totonicapán from the west, provided Mallol with a summary of his recent actions. Nasario Argueta reported that he had just received the warnings regarding Greffe and immediately put on alert all the "Indians and ladinos" of the towns in the area. He had no information about any suspicious travelers but promised to notify Mallol in the event the situation changed.[49]

The report sent to Mallol early in October from Marcos Castañeda, the juez comisionado of San Pedro Solomá, is instructive for a number of reasons.[50] First, Castañeda had jurisdiction over a particularly remote corner of Totonicapán. While Solomá and Jacaltenango were only about twenty miles apart, the road that connected them branched off the traditional route of the camino real, which kept to a low elevation as it made its way southeast toward Huehuetenango and Chiantla. The alternate path ascended the Cuchumatánes from the west through high mountain passes before reaching Solomá on the eastern slopes. A road did connect Solomá with Chiantla; however, those who used it were forced to travel along desolate terrain at more than three thousand meters above sea level. While subversives might have seen advantages to such isolation, Castañeda recognized that outsiders like Greffe would draw attention to themselves if they chose to bypass the camino real.

Yet, Castañeda made it clear to Mallol that communicating the will of the Crown to the local population was problematic. He described how he was forced "many times" to explain to his indigenous magistrates the great responsibility that had fallen to them to prevent French subversion. To be effective, communication had to occur in the local language, and it had to be followed by a warning that severe punishments would result if any "unknown traveler" were allowed to pass on the local roads without careful scrutiny. In the end, Castañeda could only promise the alcalde mayor that he would risk his own life to ensure that everyone, even those dressed as "priests, soldiers, or mendicants," was examined. He then added a postscript with a bulletin about two solitary and suspicious travelers: One had been seen entering the region from Yalixján in the direction of either San Miguel Acatán or San Sebastián Coatán; the other had aroused attention by attempting to find a route from San Miguel Acatán to the Chancob hacienda and, finally, Aguacatán without passing through Chiantla.[51]

At least in terms of senior-level communication, the colonial bureaucracy continued to function smoothly. On November 8, the captain general issued a kingdom-wide decree about French subversion which provided distinguishing characteristics about a suspected emissary, offered substantial rewards (upwards of one thousand pesos) for the discovery and apprehension of the targeted individual, and declared that those guilty of assisting this "public enemy" were subject to the death penalty and the loss of their estate.[52] Within three days, Mallol distributed a corresponding circular to "all the judges and magistrates and all the faithful subjects and heads of family" of Totonicapán. This document ordered that Bustamante's decree be published and distributed in both Spanish and the native languages of the province. For the benefit of his illiterate subjects, Mallol commanded his magistrates to explain the decree to anyone who required such service. All were put on notice to watch for strangers and inform the authorities should one appear.[53] On November 17, Joaquin Mont responded from Chiantla that the decree about the emissary had just been published "in both languages" and that town officials had put in place a system of nighttime rounds to keep watch at all hours.[54]

The pressure on colonial authorities at all levels of the bureaucracy to preserve domestic tranquility had been building in Central America since the summer of 1808. Repeated warnings about French intervention ensured that officials across the kingdom remained on guard for the next three years. In the first week of November 1811, however, the colony suffered the first major blow to the colonial order when a rebellion erupted in San Salvador that ousted the intendant and installed a pro-autonomist governing junta. Early in December, Mallol wrote to Bustamante requesting another copy of the *Gazeta Extraordinaria de Guatemala* of November 21, which described the patriotic responses from all of the "town councils, curates, military commanders, and others" who faced down the Salvadoran uprising. Perhaps expressing some insecurity about his own position, Mallol explained that he had sent his only two copies of the paper to be circulated among the communities of Totonicapán. In the future, the alcalde mayor hoped the captain general would provide him with at least four copies of all orders. Otherwise, Mallol could not be confident of disseminating critical material in a timely manner across a province "made up of two partidos and fifty-one communities spread out over more than sixty leagues of longitude and fifty of latitude."[55]

In the wake of the events of San Salvador, provincial authorities quickly shifted their concerns from the hypothetical threat posed by the French emissary to the real dangers caused by internal subversion. On December 28 Mallol ordered his local magistrates to circulate newspapers celebrating the resolution of the Salvadoran crisis. He then ordered them to pay particular attention to "anything that might disturb the peace, especially the rumors that tend to fly in such situations." Now, Mallol expected those who questioned the news or who tried to upset "peace and tranquility by word or deed" to be arrested and brought before him. Magistrates could take action against people from any class, be they "Spaniard, Ladino, or Indian, a cleric or a soldier, a regular person or someone of the greatest dignity."[56] By expanding the emergency powers of his subordinates in this manner, the alcalde mayor laid the foundations for the only significant juridical case involving subversion to come out of Totonicapán during the early years of the Spanish imperial crisis.

On December 28, Joaquin Mont, the juez comisionado of Chiantla, took into custody Manuel Paz, a native of San Martín Cuchumatán, a small satellite village northwest of Todos Santos Cuchumatán. Having failed to uncover a French emissary, the Spanish magistrate instead found his attention drawn to a fifty-eight-year-old indigenous man who served as his town's *maestro de postas* (postmaster). This was a position of significant local responsibility, not to mention public exposure, which required Paz to maintain horses at his stage along the camino real, distribute correspondence, and attend to the needs of travelers. It was, in fact, Paz's ease with outsiders that got him into serious trouble.

According to witness testimony, Paz approached the Mercederian friar Manuel Echeverria on December 27 during the latter's stop-over in San Martín Cuchumatán. The maestro de postas asked the priest about the state of affairs in San Salvador. When Echeverria responded that all appeared peaceful and tranquil again, Paz declared that the Salvadorans had done well in standing up to the European government. Echeverria expressed shock at being the recipient of such a bold statement during a casual conversation with a stranger and proceeded to scold Paz, who followed up with some "frivolous protests." Sensitive to the current political climate, the priest immediately sought out the nearest magistrate, who happened to be Mont, and made his accusation. The alcaldes of San Martín Cuchumatán then took Paz into custody.[57]

By January 18, 1812, Mallol had come to the conclusion that this was a case of infidencia which required a full investigation. He ordered Mont to be extremely careful with Paz, who remained in prison during this period, for previous records indicated that the Indian had taken a whip to two Spaniards during earlier altercations. The alcalde mayor wanted a thorough interrogation, one that would produce a legal brief "comprising all the facts that prove the hatred held by Manuel Paz for the Europeans." On the same day he sent these instructions to Mont, Mallol informed the kingdom's audiencia that he was moving forward with his prosecution of Paz "for having declared himself in opposition to the Government of the Europeans, motivated by the occurrences in San Salvador."[58]

On January 24, Mont ordered the alcaldes of San Martín Cuchumatán to send Paz to Chiantla for formal questioning. The interrogation, however, did not begin until nearly one month later, on February 17. At this time, Paz declared that he remembered talking to a Mercedarian priest back in December. In his version of events, however, Father Echeverria initiated the conversation by asking "Why haven't they captured the Emissary?" In response Paz stated that no such person had come through the area, that everyone was sensitive to the need to catch him, and that the descriptions provided by the captain general were widely available. The priest countered by arguing that this seemed a poor excuse since Hidalgo had been captured and executed in Mexico despite the fact that "eight leagues of people held him up." The priest then told Paz to be careful, for many emissaries were in fact making their way through the kingdom. Frustrated, Paz exclaimed, "Who is going to know, Father, if one of them ends up among all the *Chapetones* (Spaniards) who pass through here, since I don't speak their language?" Echeverria replied that he should examine the passports of all travelers along the route and arrest anyone lacking the required documentation. Paz answered that he had orders from the captain general to do so. The conversation then turned far from the topic of French subversion. According to the defendant, Echeverria urged Paz to sell him a horse. The Indian refused, declaring that he liked the grey horse in question. He added the fact that it had cost him fifty pesos and, besides, was his wife's property.[59]

Satisfied with the evidence uncovered in this testimony, Mallol forwarded the case to the audiencia in Guatemala City in March. The court responded two weeks later by declaring the Echeverria denunciation to be insufficient grounds for a prosecution. Paz was ordered released on April 4.[60] Back in Totonicapán, however, the colonial administration remained on high alert. In early February Mallol received his latest reminder from Bustamante to "redouble his efforts" and make sure to transmit accounts to Guatemala City of "all the people who have transited and all those who will transit" the province in the future.[61] The alcalde mayor copied this order and sent it down the bureaucratic chain to his local magistrates. Once again, Mont responded from Chiantla that he had taken the greatest care to examine all arriving and departing travelers and that he was even willing to declare that no emissary had passed through his jurisdiction, in spite of the fact that his superiors remained convinced of their presence. Willing to recommit himself to the hunt, however, Mont then recommended that two local roads around Aguacatán be blocked to force people to pass through Chiantla. With this bottleneck in place, he promised again that everyone on the road would be "scrupulously examined."[62] And so the campaign continued.

It was here, deep in the Cuchumatán Mountains of western Guatemala, that one of the more interesting though largely unreported conflicts of the Napoleonic wars was fought. For more than three years, provincial authorities waited for the French to invade Totonicapán. During this time, the colonial bureaucracy cobbled together a patchwork defensive strategy composed of roadblocks, checkpoints, mandatory travel documentation, public advisories, traveler registrations, around-the-clock surveillance, and preventive detentions. While specific counterinsurgency policies were worked out in Guatemala City, the burden of implementation fell largely upon local magistrates, the jueces comisionados.

This response also assumed that the French had managed to enter the kingdom. Multiple warnings from the Crown and detailed reports from Luís de Onís declared this the case. But, in the end, Central America turned out to be a battlefield without enemy soldiers. There was no Marengo, Austerlitz, or Waterloo here. There were no clashing armies, no glorious cavalry charges or devastating artillery bombardments. Instead, for more than three years, the colonial bureaucracy went to war with phantoms. To a great degree, the efforts undertaken by the provincial authorities of Totonicapán to defend their territory against incursions by French subversives are a measure of the reach of Napoleon at the height of his power. And while the French emperor never appeared in Spanish America in any form, while he did not design any explicit operation to destabilize provincial Guatemala, he cast a shadow across its most remote corners.

In response, the Spanish launched an insidious and self-defeating counterinsurgency campaign, one that sapped the time and energy of a bureaucratic system that never saw a return on its investment. In September 1812 Mallol issued another proclamation to the inhabitants of Totonicapán that hints at the impotence of this multiyear response to the threat of French subversion: "To this point, the published Edicts commanding each inhabitant of the communities of this jurisdiction to give timely accounts of all the people to whom they provide accommodation and the Ordinances that govern internal trade have been regarded with contempt, all of which has resulted in the concealment of evil people, fraudulent payments of the *alcabala* (sales tax), and prejudice to the public in the exchange of goods."[63] The alcalde mayor added that he had managed to repair the disdain for what his subjects likely viewed as increased and unwelcome government intrusion in their lives. However, he also found himself forced to repeat the now all too-familiar orders requiring strangers to present themselves to local magistrates and residents of the province to register anyone whom they lodged in their homes.[64]

Thus, the efforts designed to uncover the emisario francés demonstrated the clear limitations of colonial governance at this time. Local and provincial authorities went into battle with few resources, their actions effectively reduced to checking the papers of unknown travelers and keeping watch for suspicious behavior on the part of natives and strangers. Still, the move into active surveillance, however primitive, had administrative consequences. The local magistrates of Totonicapán now found themselves transforming the traditional law-and-order mandate they had long held in the colonial bureaucracy, one that prioritized supervision of behavior considered inappropriate but largely benign, into a more interventionist role in the lives of their subjects. This only became possible after 1808, in an environment in which the local maestro de postas might be a subversive. Innkeepers and priests might be traitors. Ultimately, everyone needed to be watched. In the midst of the imperial crisis, the Crown depended on the local magistrate to ensure a different kind of peace, one that provided protection against the likelihood of foreign subversion. As the official fear of French intervention declined rapidly after 1812, colonial authorities in Guatemala quickly shifted their attention toward the growing threat from the Mexican insurgency. As a result, the region remained in crisis mode for the remainder of the decade. By 1821 Spanish authority had collapsed in Totonicapán and across the kingdom, a victim in large measure of self-inflicted wounds that sapped its legitimacy to rule.

Conclusion

Spies and Shadows

I cannot provide the reality of events, I can only convey their shadow.
—Stendhal, *The Life of Henry Brulard*

Whether they serve a literal or figurative purpose, the appearance of phantoms as antagonists or agents provocateurs is a well-accepted practice in literature. The ghost of Hamlet's father is, perhaps, the classic example of how such spirits can shape events within a narrative. Unfortunately, even if such otherworldly devices are not used, the Stendhal epigraph quoted here suggests that the best a novelist can offer an audience is an impression of reality. In contrast, the historian seeks to relate demonstrable truth. Not surprisingly, History has little use for apparitions, since the light the discipline shines on the past through its reliance on verifiable sources of evidence undermines both the irrational and intangible.

How, then, should historians approach the emisario francés? Between 1808 and 1812 few subjects of Fernando VII ever claimed to have confronted any of these agents face to face. While the colonial bureaucracy was flooded with reports about them, the warnings were often built upon questionable sources, vague accusations, and unsubstantiated allegations. Even the most damning evidence uncovered against suspected subversives failed to prove the existence of the kind of vast Napoleonic conspiracy imagined by Spanish loyalists. After two centuries of scholarship many of the names associated with French espionage remain shrouded in mystery. And even if they did in fact penetrate Spanish America to the degree feared by Spanish officials at the time, they operated quite effectively in the dark corners of colonial society. For all practical purposes, the emisario francés was a shadow.

The conceit of this particular study has been to present the emisario francés as a legitimate historical agent, one who managed to leave a powerful and measurable impression across the Atlantic World despite his (or her) enigmatic nature and provenance. The Napoleonic emissary may have been at least partly imagined; however, the Spanish empire fully accepted the reality of Napoleonic espionage, and its officials reacted accordingly. While the emissary might require a novelist's touch to come fully into focus, it is possible for historians to approach the subject indirectly and assess the impact of the resulting Great Fear on the Spanish colonies by focusing on the actions of Luís de Onís, the man who was most responsible for sensitizing the colonial bureaucracy to the nature of this unique threat.

Although anti-French sentiment was pervasive in late Bourbon Spanish America, Napoleon's alleged campaign to subvert the Spanish empire required a singular voice to identify, shape, and publicize the characteristics of the figure who became known as the emisario francés. During the first three years of his residence in the United States, Luís de Onís refashioned a generalized fear of French intervention buried within the culture of the Spanish empire into a malevolent agent with sufficient shape and credibility to drive policy decisions. Stymied by the refusal of the Madison administration to accredit him, the spurned ambassador could do little to advance his diplomatic priorities following his arrival in the United States in 1809. Rather than returning to Spain or sitting idly in Philadelphia, Onís found a different outlet for his talents. By focusing his energy on blocking what he perceived to be a de facto invasion of the Spanish empire by an army of French subversives, he found a way to remain relevant during the darkest days of the imperial crisis. If he could not be an ambassador in Washington, DC, Onís found that he could still exercise significant influence across Spanish America by helping to shape colonial defense priorities. He quickly found that his legation offices in Philadelphia served as an invaluable platform for this work, one that provided both direct access to the colonial bureaucracy and an advanced position in the hunt for Napoleonic emissaries.

Despite the intense amount of time and effort he put into his campaign, the Spanish diplomat often found his efforts frustrated. From his perspective, he faced long odds against achieving his goals. He was forced to engage Napoleon and his agents on what was for all intents and purposes the hostile battlefield of the United States. Though he carried the authority of his office into this fight, he represented a government of uncertain legitimacy and with limited resources. Further, as the impact of Spain's political crisis reverberated across the Atlantic, he was required to operate within the confines of an imperial bureaucracy that was increasingly distracted by internal unrest. Onís hoped to counter the French campaign of subversion through careful investigation and reporting. In theory, this meant neutralizing foreign agents by publicizing as many names, descriptions, and plans as possible. In practice, this proved more difficult than he might have imagined, for the shadowy world of espionage resisted illumination. Desperate to represent effectively the reality and, thereby, confirm the threat of the emisario francés, Onís often found himself disseminating unconfirmed rumors, inferences, and ambiguities to his audience. As a result, his campaign had mixed results.

What, then, was the historical impact of the Napoleonic emissary on Spanish America? Here we must return to the question posed in the introduction to this book: Considering the effective collapse of the Spanish state after Bayonne, how did the colonial bureaucracy keep Spanish America together in the months and years that followed? This work suggests that Napoleon's attack on Spain and his plans for its colonies played a critical role in the fitful early stages of independence. This existential threat to the empire, comprised of both the perception and the reality of French subversion, was so great after 1808 that it became the default lens through which Spanish officials interpreted the potential for rebellion in the Americas. During the first critical years of the Independence Period (1808–1812) colonial authorities sought to protect the body politic from external contagion and in the process managed to stimulate a defensive reaction that provided the established order with some resistance against internal infection.

It is, in fact, difficult to argue that the late Bourbon colonial bureaucracy at any level could have effectively recognized the causes of native-born unrest. By 1808 twenty years of imperial decay under Carlos IV had largely paralyzed the government. During these years the Crown was in no position to initiate a systematic assessment of the state of the empire. Instead, after three centuries of Spanish rule in the Americas, the only obvious threat to the colonies came from European rivals. And, if recent history were any guide, the most likely subversives of the established order would be French inspired. By 1808 the historical memory of the colonial bureaucracy, if one existed, was shaped by people who remembered (or could read reports about) the crises of the mid 1790s. When threatened, they also had incentive to fault people and events far outside their control. In other words, the Crown and its officials had a natural inclination to project their concerns about the state of the colonies onto foreigners. Thus, by 1808 the official narrative was set: Colonial unrest could be blamed on foreign subversion; a record of such subversion existed going back to 1789; Napoleon's invasion of Hispaniola in 1802 proved that he had territorial designs on the Americas; finally, enough reports of Napoleonic espionage were now on record to justify a budding bureaucratic obsession with such perfidious emissaries.

However, even at this stage the process was hardly systematic. Shock, inertia, self-preservation, widespread loyalty to Fernando VII, and a clear consensus that France was the enemy held the colonial bureaucracy and their subjects together from in the first months after Bayonne. The colonial officials were very fortunate with the timing of this event, as it happened. Before the French intervention, a universally loathed king stepped down in favor of a universally loved heir. The empire had just enough time to give its blessing to Fernando before the Bourbon abdications. In the wake of Bayonne, the empire now had an enemy and a cause. Moreover, the resistance on the peninsula was strong enough to preserve a loyalist alternative to Joseph Bonaparte for just long enough to give the colonial bureaucracy time to regroup. Although some argued passionately that Spaniards on both sides of the Atlantic should coalesce around their common connections to a new and ill-defined vision of a Spanish nation, "Spain" did not really exist anymore for these officials, at least as a supreme authority that normally bestowed legitimacy, resources and political direction. At a time of almost unimaginable political chaos, the bureaucracy scrambled to preserve the status quo and latched on to the French threat as a legitimate excuse—however ephemeral or hypothetical—to maintain order. As it happened, Napoleonic subversion also served as a convenient explanation for the subsequent rebellions within the colonies.

At this critical moment, Luís de Onís emerged to organize and distribute across the colonies the material he had gathered on the Napoleonic emissaries. These reports had both wide reach and resonance in Spanish America, particularly across the circum-Caribbean. Colonial officials from St. Augustine to Guatemala City mobilized to defend their possessions against the French emperor and his minions. While it does not appear that substantive evidence exists to tie French agents to any major challenge to Spanish authority in the region, the Spanish bureaucracy believed in and responded to the alleged presence of subversives. Without this motivation, these officials would, perhaps, have been even less prepared than they were for the uprisings that began in earnest in 1810.

In the short term, then, the political and popular efforts to protect Spanish America from either a French invasion or French-inspired subversion helped stabilize the colonies in the wake of the Bayonne catastrophe. There was, however, a more insidious consequence to the Great Fear of 1808–1812. As chapter 6 suggests, both the Spanish bureaucracy and public opinion were destabilized by four years of repeated warnings and defensive mobilizations. Increasingly, many colonial officials found cause to suspect the loyalty of their subjects. Inevitably, many Spanish Americans resented the heavy-handed or arbitrary displays of authority that began to characterize the counterinsurgency policies of such royalist governors as José de Bustamante in Central America, Francisco Venegas and Felix María Calleja in New Spain, or José Fernando de Abascal in Peru. Anti-French measures did not directly precipitate or inspire movements for independence. At the same time, colonial officials, whose legitimacy was already tenuous after Bayonne, were tempted to impose unpopular institutional solutions to subversion. Many such policies appeared to threaten the hard-fought rights won by Americans in the political debates at Cádiz that followed the seating of the first imperial Cortes (Spanish legislative assembly) in September 1810, thereby widening the gulf between the representatives of the king and his subjects.[1]

These developments would take time to mature and feed into the currents that expanded popular support for independence. In fact, 1812 marks the end of this particular ghost story. Over the course of this fateful year, new forces emerged to shape the history of the Atlantic World and Spanish America. In Europe, the equilibrium that had for a time preserved French hegemony over the continent began to crack as Napoleon shifted his attention toward the conquest of Russia. After two years, the military stalemate on the Iberian Peninsula was finally broken when British forces led by General Arthur Wellesley, then known as Viscount Wellington, marched out of Portugal and won a series of battles on Spanish soil, culminating in the victory at Salamanca on July 22, which forced the French to withdraw from Andalusia and Madrid. Meanwhile, Spanish politicians in Cádiz began the year with a bureaucratic shakeup, seating a new Council of Regency and reorganizing a number of ministries, with José García León y Pizarro, the duque de Frías, assuming control of foreign affairs. This office reshuffling, however, was soon overshadowed by one of the most momentous events in modern Spanish history. In March the Cortes upended the loyalist political order with the promulgation of Spain's first constitution, a remarkably progressive document that would have a long-term impact on the Hispanic world.[2]

In the midst of these developments, the Napoleonic threat to Spanish America as personified by the emisario francés began to recede. Loyal Spanish subjects in the colonies could finally embrace the military and political reports streaming across the Atlantic in 1812 with the expectation that the Bonapartist regime and the French occupation were finished. Optimistic Spaniards even had reason to believe that 1812 would be remembered as the beginning of the end of the colonial rebellions. During the summer, the First Republic of Venezuela dominated by Francisco Miranda and Simón Bolívar collapsed in the face of royalist resistance. Since the defeat of Hidalgo the previous year, New Spain remained firmly in the hands of its colonial authorities, even though pockets of resistance persisted in remote areas. In addition, Central America, Cuba, and Peru all showed little or no signs of unrest. Although Buenos Aires, Santiago, and Santa Fe de Bogotá remained under the authority of autonomous governments in 1812, none had taken the decisive step of declaring independence from Spain. Most important, much of the motivation for rebellion seemed obsolete now that the new constitutional order promised Spanish Americans an unprecedented voice in a reformed and revived empire.

Ironically, as the Spanish empire appeared to stabilize in 1812, North America became a battlefield when hostilities between the United States and Great Britain finally broke out in June. In the short term, the buildup to war and its ultimate declaration had little impact on Luís de Onís. The Spanish ambassador remained at his legation offices in Philadelphia occupied with the same concerns that had filled the previous two years of his tenure. January brought reports from Natchitoches that two officers from the Mexican insurgents had arrived in New Orleans on a mission to purchase arms. Onís reported to Bardají that the rebels were accompanied by American officers and that at least one, a Colonel Bernardo, had earlier visited Washington to meet with members of Congress. He also noted that the US administration had sent an envoy to New Spain for the purpose of encouraging the insurrection.[3] A week later the ambassador began to track the movements of a recent arrival to Philadelphia, a man who styled himself the duque de Crillon. According to the Spanish consul in New York, this individual hoped to find passage to Buenos Aires in the company of two men who were known partisans of Joseph Bonaparte. Onís viewed this as part of the larger conspiracy to promote "the revolution of our Americas" and promised to distribute the necessary warnings.[4]

In the meantime, the ambassador urged his superiors to send a significant display of force to the Americas. Having heard rumors that a squadron carrying five thousand soldiers had in fact left Spain for Veracruz, Onís claimed in a private letter to Bardají that if this army were to instead land in Pensacola, it could march on Baton Rouge, Louisiana, and penetrate New Spain via Texas. In one great blow the insurgents of the region would be destroyed and Spain would be respected again by the Great Powers. While he acknowledged that this was all "a dream," Onís had come to one definite conclusion: as French influence waned, the United States was increasingly responsible for the revolutions in the Spanish colonies.[5] As he declared in a subsequent report, "energy and vigor is at once the best remedy against the emissaries of Napoleon and the machinations of this [American] government."[6]

This growing preoccupation with Madison's designs on Spanish America began to color the ambassador's understanding of the war fever that gripped the United States in early 1812. In a letter to the viceroy of Mexico, Onís reported that Congress had begun to debate the need to increase the size of the army in advance of an invasion of Canada, noting that the administration's goal was twenty-five thousand regular troops and fifty thousand militiamen. At the same time, he claimed that Madison did not want a war with Britain. Instead, he believed that the United States intended to conquer Mexico with these forces or, at a minimum, help its insurgents declare independence, for nothing mattered more to this government than incorporating "into its confederacy the Spanish provinces that have mines."[7]

Such speculation on the part of the Spanish ambassador was neither a flight of fancy nor a suggestion of prejudice. Contemporary events did suggest that the Madison administration had territorial designs on Spain's colonies. On February 12, Congress authorized the seizure of Spanish West Florida from the Pearl to the Perdido River. Formal annexation of Mobile came three months later, though the city was not occupied by US forces until the following year. Another blow to Spanish interests in the region came in March. While President Madison did not challenge Spain's claim to East Florida, his administration failed to prevent American filibusters led by the former Georgia governor George Mathews from invading Amelia Island. In fact, US troops helped garrison the fort at Fernandina before being withdrawn in May 1813, when Spanish sovereignty was restored.[8]

Onís considered these developments a natural outcome of the French-led conspiracies that had obsessed him for three years and declared in June "that the intrigues of this Government in the Floridas have all been a premeditated plan with Bonaparte."[9] Whether or not the president had consulted Napoleon, Madison did hope to acquire the entirety of East Florida at this time. In August he asked James Monroe to approach the Spanish legation about opening negotiations that might lead to the American acquisition of the colony.[10] While Monroe reported that Onís was willing to meet, substantial obstacles prevented further discussions. The president had doubts that the Spaniard was empowered to make such a treaty on behalf of the new Spanish government. He also questioned the ambassador's sincerity. A more practical concern was that Onís had not been accredited by the US government. Unwilling to take this long-delayed step, Madison let the matter drop, a decision that satisfied a Spanish government that had no desire to negotiate away territory or go to war with the United States.[11]

As the Florida unrest flared, Onís was forced to address as best he could another blatant challenge to Spanish sovereignty being hatched on American soil. In December 1811, the ambassador was alerted to the presence in Philadelphia of Tadeo Ortiz, a native of Guadalajara who had spent the previous two years in Spain. While there he fell in with supporters of colonial independence and became acquainted with the former Cortes deputy José Álvarez de Toledo. After reaching the United States, Ortiz met up again with Toledo, who had arrived some months earlier. The New Year found the men in Washington, DC, where they inquired about the possibility of American support for Mexican independence. They also plotted with José Bernardo Gutierrez de Lara, a veteran of the Hidalgo Revolt who was there for the same purpose. The two Mexicans then traveled to New Orleans, where they hoped to lay the foundations for an invasion of New Spain. Onís ordered the Spanish consul, Diego Morphy, to keep a close watch on the men.[12]

The events that followed suggest that the American government was fully prepared to take advantage of the vulnerability of the Spanish empire in 1812. In New Orleans, Governor William Claiborne brought Gutierrez de Lara together with William Shaler, who, to recall, was serving President Madison as a special agent for Cuba and Mexico. While remaining in contact with the State Department, Shaler proceeded to support the Mexican revolutionary with funds and advice and then escorted him to the border town of Natchitoches. Gutierrez de Lara made it clear that he hoped to recruit Americans in an attack against San Antonio de Béxar. In response, Shaler failed to offer official American support for the intended invasion, but at the same time he refused to condemn it outright. Instead, he encouraged a former US army lieutenant, Augustus Magee, to join the expedition as a moderating influence. The combined Gutiérrez-Magee forces entered Texas in August and soon captured Nacogdoches and La Bahía. In April 1813 Gutiérrez declared the independence of Texas after seizing San Antonio. Shortly thereafter Toledo, who arrived in Texas with the support of Shaler, seized command of the campaign, but by August a royalist counteroffensive managed to recover the territory. For the next five years the border between the United States and Spain's territories in North America remained stable.[13]

For Luís de Onís, the Spanish empire began to awaken from its long nightmare in December 1813, when Napoleon finally agreed to recognize Fernando VII as its king. The rey deseado returned to Madrid the following May to reassume his throne. This seemingly definitive act, however, had no immediate impact on the status of Spain's representative to the United States. In fact, Onís was forced to wait until December 1815, before assuming his long-delayed position as an accredited ambassador in Washington, DC.[14]

By 1817, he was deep into the negotiations that ultimately secured his enduring historical fame. On February 22, 1819, the Adams-Onís Treaty was signed, which resulted in the permanent cession of East Florida to the United States.[15]

Although the shadow of Napoleon had passed by this time, the fear of French subversion refused to die. In fact, Onís spent much of the remainder of his tenure concerned about another influx of Frenchmen to the Americas. This new threat resulted from the many hundreds of Bonapartists who crossed the Atlantic in search of new opportunities following Waterloo. Ironically, one of them was Joseph Bonaparte, the erstwhile king of Spain, who arrived in New York in August 1815.[16] In no time, Joseph's homes in Philadelphia and New Jersey attracted the kind of men who had caused the Spanish ambassador so much grief only five years earlier. But now they proved to be little more than a persistent irritation. Onís returned to Spain in 1819, secure in his reputation as a celebrated diplomat and servant of Fernando VII. He received appointments to the embassies at St. Petersburg and Naples in the years that followed but never took up these positions. Finally, in 1821 he was sent to the Court of St. James as the Spanish representative in London. After two years of service in England, Luís de Onís retired to Madrid, where he died in 1827. By this time, the overseas empire which he fought so hard to protect during his career as a Spanish statesman and ambassador had all but disappeared to history.

Appendix

The documents that follow are transcribed and translated from AHN-CD, Estado, leg. 5555, exp. 4, nos. 1–3.

Document 1: Luís de Onís to Francisco de Saavedra, Philadelphia, February 24, 1810

My Lord: From my previous reports, Your Excellency will have seen the means that I have adopted to track Mr. Desmolard, the Deputy of Joseph Napoleon now established in Baltimore. You will have seen that I have had the fortune to place various spies in his own house and on the *Tilsit*, men who make haste to inform me of all they uncover. You will have seen how, with assistance from Don Juan Bautista Bernabeu, the honorable and zealous consul for His Majesty in that port city, I have managed to learn part of the tyrant's plan as well as the names of many of the individuals employed in these plots. I have communicated these names throughout our Americas in the hopes that we can arrest and punish them immediately and thus contain the vast numbers employed in this business.

About fifteen days ago, a Spaniard, or perhaps a Portuguese, by the name of Don Francisco A. Peredo y Pereyra presented himself to me. During my stay in New York, he wrote me a letter from prison asking for my protection, as he had been jailed for debt for nearly a year. Either because of the efforts made on his behalf by our consul at my request or because he had completed the twelve-month sentence given to all miserable debtors who lack the means to pay, he finally found himself at liberty. According to my intelligence, this subject had once served the bishop of Charcas in the role of secretary, perhaps as a relation. It appears that the English captured him years ago while he was undertaking a commission for his prelate. He ended up here around the time that the news broke about Napoleon's infamous conduct at Bayonne towards our King Fernando VII. Lacking money, recommendations, or other assistance, he had to fall back on his own talent and industry in order to support himself. One scheme he undertook was designed to interest the people of this nation in the sacred cause of liberty that our courageous compatriots were now defending by convincing them to raise funds to outfit a foreign force that he himself would take to Spain and command. Although one hundred fifty men signed up and fifteen thousand pesos in subscriptions were raised, the project failed, largely because my predecessor Foronda did not support it and because Pereyra himself could not provide enough security for the fortune that would have been placed at his disposal for such a laudable object.

I was reminded of these antecedents when Pereyra humbly presented himself before me in order to thank me for the services he believes I rendered him to bring about his freedom. He asked me for an introduction to the archbishop of Baltimore, telling me that he intended to seek ordination, since it had always been his goal to become a priest and since there were so few in this country that it seemed to him to be an easy way to live honorably. I could not help but worry that this man might become very dangerous if he fell in with the French party led by Desmolard. He is talented, mischievous, and quite learned, he has many connections in our Americas, and he has nothing to lose. I understand that Desmolard seeks men with these qualities, and he pays them excessively, which would provide Pereyra with a way to make his fortune. So, I decided to see if I could prevent this outcome by carefully using him to uncover the plans and machinations of that French agent. To this purpose, I addressed him as a devoted patriot. I told him that an infamous satellite of Napoleon was in Baltimore with orders to dispatch agents to the Americas in order to spark uprisings there. Then, I said that if this Frenchman learned of Pereyra's arrival in Baltimore, he would seek him out and try to entangle him in these schemes. I told Pereyra that this would lead to his ruin, because the moment he set foot in our possessions he would certainly be hanged, since the governors of our colonies have been told that anyone landing without one of my passports should to be considered suspect and prosecuted. In fact, all agents who have recently departed will meet this fate because of the opportune warnings I have already delivered. Therefore, he needed to be careful not to expose himself to temptation. At the same time, someone with his talent, daring, ingenuity, and high level of patriotism was in a position to do a great service to the Nation. If he could introduce himself into the home of the famous Desmolard by pretending to be a supporter of Joseph and then gain his confidence, Pereyra could learn his plans, the names of the agents he employs, and their locations. He could then carefully communicate all of this information to me. And, if he did this independently in accordance with his own principles, the Fatherland would take care of him and find him a secure position, and I would pay well for his services. To this he responded: "Consider it done; provide me with some money to make the trip, since I have none, and you can rest assured that I will behave as a good Spaniard, and you will learn about all of Desmolard's plots." With that, I gave him some money and he left. And then, as I have told Your Excellency, the man who was so well suited for this work showed such skill that he won Desmolard's confidence. In fact, he would now be on the road to Paris or Mexico as one of the principal Napoleonic agents if he had not made every effort to stay behind in order to put himself even more at the center of the plans of the supposed minister of Joseph. Desmolard sought by every means possible to verify Pereyra's loyalty, including making him write to his agents without providing any letterheads. Having finally concluded that Pereyra could provide him with invaluable advice, Desmolard let him examine a list of the people he had sent to our Americas so that Pereyra could draw on his knowledge of the land and decide whether the postings were appropriate for the missions or if the men should be moved. Desmolard, who already considered Pereyra one of his principle agents, then informed him of Bonaparte's plans, and Pereyra passed everything on to me in the manner that I am now going to communicate to you.

Bonaparte, who is aware that it will be impossible to force the American colonies to recognize his brother Joseph as king of Spain and the Indies, has changed his plans. Now he is only interested in trying to induce them to declare themselves independent under his immediate protection, offering them a share in the happiness experienced by all of the countries that are under his domination by promoting a free constitution, the establishment of industry, growth in agriculture, and any other enticements that might appeal. But, what he desires most of all, and what currently preoccupies him above all else, is to find a way to prevent the flow of treasure from our possessions to Spain. "It is necessary to block the export of funds to Spain," the distinguished Desmolard states, "in order to force Spain to submit to the Legislator of the World. Once it has fallen, it will be easier to find a way to make the colonies dependent on whoever possesses Spain. Above all else, we must prevent the colonies from placing themselves under the protection of England. To ensure that they cannot provide relief to the Peninsula, His Imperial Majesty has more than five hundred agents in the Americas working to shape public opinion and win over the colonial intendants and governors. The agents have orders to spare no expense and use any means necessary, including assassination, to remove those chiefs who will not cooperate. These agents are also directed to obtain the support of the leaders of the army and the heads of the regular orders. The latter in particular should be seduced, for they can use the confessional to impress upon their congregations the advantages resulting from the liberty that awaits. They can make it clear that Napoleon has been sent by God to free humanity from the yoke of the Tyrants. They can declare that those who resist his divine and compassionate ideas are committing a mortal sin and cannot expect to receive a pardon."

In the instructions provided by Joseph Napoleon to his envoy Desmolard, which I am including here, Your Excellency will see in great detail the Tyrant of the World's Machiavellian and terrible plan, and you will see on the list attached to it the names of the vile patricians who are engaged in these machinations. I will not provide Your Excellency with an exact reproduction of every word. Since my agent was forced to make his copy hurriedly, while running in and out of the room where Desmolard was to be found, it is likely that some expressions escaped him and that his copy should not be taken as literal. However, since other agents I have employed have broadly confirmed these reports for me, I can have no doubt of their veracity. I am dispatching without delay a trustworthy subject to communicate these notices to you, because I know that I cannot put my faith in any American. Both this Government and Bonaparte's agents, who have been scattering gold all over this country, have bribed them all to keep watch on me, for Desmolard himself understands that my unexpected arrival has upset his projects considerably. He is not wrong. Although I have not said anything about the matter in my letters to Your Excellency, for fear that they might fall in the hands of this Government, I have worked very hard and with good result to establish through public opinion and the newspapers the decided partiality of this administration towards France. I even flatter myself that I have done more than anyone else to make the Federalists aware of the precipice to which this administration has brought them through the secret treaty it has made with Russia and its determination to make war on England and Spain. This is easily deduced from its decision to dismiss the English ambassador, Jackson, and its refusal to recognize me, thereby ensuring that neither of us could challenge its scandalous acquiescence to France. This level of compliance has reached the point where the administration has begun to submit to Napoleon's plan to transform this country into a kingdom for the son of the king of Westphalia, who is the nephew of Secretary of State Smith and a relative of President Madison.

Because of this news and other timely reports that I have provided to them, the Federalists understand that France, which delights in the opportunity to foment rebellion in our Americas while at the same time declaring its friendship with Spain, is attempting to seize Louisiana. This project, which is led by a Frenchman named Fouquet who resides in New Orleans, is so advanced that several deputies have gone to Paris to ask the Emperor to take them under his protection. The Federalist Party, I say again, has become so energized that it organizes daily meetings and dinners and delivers the most vehement speeches against the current administration in every city. The day before yesterday I was invited to a Protestant church to hear a eulogy for General Washington, which was given to mark that hero's birthday and which included comments that I never would have believed it possible to utter if I had not heard them.

Among these the most notable were the following: "General Washington was President of the United States, and his successors are presidents of parties. General Washington made industry, agriculture, commerce, and shipping flourish, and during his time no one ever heard anything about seizures or anti-navigation laws like the Non-Intercourse Act that has caused the ruin of this country. Washington chose men of integrity, virtue, and talent for the most important offices in government, men who had distinguished themselves in defense of the Nation. But today there is not a single man in the entire administration who doesn't owe his high position to intrigue and party. Washington preserved harmony with the great powers, and he kept the treasury full. The current administration has emptied the treasury, and it tries to sell us like slaves to the Tyrant of Europe. There have been proposals to make the presidency hereditary. Soon it will become a kingdom, and then there will be an

Emperor of America. Remember, citizens, what happened in France: first, Bonaparte was Consul, then Consul for life with the right to name his successor, then Emperor of France and now of Europe, and he wants to be the Legislator of the Universe. In the meantime, he will run our administration for you, unless you show enough energy to resist his machinations." This speech lasted for an hour and a half and was interrupted by loud acclamations. Shortly thereafter, there was a dinner for eight hundred patriots and a number of public and private balls across the city, at which multiple toasts were drunk, including one to the Spanish Patriots in the hopes that their efforts meet with success. Since getting drunk during such a commendable occasion is proof of one's patriotism, all showed themselves to be high-ranking Patriots as they toasted each other until five in the morning.

This commonwealth of Pennsylvania is particularly bound to the current Administration and thus to France. From here Your Excellency may consider what has happened in those states that favor England. New York and Massachusetts have already definitively declared that they will not fight should the Administration declare war on England. It is thought that the states of Connecticut, Rhode Island, [New] Jersey and Delaware will join them, at which point they will separate to form their own Republic. This stance has frustrated the Administration and has likely paralyzed for now its pro-Bonaparte plans.

I remain at Your Excellency's service and I pray that God grants you a long life.

Philadelphia, February 24, 1810
My Lord
Your Most Humble Servant
Kisses Your Excellency's Hands
Luís de Onís

(Dated for the record June 19, 1810
His Majesty has seen with great appreciation and satisfaction the zeal with which this business has been managed. . . . The list of the emissaries of Napoleon shall be printed in the ports that are identified in the note sent by Onís and circulated to all the Viceroys and Governors of America so that they may proceed to arrests, prosecutions, and sentencing . . . without the need for further consultations, considering the gravity of the crime with which the accused are charged.)

Document 2: A copy of the instructions given by the Usurper Joseph Napoleon to his Principle Agent or Commissioner in Baltimore, Monsieur Desmolard, and to the others who have traveled under his orders to Spanish America with the goal of inciting them to rebellion

From now on the Agents must have no other goal than to persuade the Creoles of America that His Imperial and Royal Majesty only wishes to secure the liberty of a People who have been enslaved for so many years and that he desires no other reward for such a great gift than the friendship of the natives and the right to trade in the ports of both Americas.

So that they might be free and independent of Europe, His Majesty offers all of the assistance that might be necessary, whether soldiers or military supplies, including the support of the United States of America, which is already prepared to provide them.

Every Commissary or Chief Agent, once educated about the land where he finds himself and the character of its inhabitants, will choose capable subjects who will be given the responsibility of persuading the People of the advantages of throwing off the European yoke.

The People should be made to see the wealth that will remain at their disposal in the Americas, once the ever-increasing remittances to Spain are ended. They should be made to understand that their commerce will grow once free trade is established with foreign nations. They should be told of the advantages that will benefit their nation from free agriculture, once they are able to cultivate whatever the Spanish government currently prohibits, such as saffron, flax, hemp, oil, grapes, etc.

They should understand the advantages that will result from the establishment of factories and plants of all kinds.

And the great satisfaction and advantages that will follow from the abolition of the tobacco, gunpowder, and stamp monopolies.

In order to achieve all this with ease, since these people are for the most part barbaric, the Agents should first win the respect of the governors, intendants, subdelegates, parish priests, and prelates. All expenses and means should be used to win their friendship, particularly that of the clergymen, so that they might use the confessional to persuade and advise the penitents that an independent government is good and that such an opportune moment should not be lost. The priests can make these people believe that the Emperor Napoleon has been chosen by God to punish the pride and tyranny of kings and that it is a mortal and unpardonable sin to resist the divine will.

The Agents must always remind the People how the Europeans oppose them, how horribly they treat them, and how disdainful they are of them.

They must accurately remind the Indians of the cruel means by which the Spanish conquered them, as well as the unjust and infamous treatment suffered by their legitimate lords, who were overthrown, killed, and enslaved.

They must make them aware of the injustices that they experience daily when seeking offices, which the viceroys and governors distribute to those who offer the most promises or money, thereby ignoring merit.

They should make clear the growing population of these provinces and the growing number of men of talent, and they should compare the difference in talent and abilities of the Creoles and the Europeans, between both the ecclesiastical and secular officeholders, where the injustice is most notable.

They should highlight the difference between the United States and Spanish America, emphasizing the happiness enjoyed by those Americans, their progress in commerce, agriculture, and shipping, and the pleasure they feel living free of the European yoke, alone under their elected and patriotic government. And they should assure them that once the Americas are free they will become the lawmakers of the Universe.

All Agents, including those in charge as well as the others, must make note of anyone who declares himself a friend and supporter of liberty. The subalterns will send their lists to those in charge, who will deliver them to my Envoy in the United States for the benefit of my government and a reward for each individual.

My Agents will avoid speaking out against the Inquisition or the ecclesiastical state; instead, they will take care to support the necessity of that sainted Tribunal and the benefits of the latter in any conversations.

The motto *Long Live the Roman Apostolic Catholic Religion and Death to Bad Government* will appear on the standards or banners of rebellion.

My Agents will express to the Indians how satisfying it will be for them to be lords of their country again and free of the tyrannical tribute that they send to a foreign king.

And, they will advise them that only the restorer of liberty and universal lawmaker, Napoleon, can grant this. Such power does not reside in their own hands. Finally, the Agents will strive by all necessary means to make it evident to the People the benefits of such a government.

Once the revolution is set and all the leading figures who will carry it to every city and province are in place, the principle Agents and chiefs will choose the best time for the uprising and then send timely notices to their subalterns, so that everyone will be ready on the same day and hour. This critical point will make the operations run smoothly.

The Chief Agents in each of the provinces and the subalterns in their postings will assume responsibility for the relatives of the governors, intendants, and other chief officials and by such means *poison* all those in this group who are opposed to the operations, a task which should be launched before the revolution in order to remove any obstacles.

The first goal will be to block remittances of funds to the Peninsula, something that should be easy to verify since there are fine Agents in Veracruz and other ports on the continent, though of first importance is Veracruz. Until the revolution has successfully begun, all ships arriving from Europe must be impounded, with their crews and officers imprisoned, and all ships must be prevented from leaving.

The Agents are charged with ensuring that the subalterns provide regular updates on the progress of their rebellions to their superiors. These chiefs will communicate with my Envoy in the United States by designated channels.

For this purpose, it is necessary to prepare for overland correspondence to those points on the coast where ships can always be found for whatever eventuality.

Signed Joseph Napoleon

—To my Envoy Desmolard

For the above-mentioned purpose three more schooners are being made ready in Baltimore.

Currently there are four ships traveling to different places on the continent, as the Agents know, where they will continue to inform on events. The locations that they frequent most often are New Santander and Tampico in the Kingdom of Mexico, the coast of Comayagua near Trujillo in Guatemala, and ports in Peru, Cumaná, Río de la Hacha, Cartagena, Santa Fe, Caracas, and the rest of the

Costa Firme where two ships often sail as contrabandists from Jamaica.

Based on recently arrived reports from Mexico, the Envoy Desmolard promises that the number of elite partisans who have enlisted is infinite. He is convinced that the operations in that kingdom will be successful, that everything is going to plan in Veracruz, and that this will be true for the entire expedition.

He already has a safe conduit to notify New Orleans, where all the necessary aid is standing by, but even he believes it will be useless, since his newly acquired supporters and the ineptitude of that Government, which will not take any appropriate measures when the event occurs, both promise the likelihood of success.

In addition, he has on his side powerful support from the Indian Governors of the Texpanes[1] of San Juan and Santiago in Mexico, as well as those from the provinces of Tlaxcala and Tepeaca. These lands sit on the direct path to Veracruz, which would allow them to cut all supplies and communications with Mexico City.

This Desmolard also has very gratifying reports from Agents in California as well as similar notices from Lima. Based on others received from important army officers stationed with the Veracruz garrison and the detachment in the Fortress of Perote, he will soon control this area, thereby cutting off the rest of the kingdom. He now flatters himself on the outcome of his future projects.

—Copy

Document 3: Printed list of French emissaries

Don Antonio Rentería, a native of San Sebastian in Vizcaya, Chief Deputy, destined for Mexico City, Puebla, Cuatro Villas,[2] Veracruz, and the coast down to Tampico.

Don Antonio Serrano, a native of Madrid, [appointed] to Acapulco and the southern coast of New Spain from Colima to San Blas.

Don Manuel Agudo de los Rios, a native of Córdoba, [appointed] to Valladolid, Zelaya, Guanajuato, and other neighboring cities as far as Zacatecas.

Don Torquato Medino, a native of Madrid, [appointed] to Durango and the entire kingdom of New Vizcaya, including the coast from the bay of San Bernardo,[3] New Santander to Tampico.

Don Anselmo Rodríguez, a native of Cuenca, [appointed] to San Luís Potosí.

Don Hipólito Mendieta, from Old Castile, [appointed] to the Internal Provinces, Sinaloa, and Chihuahua.

Don Sebastian Solorzano, from Madrid, [appointed] to Guadalajara, all of New Galicia, and the coast of San Blas and Tepic.

Don Santiago Parreño, a native of La Corunna, [appointed] to New Mexico and both Upper and Lower California.

Don Ignacio Saldivar, from Madrid, [appointed] to Campeche, Tabasco, and Soconusco.

Don Esteban Romero, from Granada, [appointed] to Oaxaca, Tetuan, Tepeque.[4]

THE KINGDOM OF GUATEMALA

Don Estanislao Oropesa, from Badajoz in Extremadura, [appointed] to Guatemala, Omoa, and the province of San Salvador: Chief [Deputy] for this kingdom.

Don Ciriaco Betolaza, from San Sebastian, [appointed] to Chiapas and the southern coast from Tonalá to Realejo.

Don Fermín Esparragosa, [appointed] to the area of Trujillo and the entire province of Comayagua.

Don Juan Chagaray, from Vizcaya, [appointed] to León in Nicaragua, Granada, Cartago, and Costa Rica, including El Realejo, Sontanete,[5] and Panama.

THE KINGDOM OF LIMA

Don Luis Azcarraga, from Vizcaya, [appointed] to Lima and the entire coast to Guayaquil: Chief [Deputy] for this kingdom.

Don Cristobal Espinosa, from Córdoba, [appointed] to Quito.

Don Juan Vizcarolaza, from Vizcaya, [appointed] to Panama as far as Portobelo and the coast as far as Guayaquil.

Don Remigio Aparicio, from Vitoria, [appointed] to Santiago de Chile.

Don Roque Frias, from Madrid, [appointed] to the province of La Plata.

Don Benigno Alfaro, from Pamplona, [appointed] to Buenos Aires and Montevideo.

THE KINGDOM OF SANTA FE

Don Cipriano Esparsa, from Extremadura, [appointed] to Santa Fé [de Bogotá], Cartagena, and the coast as far as Portobelo; Chief [Deputy].

Don Ermenegildo Estacheta, from Vizcaya, [appointed] to La Guaira, Caracas, and the coast of Cumaná.

Don Antonio Sánchez, from Andalusia, [appointed] to Rio Lache and the surrounding coast.

Other agents who have recently arrived from Europe have just passed through to join those listed above: specifically,

Don Juan Arevalo, from Old Castile, to meet up with Perreño in New Mexico and California.
Don Mateo Cervantes, from Madrid, to join and serve Mendieta in the Internal Provinces.
Don Raymundo Camarena, from Madrid, to go to Mexico to serve Rentería.
Two who have gone to Havana are:
Don Bernardino de Cisneros, from the Kingdom of Jaen, in order to reach Campeche.
Don Lázaro Ibarrola, from Vizcaya, to reach La Guaira.

Another by the name of Don Gregorio Anduaga, from Pamplona, who was traveling with a servant named Don Pedro Banegas de Alcarria, also embarked for Cuba in order to continue on to Portobelo.

The principal [agent] in Havana is a Spaniard and native of Bilbao who passes for an American. His real name is Don Ignacio Berrechea. He has a large following, and he travels the island visiting his subordinates. These are spread around in different places: one is in Trinidad, two are in Príncipe, one is in Sancti Spíritus, one is in Villa Clara, one is in the town of San Juan de los Remedios, another is in Holguín, another is in Baracoa, two are in [Santiago de] Cuba, and another is in Matanzas.

One is in San Juan, Puerto Rico, and another in la Aguada de San Francisco.[6] Two travel to St. Croix and St. Thomas as contrabandists in order to pick up information from Curaçao. There are letters from those agents from Caracas and all along the coast.

Three are based in Jamaica. They are able to gather significant information from the kingdom of Santa Fé [de Bogotá] and Peru, via Portobelo, as well as the kingdom of Guatemala and New Spain with the assistance of six more who travel as contrabandists to these areas.

There are two agents in Curaçao and one in Trinidad de Sotavento.[7]

The agent and correspondent in Charleston is Don Juan Tineo, a native of Valladolid.

Don Estanislao Morales, from New Castile, is in New Orleans.

The chief agent in Jamaica is Don José Martínez Gallego.

Don Santiago Antonin[8] and Mr. Lacroissé or St. Croix have left on the American schooner the *Fly* to join Frias and Alfaro in the province of La Plata, Buenos Aires, and Montevideo. It is believed that a Mr. Duclos, a Frenchman about forty-five to fifty years old, who served Carlos IV as a naval officer and currently holds the rank of post captain under Joseph, intends to follow them.

Mr. Leger, a Frenchman from the region bordering Germany who speaks both languages fluently as well as Spanish, left Baltimore a few days ago for the Louisiana frontier and to ally himself with the Germans who have settled in that area. His goal is to establish a means of communications with Mexico. Three wagons full of merchandise follow him, for he intends to set himself up as a merchant in Ouachita[9] or its environs. When [Leger] said goodbye to Desmolard, the Chief Agent told him to be sure to follow the instructions that he had given him.

Three Frenchmen have recently left for Augusta in Georgia, without doubt intending to continue from there into Florida. Their names are Desmoyes, Carolle, and Kinglin.

Three Spaniards named Manuel, Diego Sayo, and Domingo André have also left Baltimore, but no one knows their destination.

A creole from Lastibouite[10] on the island of Santo Domingo has also gone to Jamaica.

Notes

Introduction

Epigraph: Isidro Sicilia, *Nos el Doctor Don Isidro Sicilia Arce-Dean de esta Santa Metropolitana Yglesia, Provisor Gobernador y Vicario capitular de este Arzobispado*, decree, May 23, 1810, Papers of Alejandro Marure, Ayer Collection, Newberry Library, Chicago.

1. Credit for this phrase goes to Louis E. Bumgartner, whose book *José del Valle of Central America* (Durham, NC: Duke University Press, 1963) was written at the height of the Red Scare in the United States.

2. Rafe Blaufarb, "The Western Question: The Geopolitics of Latin American Independence." *American Historical Review* 112, no. 3 (June 2007): 742–63; Timothy E. Anna, *Spain and the Loss of America* (Lincoln: University of Nebraska Press, 1983), 1.

3. The term "counterinsurgency" is most often associated with the carefully delineated military and political responses to Cold War-era communist movements in Southeast Asia and Latin America. No equivalent blueprint existed within the Spanish state in the early nineteenth century. However, colonial authorities did anticipate that subversion would precipitate insurgency. They learned from each other's actions and coordinated strategies designed to prevent unrest. As shall be seen, Spanish diplomats and colonial officials easily adapted already widespread counterintelligence practices into counterespionage operations against the French. These then supported much of the subsequent counterinsurgency campaigns. For these reasons, I believe it is appropriate to use the word in this particular historical context. See Hugh Hamill, "Royalist Counterinsurgency in the Mexican War for Independence: The Lessons of 1811," *Hispanic American Historical Review* 53, no. 3 (August 1973): 470–89.

4. The historical scholarship dedicated to French intervention in Latin American independence began effectively with the publication of Carlos Villanueva's *Historia y diplomacia: Napoleón y la independencia de América* in 1911. This work, which drew heavily on printed correspondence and unpublished documents from the French Ministry of Foreign Affairs, provided inspiration for many subsequent ac-

counts of French policy in the region. Villanueva sought to demonstrate an interest by Napoleon in Spanish America dating to the months preceding the Bourbon abdications. He identified records which suggested that Napoleon had sent thirty agents to the region prior to May 1808; furthermore, he found correspondence from the emperor indicating that an additional thirty-two departed during the summer after Bayonne. Most of these were afrancesado Spaniards charged with persuading official and public opinion that the new Bonapartist regime in Spain was legitimate. *Historia y diplomacia*: *Napoleón y la independencia de América* (Paris: Garnier, 1911), 172.

5. Villanueva also established an analytical framework for charting the evolution of French foreign policy toward Spanish America during this period. Arguing that Napoleon initially expected little resistance from either Spain or the colonies, he highlighted communications from the French to Spanish colonial officials that incorporated multiple documents—often including the acts of abdication and related correspondence between the Spanish Bourbons and Napoleon—all designed to establish the legality of the transfer of sovereignty. If the agents sent by Napoleon hoped for a receptive audience when they arrived in Spanish America, they were largely disappointed. By the end of 1808, the colonies had overwhelmingly declared their continued loyalty to Fernando VII. Nevertheless, according to Villanueva, the government of José I in Spain remained convinced into 1809 that the colonies would eventually support the new regime, especially if French armies could quickly eliminate the last vestiges of loyalist resistance. In March 1809, buoyed by recent military gains, Joseph and his ministers prepared a new wave of royal decrees, orders, and proclamations for the colonial bureaucracy in an effort to assert the authority of the new regime over the Americas. Among the emissaries charged with delivering the correspondence were Antonio Suárez, Gustavo Nording de Witt, and various unnamed friends of Santiago Liniers, the French-born viceroy of the Río de la Plata. Villanueva argued that this first, optimistic phase of Napoleonic intervention in Spanish colonial affairs collapsed by the end of 1809. Despite consistent military successes and the occupation of almost all the Iberian Peninsula, the French and their afrancesado allies could not undermine Spanish opposition to the Bonapartist regime. According to Villanueva, Napoleon now unilaterally changed imperial policy toward the Americas by declaring his support for Spanish-American independence in a speech to the French Chamber of Deputies on December 12, 1809. Convinced that his brother would never be accepted as king by the colonies, Napoleon decided that peace in Spain was paramount to his European interests. If Spanish-American financial aid sustained the loyalist government, thereby prolonging the Peninsular War and preventing France from directing all its forces against Britain, then it would be best to foster revolutionary movements in the Americas. The presumed newly independent nations would be beholden to Napoleon for his support and their leaders might then seek imperial protection and commerce. If Joseph, who was apparently not consulted about this policy shift, had to lose the colonies to keep Spain, that was an acceptable outcome for the emperor. *Historia y diplomacia*, 172–76, 229–32.

6. Five years after Villanueva's monograph appeared, William Spence Robertson published an article that also sought to delineate the role played by Napoleon during the early days of Spain's imperial crisis. Robertson argued that French intervention in Spain was critical for the subsequent revolutions in the colonies: the "inflammable tinder that lay scattered throughout the vast dominions of Spain in America was lighted by Napoleon's hand." "The Juntas of 1808 and the Spanish Colonies," *English Historical Review* 21, no. 124 (October 1916): 585.

7. In *Napoleón y la independencia de América*, Enrique de Gandía returned to the enduring questions concerning the French impact on Latin American independence. This account held with the prevailing historiographical consensus that Napoleon actively used an army of emissaries to destabilize Spanish America. Gandía was also one of a number of historians who highlighted suspected connections between Napoleonic France and such heroes of independence as Francisco Miranda, José de San Martín, and Miguel Hidalgo, arguing for example that San Martín was one of a number of French partisans whose arrival in Buenos Aires in 1812 precipitated the fall of its autonomist government. As a result, he concluded "we can consider Napoleon to be the European founder of the independence of Spanish America." *Napoleón y la independencia de América* (Buenos Aires: Editorial Antonio Zamora, 1955), 207, 213.

8. For example, see J. I. Rubio Mañé, "Juan (Emilio) Gustavo de Witt, emisario del Ministro M. J. de Azanza, al servicio de José Bonaparte, que llegó a Yucatán en el año de 1810," *Boletín del Archivo General de la Nación* 15, no. 3 (July–September 1944). See also Jacques Houdaille, "Gaetan Souchet d'Alvimart, the Alleged Envoy of Napoleon to Mexico, 1807–1809," *The Americas* 16, no. 2 (October 1959): 109–31; and Houdaille, "La Mission de Monsieur Greffe, 1810," *Revista de historia de América,* no. 50 (December 1960): 475–83.

9. See Fernand Braudel, *La Méditerranée et le monde méditerranéen à l'époque de Philippe II* (Paris: A. Colin, 1949). World War II also shaped Atlantic studies, as this conflict and the succeeding Cold War inspired both a movement for increased hemispheric cooperation and a transatlantic alliance. See Michael Kraus, *The Atlantic Civilization: Eighteenth-Century Origins* (Ithaca, NY: Cornell University Press, 1949).

10. A fully comprehensive bibliography for Atlantic World studies is beyond the scope of this discussion. In 1995 Harvard University launched what became known as the International Seminar on the History of the Atlantic World, 1500–1825. Its online list of Recent Works in Atlantic History—which covers more than a decade of scholarship and may be found at http://www.fas.harvard.edu/~atlantic/Resources/resourcesrecentworks.html—is a valuable resource for students engaged in research in all aspects of the Atlantic World.

11. A selection of recent works on the relations between the United States and Spain includes J. C. A. Stagg, *Borderlines in Borderlands: James Madison and the Spanish-American Frontier, 1776–1821* (New Haven, CT: Yale University Press, 2009); James E. Lewis, *The American Union and the Problem of Neighborhood: The United States and the Collapse of the Spanish Empire, 1783–1829* (Chapel Hill: University of

North Carolina Press, 1998); Andrew McMichael, *Atlantic Loyalties: Americans in Spanish West Florida, 1785–1810* (Athens: University of Georgia Press, 2008); and James G. Cusick, *The Other War of 1812: The Patriot War and the American Invasion of Spanish East Florida* (Gainesville: University Press of Florida, 2003).

12. Victor M. Uribe-Uran credits Eric J. Hobsbawm with coining the phrase "Age of Revolution" in 1962 and notes the use of the similar "Age of Democratic Revolutions" by R. R. Palmer around the same time. See Victor M. Uribe-Uran, ed., *State and Society in Spanish America during the Age of Revolution* (Wilmington, DE: Scholarly Resources, 2001), xi.

13. For example, see the works of the major figures of nineteenth-century Latin American historiography, including Carlos María Bustamante, Lucas Alamán, Benjamín Vicuña MacKenna, Miguel Luís Amunátegui, and Bartolomé Mitre. Examples for each are cited in the bibliography.

14. William R. Manning, ed., *Diplomatic Correspondence of the United States concerning Independence of the Latin-American Nations*, 3 vols. (New York: Oxford University Press, 1925–1926); C. K. Webster, ed., *Britain and the Independence of Latin America, 1812–1830: Select Documents from the Foreign Office Archives*, 2 vols. (London: Oxford University Press, 1938).

15. See, for example, Charles C. Griffin, *The United States and the Disruption of the Spanish Empire, 1810–1822* (New York: Columbia University Press, 1937); Arthur P. Whitaker, *The United States and the Independence of Latin America, 1800–1830* (Baltimore: Johns Hopkins University Press, 1941); and Samuel Flagg Bemis, *The Latin American Policy of the United States, an Historical Interpretation* (New York: Harcourt, Brace, 1943).

16. As Rafe Blaufarb notes, an argument can be made that the historiography of the last half century continues to reflect political narratives shaped by elite actors. Prime examples are John Lynch, *The Spanish-American Revolutions, 1808–1826* (New York: W. W. Norton, 1973); Lester D. Langley, *The Americas in the Age of Revolution, 1750–1850* (New Haven, CT: Yale University Press, 1996); Jay Kinsbruner, *Independence in Spanish America: Civil Wars, Revolutions, and Underdevelopment*, 2nd ed. (Albuquerque: University of New Mexico Press, 2000); John Lynch, *Simón Bolívar: A Life* (New Haven, CT: Yale University Press, 2006); and Robert Harvey, *Liberators: Latin America's Struggle for Independence* (New York: Overlook Press, 2000). However, one can also point out many other examples of a parallel historiographical movement that has engaged the period from a different perspective, one that increasingly addresses issues of culture, gender, and race. See, for example, Peter Guardino, *Peasants, Politics, and the Formation of Mexico's National State: Guerrero, 1800–1857* (Stanford, CA: Stanford University Press, 1996); John Tutino, *From Insurrection to Revolution in Mexico: Social Bases of Agrarian Violence, 1750–1940* (Princeton, NJ: Princeton University Press, 1986); Sarah H. Chambers, *From Subjects to Citizens: Honor, Gender, and Politics in Arequipa, Peru, 1780–1854* (University Park, PA: Penn State University Press, 1999); Eric Van Young, *The Other Rebellion: Popular Violence, Ideology, and the Mexican Struggle for Independence, 1810–1821* (Stanford, CA: Stanford University Press, 2001); and Marixa Lasso, *Myths of*

Harmony: Race and Republicanism during the Age of Revolution, Colombia 1795–1831 (Pittsburgh: University of Pittsburgh Press, 2007). For more on this discussion see Blaufarb, "The Western Question."

17. The New Diplomatic History can be defined as a scholarly movement that returns the state and foreign relations to the forefront of historical inquiry by concentrating on diplomats (both formal and informal) as a distinct social group with a unique language, customs, and institutions. It explores their influences, methods, and actions and seeks to explain their behavior and impact on the broader society by incorporating such modern historical methods as gender theory and cultural studies. It utilizes the traditional sources of diplomatic history, such as diplomatic correspondence, foreign ministry records, and treaties but also incorporates more esoteric material in the hopes of constructing a multifaceted perspective. See Thomas W. Zeiler, "The Diplomatic History Bandwagon: A State of the Field," *Journal of American History* 95, no. 4 (March 2009): 1053–73. In "The Western Question," Blaufarb cites Karen Racine, *Francisco de Miranda: A Transatlantic Life in the Age of Revolution* (Wilmington, DE: Scholarly Resources, 2003) as one example of this new diplomatic history. I would also include Jeremy Adelman, *Sovereignty and Revolution in the Iberian Atlantic* (Princeton, NJ: Princeton University Press, 2006), along with recent works on the relations between the United States and Spain from J. C. A. Stagg, James E. Lewis, and, Andrew McMichael. See this volume, introduction, n. 11.

18. A classic example would be Napoleon Bonaparte, *Correspondence de Napoléon Ier: Publiée par ordre de l'empereur Napoléon III*, 32 vols. (Paris: H. Plon, J. Dumaine, 1864–1866).

19. Villanueva, *Historia y diplomacia*; William Spence Robertson, *France and Latin-American Independence* (Baltimore: Johns Hopkins University Press, 1939); and John Rydjord, *Foreign Interest in the Independence of New Spain* (Durham, NC: Duke University Press, 1935).

20. For example, one account noted that "[Joseph Bonaparte] despatched agents to America for the purpose of exciting and encouraging the revolution there." *A view of South America and Mexico, comprising their history, the political condition, geography, agriculture, commerce, &c. of the republics of Mexico, Guatemala, Columbia, Peru, the United provinces of South America and Chili, with a complete history of the revolution in each of these independent states* (New York: H. Huntington Jr., 1826), 159. An earlier account, *Outline of the Revolution in Spanish America; or, An account of the origin, progress, and actual state of the war carried on between Spain and Spanish America, containing the principal facts which have marked the struggle, by a South-American* (London: Longman, Hurst, Rees, Orme, and Brown, 1817), printed a translation of the Desmolard Instructions. See pp. 79–87.

21. Twenty years of research in the national archives of France, Spain, Mexico, Portugal, Britain, and the United States led Robertson to attempt a definitive statement about French policy in the Americas from the Revolution to Louis Philippe. His *France and Latin-American Independence* expanded on Villanueva's earlier conclusions about Napoleon's interest in the American colonies, citing extensive cor-

respondence between senior French officials—including the emperor himself—during the spring and summer of 1808 that sought to construct a viable strategy for winning the loyalty of Spanish America in the wake of Bayonne. Robertson showed how a propaganda war quickly came to define the early phase of French activity in the Americas, as multiple waves of emissaries were sent across the Atlantic to influence public opinion. By documenting letters from Foreign Minister Jean-Baptiste de Champagny to Victor Hugues, the French governor at Cayenne, he illuminated Napoleon's decision to establish a Caribbean base of operations by transforming the colonies of French Guiana, Martinique, and Guadeloupe into diplomatic, intelligence, and distribution centers for Spanish America. In addition to Claude Henri Étienne Bernard de Sassenay, who appeared in his earlier work, Robertson named a number of French emissaries, including one Octavio d'Alvimart, also known as General Alvina, a Colonel Cabello, and an "agent" Suárez who actively promoted the Bonapartist cause in the Americas into the spring of 1809. As for their short-term impact, Robertson argued that British warships, the colonial bureaucracy, and Spanish American loyalism succeeded in eliminating these real, and other rumored, French threats by the first anniversary of the overthrow of Fernando VII. Robertson demonstrated the stubborn French interest in the Americas by highlighting the arrival of a new wave of revolutionary agents in late 1809. As Napoleon shifted his policy toward destabilization of the Spanish colonies, a "center of agitation" emerged in the United States with the arrival of Joseph Desmolard in December 1809. The next year, Robertson notes, saw the capture and execution of suspected French agents Manuel Rodríguez Alemán de Peña in Cuba and Gustavo Nording de Witt in the Yucatan. Subsequent emissaries, including Jacques Athanase d'Amblimont and Louis Jean Marie Ledreznech, managed to operate without interruption. After 1812, however, as Napoleon's fortunes in Europe began to collapse, active French intervention in the American revolutions contracted. Robertson concluded that French interest in Spanish America was persistent enough during this period to have an impact on colonial independence movements. Unable to produce a direct causal link between the actions of French agents in the colonies and the outbreak of rebellion, he implied both a positive and a negative connection: In one sense, France introduced and sustained revolutionary sentiment among some Spanish Americans, a spark that would grow into a fire long after the withdrawal of Napoleonic agents; in another sense, anti-French sentiments led to popular uprisings against Spanish colonial officials, many of whom were tainted by suspected connections to Napoleon or Joseph. Ultimately, Robertson argued that the French agents and emissaries were important because they reflected Napoleon's reach and potential influence in the Americas at a time when the established order was breaking down. See *France and Latin-American Independence*, 51–63, 74–75, 78–86.

22. Already well-known were the official American agents William Shaler, Joel Poinsett, and Robert Lowry, who received appointments from Madison to represent US interests in Spanish America. Whitaker described the three different kinds of executive agents employed by the US government: "special agents, agents for commerce and seamen, and consuls" (*The United States*, 63–65). British inter-

ests were represented by an extensive diplomatic service in the Americas. In 1807, for example, when the Portuguese court fled Lisbon for Río de Janeiro, the British envoy Lord Strangford followed and proceeded to involve himself in much of the regional unrest over the next six years. See Webster, *Britain and the Independence of Latin America.*

23. In a series of works that culminated in *Foreign Interest in the Independence of New Spain* (see this volume, introduction, n. 19), Rydjord focused on the actions of French agents in the Americas. Addressing the overall impact of French policy on the region, he concluded that Napoleon was responsible for the outbreak of rebellion in Mexico "indirectly by his invasion of Spain, and directly through the activities of his agents." Rydjord also introduced Luís de Onís as a major character in the emerging historical narrative, describing him as "the most vigilant and tireless worker against the machinations of Napoleon in America." See John Rydjord, "Napoleon and the Independence of New Spain," in *New Spain and the Anglo-American West: Historical Contributions Presented to Herbert Eugene Bolton*, ed. Charles W. Hackett (Los Angeles: Lancaster Press, 1932), 293–308.

24. In the 1940s Miguel Artola began his decades-long exploration of the group comprised of both Spanish Francophiles in general and adherents to the Bonapartist cause in particular. His primary historiographical achievement, reflected in *Los afrancesados y América* (Madrid: Instituto Gonzalo Fernández de Oviedo, 1949), was to classify and categorize the followers of Joseph Bonaparte. This effort added a fresh perspective to the traditional narrative of French intervention in Spanish America. Artola's predecessors had been satisfied with a two-phase account of Napoleon's Spanish American policy, which established December 1809 as the pivot point between French efforts to win over the Spanish colonies and a campaign to encourage outright independence. In contrast, Artola's essay posited four distinct periods. Specifically, between 1804 and April 1808 Napoleon found multiple reasons to consider Spanish America a likely arena for his ambitions, even after the collapse of his Haitian scheme and the sale of Louisiana to the United States in 1803. Even in these circumstances, the weakness of Spain allowed Napoleon to indulge in a belief that the colonies might be ripe for annexation. The more so since, as Artola demonstrated, he already had French agents in the region to keep him informed of developments. After Bayonne, the emperor and his senior officials directed a new wave of emissaries to the region with the specific goal of convincing Spanish Americans of the legitimacy of King Joseph. (Here, Artola referred once more to the by now familiar list of suspects: Sassenay, Hugues, d'Alvimart, and Paul de Lamanon.) By the end of the year, however, this campaign had effectively failed. Few French ships were available for transporting the news, agents, soldiers, and munitions that Napoleon wanted. Fewer avoided interception by English warships. Moreover, those emissaries who made it to the colonies found themselves rejected or imprisoned by local authorities. As a result, a new effort to win over Spanish America was launched in March 1809. In this third phase of the Bonapartist foreign policy, the afrancesado government of King Joseph stepped forward to lead the campaign, though it remained dependent upon French lines of communica-

tion and diplomatic infrastructure. At this point, the French recognized the United States as an important battlefield in the campaign between the rey intruso and the loyalist Junta Central for the hearts and minds of the colonies. According to Artola, Joseph's foreign minister commissioned three new agents (Cabello, Rodríguez Alemán, and Santiago Antonini) and ordered them to depart Madrid in April. A fourth, Noording de Witt, also apparently left for the Americas at this time. Again, this campaign failed to win American support. By 1809 the Junta Central was well aware of the existence of the emissaries and taking active countermeasures to warn colonial authorities of their plans and secure the colonies, even as French armies advanced on the battlefields in Spain itself. Antonini reached the United States in December. Alemán and de Witt reached the colonies in 1810 (in July and November respectively) and were executed upon arrival. In the meantime, the final phase of French strategy unfolded as Napoleon decided to reassert his unilateral control over the American policy by declaring his support for Spanish American independence. In this environment, new agents provocateurs—including Desmolard, d'Amblimont, and Ledrezenech—made their appearance, taking their orders from Paris and supervising the introduction of scores of subversives into the Spanish colonies over the course of the next two years. Transcriptions of many of the letters from Napoleon to his officials and agents were published in Caracciolo Parra Pérez, *Bayona y la política de Napoleón en America* (Caracas: Tip. Americana, 1959). It should be noted that Lyman Johnson casts doubt upon some of the details of the Artola narrative in his research on Antonini; see his *Workshop of Revolution: Plebeian Buenos Aires and the Atlantic World, 1776–1810* (Durham, NC: Duke University Press, 2011), 267.

25. Specifically, "The action of these emissaries and the impact they may have had on the independence movement in Spanish America have so far received little attention. . . . It is certain, however, that the documents of the time and especially the Mexican newspapers, both loyalist and revolutionary, often mention Napoleon's designs against New Spain and it is quite possible that this threat created the war psychosis which was to cause the first uprisings against the Spanish domination" (Houdaille, "Gaetan Souchet d'Alvimart," 109). Elsewhere, Houdaille summarized the previous research on the topic and contributed additional names to the growing list of suspected French agents: Francisco Zápari, José María Navarro, José Bocony, Fausto Turbini, Manuel de Inca Jupánguez, and José Estonlinque ("Frenchmen and Francophiles in New Spain from 1760 to 1810," *The Americas* 13, no. 1 [July 1956]: 1–29). Houdaille's essays on d'Alvimart and Monsieur Greffe, respectively, shine a spotlight on two mysterious figures whose notoriety in contemporary sources and suspected intrigues shaped much of the early bureaucratic reaction to potential threats from France. In "Gaetan Souchet d'Alvimart," Houdaille concluded that d'Alvimart was likely not an official emissary of Napoleon but rather someone who considered himself a legitimate spokesman for the emperor while on private business to Spanish America. The evidence for Monsieur Greffe also came back inconclusive. Seeking some confirmation of his identity and backstory, Houdaille traced a likely candidate in one François Denis de Greffé (an officer in a Hussars regiment

that was sent to Spain in 1809 and who later found his way to the United States) but also questioned the accuracy of the claims made against this individual. In fact, Houdaille believed that the evidence against many of the people suspected of being French emissaries would not hold up to careful scrutiny: "We were unable to identify a single one with the exception of de Greffe by viewing files of the Ministry of War. There are a dozen Desmolard, all originating in the Dauphiné. None of the information given in the records allows us to discern which came to Baltimore to organize the sending of the emissaries of Napoleon into Spanish America. There is a family Fuchsamberg of Amblimont but Jacques Athanase of Amblimont does not obviously belong" ("La Mission de Monsieur Greffe," 483).

Chapter 1

Epigraph: "La voz del Patricio leal a sus hermanos con el motive de la real proclamación del S. D. Fernando VII, y la funesta crisis en que se halla la Monarquía." Quoted in Isidro Vanegas Useche, ed., *Plenitud y disolución del poder monárquico en la Nueva Granada: Documentos 1807–1819* (Bucaramanga: Universidad Industrial de Santander, Colección Bicentenario, 2010), 112–13.

1. For an overview of this period, see John Lynch, *The Hispanic World in Crisis and Change, 1598–1700*, vol. 2, *A History of Spain* (Oxford: Blackwell Press, 1992).

2. For a general overview and individual case studies of the Bourbon Reforms, see Jordana Dym and Christophe Belaubre, eds., *Politics, Economy and Society in Bourbon Central America, 1759–1821* (Boulder: University Press of Colorado, 2007). The classic monograph on the topic is Richard Herr, *The Eighteenth-Century Revolution in Spain* (Princeton, NJ: Princeton University Press, 1958).

3. José de Bustamante, the then captain general of Guatemala, used the phrase "*la destructora alianza*" in his first public decree to his new subjects as he recounted a decisive event that had happened during his earlier posting as the governor of Montevideo. In an incident suggestive of the unequal relationship between the two allies, a small French squadron attempted to dock at the port in 1802 without the customary salute to the Spanish flag. By refusing to accept the slight, Bustamante won significant popular support for his stand in defense of Spanish rights. See José de Bustamante, *El Presidente Gobernador y Capitán General de Guatemala*, decree, April 13, 1811, Latin American Library, Tulane University (hereafter TU-LAL), 1.

4. Claudia Rosas Lauro discusses the theme of fear directly in *Del trono a la guillotina: El impacto de la Revolución Francesa en el Perú (1789–1808)* (Lima: Institut français d'études andines, Embajada de Francia en el Perú, Fondo Editorial de la Pontificia Universidad Católica del Perú, 2006), 167–78. As she notes, a study of fear in history begins with Georges Lefebvre, *The Great Fear of 1789: Rural Panic in Revolutionary France* (New York: Pantheon Books, 1973). See also Herr, *Eighteenth-Century Revolution*, 239–68.

5. Respectively, Zenón de Somodevilla (1702–1781), Pedro Rodríguez de Campomanes (1723–1802), José Moñino y Redondo (1728–1808), and Pedro Pablo Abarca de Bolea y Jiménez de Urrea (1718–1798).

6. Herr, *Eighteenth-Century Revolution*, 154–200.

7. Herr cites more than thirteen thousand French heads of families resident in Spain and more than four thousand French travelers at the beginning of the 1790s (*Eighteenth-Century Revolution*, 257). Houdaille cites a native French population of four thousand in Cadiz and ten thousand in Madrid by the end of the century. According to his research, New Spain saw more than seven hundred immigrants from France over the 1700s ("Frenchmen and Francophiles," 3–6). Of course, most of Spanish Louisiana was French in ancestry, culture, and language. Dislocations from the Haitian Revolution would disperse another large wave of French migrants across Spanish America in the 1790s. See Nathalie Dessens, "Napoleon and Louisiana: New Atlantic Perspectives," in *Napoleon's Atlantic: The Impact of Napoleonic Empire in the Atlantic World*, ed. Christophe Belaubre, Jordana Dym, and John Savage (Leiden: Brill, 2010), 63–77.

8. Herr, *Eighteenth-Century Revolution*, 240–48; 256–65.

9. Quoted in Rosas Lauro, *Del trono a la guillotina*, 181.

10. This "propaganda campaign" is the subject of chapter 9 in Herr, *Eighteenth-Century Revolution*, 269–96.

11. For an overview, see David Barry Gaspar and David P. Geggus, eds., *A Turbulent Time: The French Revolution and the Greater Caribbean* (Bloomington: Indiana University Press, 1997); and Rosario Sevilla Soler, "Las repercusiones de la Revolución Francesa en el Caribe español: Los casos de Santo Domingo y Trinidad," *Cuadernos Americanos de Historia Nueva Época* 5, no. 17 (September–October 1989): 126–30.

12. "Si entriegan la Plaza los dejamos / y si no la entriegan los matamos / lo ablamos con suffisiensia / Por que emos de pregonár, / la libertad de consiensia / no asperen a questa rruina / por que emos de hacer poner / en la plaza, Guillotina. / Viva la Nasion francesa / ¿Esta bien aquesta pieza?" Quoted in Ricardo Caillet-Bois, *La América española y la revolución francesa* (Buenos Aires: Talleres gráficos Rodríguez Giles, 1940), 172.

13. In 1804, Captain General Someruelos put the number of immigrants at eighteen thousand. See Matt D. Childs, "'The Revolution against the French': Race and Patriotism in the 1809 Riot in Havana," in Belaubre, Dym, and Savage, *Napoleon's Atlantic*, 124.

14. Quoted in Caillet-Bois, *La América española*, 174.

15. John Rydjord, "The French Revolution and Mexico," *Hispanic American Historical Review* (hereafter *HAHR*) 9, no. 1 (1929): 80. See also Kimberly S. Hanger, "Conflicting Loyalties: The French Revolution and Free People of Color in Spanish New Orleans," in Gaspar and Geggus, *A Turbulent Time*, 178–203.

16. Quoted in Rydjord, "French Revolution and Mexico," 62–63.

17. Houdaille, "Frenchmen and Francophiles," 13–15; Rydjord, "French Revolution and Mexico," 82–84. A 1791 report included warnings about an American agent named Folney who intended to travel from Bordeaux to New Spain in order to subvert the Spanish regime. Another suspected agent, Mateo Coste, became the focus of an intensive search around Acayucan in 1792. Rydjord describes the French

community as including barbers, cooks, soldiers, merchants, and farmers ("French Revolution and Mexico," 87).

18. The pasquinade reads: "Los más sabios / Son los franceses. / El seguirles en sus / Dictámenes, no es absurdo. / Por mucho que hagan las leyes / Nunca podrá sofocar los gritos / Que inspira la Naturaleza." Quoted in Caillet-Bois, *La América española*, 167.

19. Rydjord, "French Revolution and Mexico," 63, 89–91. Trial records indicated that the suspects held frequent meetings where they discussed news from France, sang the "Marseillaise," and shared revolutionary documents.

20. Rydjord, *Foreign Interest*, 141.

21. Houdaille, "Frenchmen and Francophiles," 14–15. According to his sources, one of the exiles was Juan Lafita y Miramón, who moved to Louisiana and became infamous as the privateer/pirate Jean Lafitte. See also Rydjord, "French Revolution and Mexico," 93–96; Rydjord, *Foreign Interest*, 143–46.

22. José Domás y Valle to Junta Superior, Guatemala, October 21, 1794, Archivo General de Centroámerica (hereafter AGCA), A3, leg. 2165, exp. 32519.

23. Caillet-Bois, *La América española*, 171.

24. *La América española*, 181–84.

25. *La América española*, 176.

26. Quoted in Caillet-Bois, *La América española*, 198.

27. *La América española*, 198–99. For more on Espejo see Carlos Paladines, *Juicio a Eugenio Espejo* (Quito: Casa de la Cultura Ecuatoriana, 2007).

28. Quoted in Caillet-Bois, *La América española*, 185.

29. David Geggus, "Slave Rebellion during the Age of Revolution," in *Curacao in the Age of Revolutions, 1795–1800*, ed. Wim Klooster and Gert Oostindie (Leiden: BRILL, 2011), 23–56.

30. Carmen L. Michelena, *Luces revolucionarias: De la rebelión de Madrid (1795) a la rebelión de La Guaira (1797)* (Caracas: Fundación Centro de Estudios Latinoamericanos Rómulo Gallegos, 2010), 290. See also Ineke Phaf-Rheinberger, *The "Air of Liberty": Narratives of the South Atlantic Past* (Amsterdam: Editions Rodopi B. V.), 95.

31. For more on this period in Peru see in particular Rosas Lauro, *Del trono a la guillotina*, 156–226.

32. *Del trono a la guillotina*, 187. Rosas Lauro identifies ninety six people charged with reading prohibited books in the period between 1780 and 1808. Inevitably, many members of the intellectual elite, including military officers, bureaucrats, clerics, and titled noblemen were implicated.

33. Rosas Lauro identifies a small but visible French community in Lima, most of whom were members of the plebe, working as barbers, cooks, surgeons, waiters, and shopkeepers. Other provinces also had small concentrations of French immigrants (*Del trono a la guillotina*, 199–200).

34. *Del trono a la guillotina*, 203, and Carta del Virrey Gil de Taboaba al Duque de Alcudia, September 23, 1794, quoted in the same book, 204. See Caillet-Bois, *La América española*, 194–96.

35. Caillet-Bois, *La América española*, 196–97.

36. *La América española*, 199–206.

37. *La América española*, 202.

38. Johnson, *Workshop of Revolution*, 155.

39. *Workshop of Revolution*, 149–78.

40. *Workshop of Revolution*, 149.

41. The Archivo General de la Nación in Buenos Aires (hereafter AGN-BA) holds records from the case in Tribunales 36-1-5; leg. 60, exp. 6.

42. See Childs, "'Revolution against the French,'" 119–38. See also Sigfrido Vázquez Cienfuegos, "*Víboras en nuestro seno*: Franceses y afrancesados en Cuba durante la Guerra de la independencia," in *El comienzo de la Guerra de la Independencia*, ed. José Luis Martínez Sanz and Emilio de Diego (Madrid: Congreso Internacional del Bicentenario, 2008), 1–13. Vázquez Cienfuegos estimates that about 6 percent of Cuba's five hundred thousand inhabitants in 1808 were French refugees, a percentage that reached as high as 22 percent on the eastern part of the island.

43. *Proclama del Sor Capitn Gral a los habitantes de la Ysla de Cuba y de esta Provincia*, July 17, 1808. Included in Enrique White to the Inhabitants of East Florida, decree, September 5, 1808, University of Florida, East Florida Papers (hereafter UF-EFP), reel 118.

44. This event was summarized by the royal notary three days later. See José de Zubizarreta, September 6, 1808, UF-EFP, reel 118. The governor then sent the report on to the captain general. See Enrique White to Someruelos, St. Augustine, September 10, 1808, UF-EFP, reel 11. Such sentiment was not unanimous, it appears. On September 7, Zubizarreta was forced to issue a public statement offering a reward of one hundred pesos for information that would lead to the arrest of the person responsible for removing the official decree announcing the war against France that had been "attached to the corner of the house occupied by Gabriel González on the Plazuela del Cuartel de Cuba." See José de Zubizarreta, *Aviso al publico*, St. Augustine, September 7, 1808, UF-EFP, reel 118.

45. Childs, "'Revolution against the French,'" 125.

46. Enrique White to Someruelos, St. Augustine, September 10, 1808, UF-EFP, reel 15. James Cusick estimates the total population of the colony in 1811 at 3690, half of whom lived in St. Augustine itself. Cusick, *The Other War*, 41.

47. White to Someruelos, St. Augustine, September 16, 1808, UF-EFP, reel 11. Pleas for clemency from French residents of St. Augustine, including Guillermo Gigant and Simon Le Roy, are common in the records of this period. See for example Bernardo Segur to White, St. Augustine, September 1, 1808, UF-EFP, reel 80.

48. This decree was written by Pedro Cevallos, who also reported on recent decisions by the Junta, the Council of Castile, and the Council of the Indies to declare null and void the "acts of sovereignty exercised by the intrusive government." He announced that colonial officials should suspend all "orders, elections, nominations, bills of exchange, proclamations, and other rulings emanating from that illegitimate authority" and emphasized that colonial officials be sure not to admit "French emissaries or partisans to their cause, nor the incendiary papers they are accustomed to distribute." *Real Orden*, decree, Aranjuez, November 1, 1808, UF-EFP, reel 118.

49. Someruelos, "A las dos Floridas," Havana, February 21, 1809, UF Papeles de Cuba (hereafter UF-PC), leg. 1566, reel 68. East Floridians received the Junta orders on March 14, 1809. See Enrique White, proclamation, St. Augustine, March 14, 1809, UF-EFP, reel 118.

50. Vicente Folch to Someruelos, Pensacola, February 21, 1809, UF-PC, leg. 1566, reel 66.

51. Quoted in Vázquez Cienfuegos, "*Víboras en nuestro seno*," 5–6.

52. Childs, "'Revolution against the French,'" 126.

53. Someruelos, decree, Havana, March 12, 1809, UF-PC, leg. 1566, reel 68. Governor White acknowledged his receipt of these orders in May. He wrote: "The French established here have been removed to the United States of America, and I have no reason to be suspicious of the few who remain: but, nevertheless, I will keep a scrupulous watch over their conduct, and anyone who does not conform to our religion and national laws will be expelled from the Province; and at the same time I will take care of public tranquility and not allow the introduction of any French emissaries or those addicted to their cause." White to Someruelos, St. Augustine, May 12, 1809, UF-PC, leg. 1566, reel 68.

54. White to Someruelos, May 12, 1809.

55. By March, the captain general had already fought off numerous charges questioning his own loyalty emanating from the former intendant of Havana, Rafael Gómez Roubaud. Someruelos found himself in the difficult position of having close ties to three of Joseph Bonaparte's closest ministers: Secretary of State Urquijo, Secretary of War O'Farrill, and Secretary of the Indies Azanza. Even his stepfather, Antonio de los Heros, the conde de Montarco, had joined the Bonapartist court. See Vázquez Cienfuegos, "*Víboras en nuestro seno*," 4. According to Vázquez Cienfuegos, the Havana *junta de vigilancia* investigated 563 people between March 18 and July 21 ("*Víboras en nuestro seno*," 6).

56. See the analysis of the Havana riots in Childs, "'Revolution against the French,'" 127–35. Forty ships transported more than six thousand refugees to New Orleans during the summer of 1809. Vázquez Cienfuegos, "*Víboras en nuestro seno*," 6.

57. The *Gazeta de México* published the news that Joseph Bonaparte had assumed the Spanish throne on July 16. See Timothy E. Anna, *The Fall of the Royal Government in Mexico City* (Lincoln: University of Nebraska Press, 1978), 37–38. The *Centinelle* also brought correspondence from Prince Murat to Viceroy José de Iturrigaray, who ordered that the documents be destroyed. See Artola, *Los afrancesados*, 553.

58. Anna, *Fall of the Royal Government (Mexico)*, 39–56. See also Brian Hamnett, "Mexico's Royalist Coalition," *Journal of Latin American Studies* 12, no. 1 (May 1980): 61–63.

59. Anna, *Fall of the Royal Government (Mexico)*, 40. Demonstrating his own interest in the colony, on May 25 Napoleon personally appointed a Spanish general, Gregorio de la Cuesta, to be the new viceroy of New Spain. Cuesta declined the position, however. See Artola, *Los afrancesados*, 547.

60. Many in the city believed that the newly appointed viceroy was Miguel José de Azanza, who had served as viceroy of New Spain only a decade earlier. This summary of the August 10 uprising at Veracruz is drawn largely from Miguel Lerdo de

Tejada, *Apuntes históricos de la heróica ciudad de Vera-Cruz,* vol. 2 (Mexico City: Imprenta de Vicente García Torres, 1857), 28–42.

61. See Christon I. Archer, "Mexico en 1810: El fin del principio, el principio del fin," in *Mexico en tres momentos, 1810-1910-2010: Hacia la conmemoración del bicentenario de la Independencia y del centenario de la Revolución Mexicana: Retos y perspectivas*, vol. 1, ed. Alicia Mayer (Mexico City: UNAM, 2007), 26–27; Artola, *Los afrancesados*, 554. The quote comes from Robertson, *France and Latin-American Independence*, 56.

62. The most comprehensive account of his life is found in Houdaille, "Gaetan Souchet d'Alvimart," 109–31. See also the documents collected in "El aventurero conde Octaviano d'Alvimar espia de Napoleon," *Boletín del Archivo General de la Nación* 7, no. 2 (April/May/June 1936): 161–75.

63. Folch to Someruelos, January 24, 1809, UF-PC, leg. 1566, reel 66. These documents include the parts of the case that were referred by the governor of Baton Rouge to the governor of Pensacola and finally to the captain general in Cuba. See also Houdaille, "Gaetan Souchet d'Alvimart," 120–21.

64. Folch to Someruelos, January 24, 1809.

65. Houdaille, "Gaetan Souchet d'Alvimart," 122–24.

66. Robertson, *France and Latin-American Independence*, 59.

67. Anna, *Fall of the Royal Government (Mexico)*, 67.

68. See the case against fray Mariano Fernández de Córdoba from May 1809, as summarized in Antonio Ibarra, "Crimenes y castigos politicos en la Nueva España borbónica," in *Las guerras de independencia en la América española*, ed. Marta Terán and José Antonio Serrano Ortega (Morelia: El Colegio de Michoacán, 2002), 261–62.

69. Anna, *Fall of the Royal Government (Mexico)*, 60, 66–67. See also Ibarra, "Crimenes y castigos," 258–60; and Brian R. Hamnett, *Revolución y contrarevolucion en México y el Perú: Liberalismo, realeza y separatismo (1800–1824)* (Mexico: Fondo de Cultura Económica, 1978).

70. Caracciolo Parra Pérez, *Historia de la primera República de Venezuela* (Caracas: Tip. Americana, 1939), 145.

71. Pérez, *Historia*, 146.

72. Pérez, *Historia*, 146–52; Artola, *Los afrancesados*, 552–53.

73. Quoted in Robertson, *France and Latin-American Independence*, 59.

74. Parra Pérez, *Historia*, 157–58.

75. Racine, *Francisco de Miranda*, 173–85; Parra Pérez, *Historia*, 160–61.

76. Parra Pérez, *Historia*, 189–90. Emparán arrived under unusual circumstances. He knew the colony well, having served as the governor of Cumaná from 1792 to 1804. In May 1808, this experience brought him to the attention of Prince Joachim Murat, who sought to appoint him captain general of Venezuela under Joseph's evolving government. Emparán declared for the loyalists, however, and received the posting from the Junta Central in January 1809. Many in Spanish America continued to link him to Napoleon, however, using that stain on his reputation to question his loyalty.

77. See the collection of primary sources in Vanegas Useche, *Plenitud y disolución* (see note to epigraph, this chapter).

78. Quoted in Magali Carrillo Rocha, "Comienzos de una desilusión: Noticias públicas y lealismo, Nueva Granada, 1808," *Historia y sociedad* 21 (July–December 2011): 102. Here, Carrillo Rocha highlights the many colorful invectives that emerged in the media to refer to the newly tyrannical Napoleon.

79. Carrillo Rocha, "Comienzos de una desilusión," 102.

80. Cartagena declared its allegiance on August 14, followed by Mompós and Santa Marta on August 21; Bogotá declared on September 11, followed by Tunja on October 11 and Popayán on October 29; the towns of Honda (on December 25) and Cúcuta (on December 28), were two of the last to complete this demonstration of loyalty in 1808. See the table produced by Vanegas Useche in *Plenitud y disolución*, 39. See also the *Noticia dada por el Cabildo de Cartagena a las autoridades eclesiásticas respecto a la jura de Fernando 7º en esa ciudad* from August 11, 1808 (published in Vanegas Useche, 60–62). The city council of Bogotá discussed the oath on September 6. See the material relating to the capital in Vanegas Useche, 71–87. Documents relating to the ceremonies in Tunja, Cartagena, Simití, Mompós, and Popayán, among other towns, are also included.

81. Vanegas Useche, *Plenitud y disolución*, 104–6.

82. *Plenitud y disolución*, 106–8.

83. Camilo Torres, *Representación del Cabildo de Bogotá Capital del Nuevo Reino de Granada a la Suprema Junta Central de España, en el año de 1809* (Santafé de Bogotá: Imprenta de N. Lora, 1832), 31.

Chapter 2

Epigraph: Luís de Onís to Mauricio de Onís, Philadelphia, March 29, 1810. Quoted in Ángel del Río, *La misión de don Luís de Onís en los estados unidos (1809–1819)* (New York, 1981), 212.

1. Stagg, *Borderlines in Borderlands*, 42 (see this volume, introduction, n. 11). As Stagg notes, Irujo clashed with the US government over its aggressive interpretation of the treaties that produced the Louisiana Purchase, in particular the disposition of the land along the northern Gulf coast known as West Florida. This territory between New Orleans and the Perdido River was held by Spain but claimed by the US as a result of the Louisiana cession. As the son-in-law of the governor of Pennsylvania, Irujo may also have allowed personal relationships to influence his official duties.

2. By the beginning of the nineteenth century, foreign diplomatic posts had coalesced into three widely accepted categories: First in rank were the *embassies*, to which was appointed an accredited ambassador or ambassador extraordinary; second were the *legations*, which were headed by an accredited minister, a minister plenipotentiary, a minister extraordinary, a minister plenipotentiary or envoy extraordinary, or, in the absence of such a senior officer, a chargé d'affairs ad interim; and, finally, came the *residences*, which was a lesser post entrusted to a resi-

dent or a chargé d'affairs *en titre*. Below these missions, all designed for direct government-to-government communication, spread a network of consulates with appointed consular officers. See Edward A. Whitcomb, *Napoleon's Diplomatic Service* (Durham, NC: Duke University Press, 1979), 4.

3. Valentín de Foronda to James Madison, Philadelphia, December 31, 1808, National Archives, United States (hereafter NA-NSL), Notes from the Spanish Legation in the United States to the Department of State, 1790–1906, r. 4, vol. 2A.

4. Foronda was himself a master at this particular duty. In 1804 he prepared his *Apuntes ligeros sobre los Estados Unidos de la America Septentrional* for the benefit of his superiors. A well-respected public intellectual in Spain and the United States, Foronda published many works on politics and economics during his lifetime and, among other honors, was elected to the American Philosophical Association. See José de Onís, "Valentín de Foronda's Memoir on the United States of North America, 1804," *The Americas* 4, no. 3 (1947–1948): 351–62.

5. Sean T. Perrone has done extensive work on the operations of the Spanish consulates in the United States during the early Republic. See "The Role of Spanish Consuls in the United States, 1795–1898," in *Nation and Conflict in Modern Spain: Essays in Honor of Stanley G. Payne*, ed. Brian D. Bunk, Sasha D. Pack, and Carl-Gustaf Scott (Madison: Parallel Press, 2008), 81–102. See also Whitcomb, *Napoleon's Diplomatic Service*, 94–108.

6. Sean T. Perrone, "Spanish Consuls and Trade Networks between Spain and the United States, 1795–1820," *Bulletin for Spanish and Portuguese Historical Studies* 38, no. 1 (2013): 76. According to Karen Racine, Carlos de Irujo had an energetic intelligence network that provided detailed information about the activities of Francisco de Miranda during his visit to the United States in 1805 (*Francisco de Miranda*, 158). For more on Irujo, see Eric Beerman, "Spanish Envoy to the United States (1796–1809): Marques de Casa Irujo and His Philadelphia Wife Sally McKean," *The Americas*, 37, no. 4 (April 1981): 445–56.

7. As compensation for this earlier loss, Spain received the Louisiana territory from its French ally, thereby dramatically expanding its territorial holdings in North America.

8. An excellent summary of these developments can be found in John Lynch, *Bourbon Spain, 1700–1808* (Oxford: Basil Blackwell, 1989), 375–421.

9. See Stagg, *Borderlines in Borderlands*, 13–51; also Lewis, *The American Union*, 12–40 (see this volume, introduction, n. 11).

10. In February 1804, Congress passed the Mobile Act, which formalized the US claim to West Florida. For historical context, see Stagg, *Borderlines in Borderlands*, 42.

11. Jefferson to Robert Livingston, Washington DC, April 18, 1802, Library of Congress, Digital Collections, Thomas Jefferson Papers (hereafter LC-TJP), https://www.loc.gov/collections/thomas-jefferson-papers/.

12. See François Furstenburg, *When the United States Spoke French: Five Refugees Who Shaped a Nation* (New York: Penguin Press, 2014). See also Robert J. Alderson Jr., *This Bright Era of Happy Revolutions: French Consul Michel-Ange-Bernard Man-*

gourit and International Republicanism in Charleston, 1792–1794 (Columbia: University of South Carolina Press, 2008). Alderson's book identifies both Genêt and Mangourit as leading agents in an early French effort to use the United States as a base from which to spread revolutionary ideology into Spanish America (xi).

13. See Dessens, "Napoleon and Louisiana," 68–69 (see this volume, ch. 1, n. 7). An 1805 census in New Orleans counted 8475 permanent residents. Between 1809 and 1810, approximately ten thousand French-speaking refugees from Cuba and the French Caribbean arrived in the city. See John T. Magill, Pamela D. Arceneaux, and John H. Lawrence, "Between Colony and State: Louisiana in the Territorial Period, 1803–1812," *Historic New Orleans Collection Quarterly*, 26, no. 4 (Fall 2009): 12.

14. See Peter P. Hill, *Napoleon's Troublesome Americans: Franco-American Relations, 1804–1815* (Washington, DC: Potomac Books, 2005).

15. Foronda to secretario de estado, Philadelphia, August 2, 1808, Archivo Histórico Nacional, Madrid, Spain (hereafter AHN-CD), Estado, leg. 5634, exp. 508, no. 182.

16. Foronda learned of the formation of the Junta Central in October 1808. See Foronda to secretario de estado, Philadelphia, October 10, 1808, AHN-CD, Estado, leg. 5634, exp. 510, no. 185.

17. Enrique White to the marqués de Someruelos, St. Augustine, August 27, 1808, UF-EFP, reel 11.

18. White to Someruelos, August 27, 1808.

19. White to Someruelos, August 27, 1808.

20. By the beginning of the century, a new town, later named Fernandina in honor of Fernando VII, had emerged on Amelia Island to support the burgeoning commercial potential of the coast. Cusick, *The Other War*, 41 (see this volume, ch. 1, n. 11).

21. Foronda to Cevallos, Philadelphia, October 25, 1808, AHN-CD, Estado, leg. 5634, exp. 511, no. 187.

22. The appointments were as follows: Luís de Onís as minister plenipotentiary and envoy extraordinary; Diego Morphy as consul in New Orleans (Morphy at the time held this post in Charleston); Carlos Mulvey as vice-consul in Savannah; Narciso de Heredia as secretary to the consulate general; Felipe Fatio as consul in Charleston (he had been vice-consul in Savannah); José Ignacio de Vilar as vice-consul general in Philadelphia. Foronda gave official notification of these appointments to the State Department on May 3, 1809 and suggested that the Junta had made them in order to reaffirm its commitment to preserving "peace and harmony" with the United States. Viar, who had served in the early 1790s as chargé d'affaires of the Spanish mission to the United States, was particularly recommended as someone who might foster better relations. See Foronda to Smith, Philadelphia, May 3, 1809, NA-NSL, r. 4, vol. 2A. Because of the arrival in the US of a minister plenipotentiary, the Junta Central decided to downgrade Philadelphia from a consulate general to a consulate, equal in status to all the others. Bartholomé de Renguenet received the appointment as the new consul there. See Luís de Onís to Enrique White, Philadelphia, November 4, 1809, UF-EFP, reel 40.

See also the Spanish diplomatic correspondence located in Foronda to secretario de estado, Philadelphia, May 1, 1809, AHN-CD, Estado, leg. 5635, exp. 580, no. 264; leg. 5635, exp. 583, no. 265.

23. For Madison's foreign policy see J. C. A. Stagg's large body of work; see also Hill, *Napoleon's Troublesome Americans*, and Lewis, *The American Union*.

24. In a letter to Smith dated March 9, Foronda informed the American secretary of state that he had been told by the captain general of Cuba that the American navy was stopping Spanish shipping in the Gulf of Mexico. Foronda to Smith, Philadelphia, March 9, 1809, NA-NSL, r. 4, vol. 2A.

25. In this particular letter Foronda complained to Smith that the Non-Intercourse Act required Spanish vessels to post massive bonds—four times the value of the merchandise in question, or in his example two hundred thousand dollars against a value of fifty thousand dollars—as a guarantee that they would not sail to ports in France or England. Foronda to Smith, Philadelphia, March 11, 1809, NA-NSL, r. 4, vol. 2A.

26. He cited correspondence between Governor Claiborne and Vicente Folch, the Spanish governor in Pensacola, as evidence to support his claims. Foronda to Smith, Philadelphia, March 14, 1809, NA-NSL, r. 4, vol. 2A. On August 3, Foronda wrote to the Junta Central that he would ask the administration for an explanation regarding reports of the deployment of four thousand soldiers to New Orleans, as well as a project pending in Congress to raise fifty thousand volunteers there. He ordered the Spanish consul in Louisiana to follow these developments carefully, provide updates to the Junta Central as needed, and notify the captain general of Cuba, the viceroy of New Spain, and the governor of the province of Tejas. Foronda to the Junta Central, AHN-CD, Estado, leg. 5635, exp. 651, no. 30.

27. Foronda to Smith, Philadelphia, April 24, 1809, NA-NSL, r. 4, vol. 2A. The decree dates to September 1808.

28. Foronda to the Junta Central, Philadelphia, May 4, 1809, AHN-CD, Estado, leg. 5635, exp. 584, no. 269.

29. Foronda's letter to Smith from June 24, 1809, is found in NA-NSL, r. 4, vol. 2A. His correspondence with Spain is dated July 9 (with Smith's response from July 6 enclosed) and found in AHN-CD, Estado, leg. 5635, exp. 598, no. 285. In fact, Foronda considered Viar to be an ally of his "enemies" in the United States, a list that included former ambassador Irujo, Governor Folch of Pensacola, and the gazetteer "Sarmiento" who attacked Foronda in local newspapers under the nom de plume "El patriota español." See AHN-CD, Estado, leg. 5635, exp. 599, no. 286; leg. 5635, exp. 583, no. 267; and leg. 5635, exp. 542, no. 216.

30. Foronda to Smith, Philadelphia, June 28, 1809, NA-NSL, r. 4, vol. 2A. The article in *Gazeta del Gobierno* was published on February 24.

31. Foronda to Smith, Philadelphia, June 10, 1809, NA-NSL, r. 4, vol. 2A.

32. Foronda to the Junta Central, Philadelphia, January 19, 1809. AHN-CD, Estado, leg. 5635, exp. 540, no. 213. In all, Foronda collected eight letters from ministers of Joseph Bonaparte and delivered them to the Junta on August 2, 1809. AHN-CD, Estado, leg. 5635, exp. 600, no. 287.

33. Foronda to the Junta Central, Philadelphia, June 28, 1809, AHN-CD, Estado, leg. 5635, exp. 639, no. 17.

34. Foronda to the Junta Central, Philadelphia, June 28, 1809, AHN-CD, Estado, leg. 5635, exp. 640, no. 18.

35. J. C. A. Stagg, *Mr. Madison's War: Politics, Diplomacy, and Warfare in the Early American Republic, 1783–1830* (Princeton, NJ: Princeton University Press, 1983), 25–26; Hill, *Napoleon's Troublesome Americans*, 65–74. See also James Madison to Thomas Jefferson, Washington, DC, April 24, 1809, in *The Papers of James Madison*, Presidential Series (hereafter *PJM*), vol. 1, ed. Robert Rutland et al. (Charlottesville: University of Virginia Press, 1984), 135–36.

36. Foronda to Smith, Philadelphia, September 2, 1809, NA-NSL, r. 4, vol. 2A. Two weeks later, Foronda still had not received a reply to his letter. He asked Consul Bernabeu to hand deliver a copy to the secretary of state. Unfortunately, Smith was out of town when Bernabeu visited. Bernabeu to Smith, Baltimore, September 25, 1809, NA-NSL, r. 4, vol. 2A.

37. Foronda to Smith, Philadelphia, September 26, 1809, NA-NSL, r. 4, vol. 2A.

38. Onís to Junta Central, New York, October 14, 1809, AHN-CD, Estado, leg. 5635, exp. 667, no. 1. Foronda departed on November 1. See the *Maryland Gazette*, November 8, 1809, 66, no. 3278, Maryland State Archives, Early State Records Online (hereafter MSA-ESR). He returned to Spain and spent the next four years in La Coruña, where he continued his political writings. His progressive ideas created powerful enemies upon the restoration of absolutism under Fernando VII, and he spent much of the remainder of the decade under confinement. Back in favor with the liberal revolution of 1820, Foronda died in Pamplona in 1821 at the age of seventy. See the entry for "Foronda y González de Echáverri, Valentín Tadeo de," in *Diccionario Biografíco Español*, vol. 20 (Madrid: Real Academia de la Historia, 2009–2013), 487–89.

Chapter 3

Epigraph: Luís de Onís to Enrique White, Philadelphia, October 31, 1809, UF-EFP, reel 40.

1. This biographical sketch is drawn from the following sources: Luís de Onís, *Memoria sobre las Negociaciones entre España y los Estados Unidos de América* (Madrid: Ediciones José Porrua Turanzas, 1969). See in particular the introduction by Jack D. L. Holmes, xv–xvi. Also, del Río, *La misión*, 39–45, 193–208. Holmes and del Río both appear to have relied heavily upon an anonymous manuscript that was written following the death of Onís in 1827 and traced the highlights of his career. Del Río credits this biography to Onís's son, Mauricio, and reprints it in full in his own study. See also the entry for "Onís y González Vara, Luís José de," *Diccionario Biográfico Español*, vol. 38 (Madrid: Real Academia de la Historia, 2009–2013), 552–53.

2. An excellent summary of these developments can be found in Lynch, *Bourbon Spain*, 375–421.

3. For more on the *motín de Aranjuez*, as these events became known, see Barbara H. Stein and Stanley J. Stein, *Crisis in an Atlantic Empire: Spain and New Spain, 1808–1810* (New York: Johns Hopkins University Press, 2014), 7–44.

4. Juan de Escoiquiz, *Memorias (1807–1808)* (Seville: Editorial Renacimiento, 2007), 214.

5. Del Río suggests that Onís may have been dispatched to Paris on a secret mission and did not join the Spanish retinue until Vitoria (*La misión*, 43).

6. Escoiquiz, *Memorias*, 214–17.

7. See Stein and Stein, *Crisis*, 45–74.

8. Escoiquiz, *Memorias*, 229.

9. "Biografá de Don Luís de Onís," quoted in del Río, *La misión*, 198.

10. Del Río, *La misión*, 43–44.

11. Napoleon formally transferred the crown to Joseph on June 4.

12. See Stein and Stein, *Crisis*, 75–93.

13. This constitution abolished such pillars of the old order as the Inquisition, feudalism, the military orders, the Mesta, and the Council of Castile. It created a reformed legislative assembly (the *Cortes Generales*), introduced the Napoleonic Code into Spain, and reorganized the country into new departments. Because of the opposition to the Bonapartist regime, its provisions were largely ignored and, as a result, the charter had very little sustained influence on Spanish political culture. See Alfonso Bullón de Mendoza and Gomez de Valugera, "Revolución y contrarevolución en España y América (1808–1840)," in *España siglo XIX*, ed. Javier Parades Alonso (Madrid: ACTAS, 1991), 71–75.

14. Urquijo, an unabashed Francophile, held the position of secretario de estado from February 1799 to December 1800 under Carlos IV. He recovered this position under Joseph and retained it throughout the Bonapartist regime. Azanza had served in a variety of diplomatic posts under Carlos III. In 1793 he became secretario de guerra and held the office for three years, before serving as viceroy of New Spain from 1798 to 1800. Upon the ascension of Fernando VII, he became minister of the treasury and then transferred his loyalty to Napoleon at Bayonne. He served Joseph in the Ministry of the Indies, the Ministry of State, the Foreign Ministry, and the Ministry of Religious Affairs over the next five years. For more on Azanza and other notorious josefinos, see Víctor Peralta Ruiz, "From Indiano Bureaucrats to Afrancesado Politicians in the Spanish Bonapartist State: The Cases of Azanza and Mata Linares," in Belaubre, Dym, and Savage, *Napoleon's Atlantic*, 173–91.

15. The provincial juntas were: Aragón, Asturias, Canarias, Castilla la Vieja, Catalonia, Córdoba, Extremadura, Galicia, Granada, Jaén, León, Madrid, Mallorca, Murcia, Navarra, Sevilla, Toledo, and Valencia. From the beginning of the formal resistance to José I, the Junta de Sevilla asserted itself as the first among equals in the inevitable competition for support between the provincial juntas. This presumption of preeminence was largely based on the monopoly held by Seville-Cádiz merchants over the Spanish imperial economy and their strong links to the colonies. See Stein and Stein, *Crisis*, 94–128.

16. A contemporary account of these events can be found in Francisco de Saa-

vedra, *Rebelión de las provincias en España: Los grandes días de la Junta Suprema de Sevilla, 1808–1810* (Madrid: Ediciones Alfar, 2011).

17. For more on the leading figures of the Junta Central and the transition from provincial juntas to the Junta Central see Stein and Stein, *Crisis*, 378–402.

18. This was the *Exposición de los hechos y maquinaciones que han preparado la usurpación de la corona de España, y los medios que el emperador de los franceses ha puesto en obra para realizarla* (Cádiz, 1808). At least two scholars of Spanish diplomacy during this period have argued that the *Exposición* was the work of Onís and Pérez de Castro. See del Río, *La misión*, 43, note 5.

19. Del Río, *La misión*, 43–44. The political positioning after September 25 was complicated. Floridablanca held the title of *presidente* of the Junta Central and secretario de estado, the most important of five government portfolios—including Guerra (War), Hacienda (Treasury), Marina (Navy), and Justicia (Justice)—that made up the Bourbon-era executive branch. In October the position of secretario de estado was assigned to Cevallos but was then exercised by Garay. When Floridablanca died in December, Garay possessed the most powerful executive office within the Junta Central.

20. See del Río, *La misión*, 43–44, 198.

21. Onís, *Memoria*, 5–6.

22. Onís to Junta Central, New York, October 4, 1809, AHN-CD, Estado, leg. 5635, exp. 667, no. 1. The *Cornelia* docked in the port of New York on October 3. In addition to Onís, she carried Bartolomé Rengenet, the newly appointed Spanish consul for Philadelphia, and the families of both men, along with a large retinue of domestic and official servants. *Maryland Gazette*, October 11, 1809, 66, no. 3274, MSA-ESR. The ship was a forty-four-gun frigate, of French origin, and reputedly "the same vessel in which Bonaparte came from Egypt." *Maryland Gazette*, October 18, 1809, 66, no. 3275; and November 8, 1809, 66, no. 3278, MSA-ESR.

23. According to the *Maryland Gazette*, the trouble started with the docking of the ship: "Some misapprehension of etiquette as to the salute at first took place, as it seems to have been expected by the Spanish officers that the first salute would come from the American batteries; upon some explanation with an officer of the United States army and the Spanish consul the established form of proceeding in such cases was understood—and a communication was made to Fort Columbus with the intention to offer the usual salute. The usage is not to salute any but national ships unless previous intimation is given. Had the Spanish vessel passed the river with sails set, she would have been saluted by commodore Rogers, but as she took in sail and came to anchor, the usages of the navy it seems consider her only as a battery when not under sail. Some silly rumors were afloat on the occasion, and much talk about it, but all really meaning nothing, but talk." *Maryland Gazette*, October 11, 1809, 66, no. 3274, MSA-ESR. Onís's version of these events was recorded in a letter to his son. See Luís de Onís to Mauricio de Onís, New York, October 5, 1809. Quoted in del Río, *La misión*, 208.

24. Onís to Robert Smith, New York, October 7, 1809, NA-NSL, r. 4, vol. 2A.

25. Onís made these arguments in a letter to the secretary of state two weeks

after his arrival in the United States. See Onís to Smith, Washington, DC, October 20, 1809, NA-NSL, r. 4, vol. 2A.

26. The *Maryland Gazette* anticipated the administration's official response by a full two weeks: "It is not for the United States to question the existence or nonexistence of either of the nominal kings of Spain, whether it be Joseph at Madrid or Ferdinand at Orleans" (October 11, 1809, 66, no. 3274, MSA-ESR). In his correspondence, Madison claimed to base this decision on a number of factors. First and foremost, he told Caesar Rodney, "Is Ferdinand or the Junta, in actual possession of the Govt.? . . . [A]ll the most recent & authentic information decides in the negative." Madison to Caesar A. Rodney, Washington, DC, October 22, 1809, *PJM,* vol. 2, ed. J. C. A. Stagg et al. (Charlottesville: University of Virginia Press, 1992), 26–27. One day later, he suggested to William Pinkney that the "principle of neutrality on one hand, and on the other, the limited authority of the Executive which does not extend beyond the point of fact, could never permit the reception of Mr. Onis in the actual state of things in Spain." He noted his surprise that the Junta had even gone ahead with the appointment and added that many in the US believed that the British had instigated the move in the hopes of forcing Washington to recognize Onís, a step that would lead the United States into a public and costly rupture with France. Madison to Pinkney, Washington, DC, October 23, 1809, *PJM,* 2:27–29. Others assumed that party politics were a factor. At the end of October, President Madison received a letter from an unidentified member of the Democratic Party expressing his hope that rumors of the administration's decision not to recognize Onís were in fact a "federal fabrication." The author continued by suggesting that Secretary Smith had significant personal interests "in the overthrow of the Old Spanish Government" and could not, therefore, be objective. See unsigned letter to Madison, Philadelphia, (ca. 30) October (1809), *PJM,* 2:50–51.

27. Onís also took some time on this day to write a letter to Thomas Jefferson. See Jefferson to Madison, Monticello, November 6, 1809, *PJM,* 2:56. Initially, Onís reported to his son that American officials were "muy embarazados con mi llegada" and had not decided whether to recognize him. He suspected that a refusal would lead to war between Spain and the United States. As an aside, he remarked that the countryside was quite beautiful and that it reminded him of Saxony. Luís de Onís to Mauricio de Onís, October 20, 1809, Georgetown. Quoted in del Río, *La misión,* 200.

28. Onís to Junta Central, Baltimore, October 15, 1809, AHN-CD, Estado, leg. 5635, exp. 668, no. 2; Onís to Smith, Washington, DC, October 17, 1809, NA-NSL; Onís to Junta Central, Baltimore, October 19, 1809, AHN-CD, Estado, leg. 5635, exp. 669, no. 3; Onis to Junta Central, Washington, DC, October 21, 1809, AHN-CD, Estado, leg. 5635, exp. 670, no. 4; Onís to Smith, Philadelphia, November 20, 1809, NA-NSL, r. 4, vol. 2A. The *Maryland Gazette* published the official news on November 1, after receiving the news late on October 24. It declared that Onís "has, however, been treated with the utmost attention by the President of the United States, who assured him that it gave him infinite pain not to be able to receive him as minister, which could not be done while Spain remained in its present unsettled

state; and assured him at the same time, that no minister from King Joseph could be received" (November 1, 1809, 66, no. 3277, MSA-ESR).

29. Onís sought to justify his demand for a written explanation by blaming his poor English: "temo que tal vez no habré podido explicarme bien en Ingles en el discurso que he tenido con VS o quizá no habré entendido con la claridad necesaria sus expresiones cuando se negó a recibir la copia de mis credenciales." Onís to Smith, Washington, DC, October 20, 1809, NA-NSL, r. 4, vol. 2A.

30. Onis to the Junta Central, Washington, DC, October 21, 1809, AHN-CD, leg. 5635, exp. 670, no. 4.

31. Luís de Onís to Mauricio de Onís, undated postscript, New York, October 20, 1809, quoted in del Río, *La misión*, 210. The meeting occurred at the Georgetown races on October 24, according to Stagg. See Madison to Rodney, Washington, October 22, 1809, *PJM*, 2:26–27, note 2. Onís was acquainted with the Jackson family before his arrival in the United States. Sir George Jackson, Francis's brother, served as one of the secretaries of legation of the British mission to the Junta Central. Writing to his brother, Francis declared, "I have done what I could for Onis, but Madison refuses to receive him. This resolution was taken, it appears, some time before his arrival, and might have been foreseen from the treatment experienced by Foronda and [Viar]. A bad effect is produced by the minister of the Junta remaining here, even till he can receive fresh orders." Quoted in a letter from Francis Jackson to George Jackson, Washington, DC, October 28, 1809, in George Jackson and Catherine Charlotte Jackson, *The Bath Archives: A Further Selection from the Diaries and Letters of Sir George Jackson, K.C.H.* (London: R. Bentley and Son, 1873), 29.

32. Onís to Junta Central, Washington, DC, October 27, 1809, AHN-CD, Estado, leg. 5635, exp. 682, no. 18.

33. Onís to Junta Central, Washington, DC, October 26, 1809, AHN-CD, Estado, leg. 5635, exp. 683, no. 19.

34. Onís to Junta Central, Philadelphia, November 15, 1809, AHN-CD, Estado, leg. 5635, exp. 685, no. 21; Onís to Junta Central, Philadelphia, November 16, 1809, AHN-CD, Estado, leg. 5635, exp. 684, no. 20; Onís to Junta Central, Philadelphia, November 16, 1809, AHN-CD, Estado, leg. 5635, exp. 687, no. 24; Onís to Junta Central, Philadelphia, November 15, 1809, AHN-CD, Estado, leg. 5635, exp. 689, no. 26. Some months later, Onís received a response from Spain that gave him permission to try and befriend the First Lady and Mrs. Monroe if he believed them to be corruptible. However, he was warned that the poverty of the Spanish state prevented any significant outlay on their behalf.

35. Onís to Junta Central, Philadelphia, November 16, 1809, AHN-CD, Estado, leg. 5635, exp. 686, no. 23; exp. 688, no. 25.

36. Onís to White, Philadelphia, November 21, 1809, UF-EFP, Reel 40.

37. Onís to Garay, Philadelphia, November 28, 1809, AHN-CD, Estado, leg. 5635, exp. 691, no. 28.

38. Onís to Garay, November 28, 1809.

39. Among other complaints, Onís wanted to remind Smith that the recent de-

parture of Minister Jackson from Washington would "interrupt the method proposed . . . of communication between the United States & Spain." Onís to Smith, Philadelphia, November 20, 1809, NA-NSL, r. 4, vol. 2A.

40. Morphy would not reach New Orleans until February 1810. See Diego Morphy to Manuel de Salcedo, New Orleans, February 18, 1810, University of Texas, The Bexar Archives, General Manuscript Series, Briscoe Center for American History (hereafter UT-BA), roll 44, frame 279. Manuel de Salcedo served as the governor of Spanish Texas; his uncle, Nemesio de Salcedo, was the commandant general of the Provincias Internas.

41. Onís to Garay, Philadelphia, December 13, 1809, AHN-CD, Estado, leg. 5635, exp. 699, no. 37.

42. Bernabeu to Leandro Moxó, Baltimore, November 21, 1809, AHN-CD, Estado, leg. 5635, exp. 699, no. 37. It appears that the consul was referring to Ciriaco de Cevallos, a distinguished Spanish naval captain who served as the port commander in Veracruz in 1808. On August 10, the French warship *Vaillant*, under the command of Lt. Charpantier, brought correspondence from the French foreign minister to Mexican authorities announcing the events at Bayonne. Cevallos quarantined the ship from a mob that formed under the impression that the ship carried a French-appointed viceroy. He then confiscated the papers and imprisoned the French crew at San Juan de Ulúa. Cevallos then found himself implicated in the rumors of French intrigue that swept the town and fled the next day for New Orleans. See Lerdo de Tejada, *Apuntes históricos*, 37–38; see also Archer, "Mexico en 1810," 26 (see this volume, ch. 1, n. 61).

43. Bernabeu to Smith, Baltimore, November 28, 1809, NA-NSL, r. 4, vol. 2A.

44. Bernabeu to Smith, November 28, 1809.

45. Bernabeu to Smith, November 28, 1809.

46. Bernabeu to Onís, Baltimore, November 30, 1809, AHN-CD, Estado, leg. 5635, exp. 695, no. 32.

47. Onís to Junta Central, Philadelphia, December 1, 1809, AHN-CD, Estado, leg. 5635, exp. 695, no. 32.

48. Onís to Garay, Philadelphia, December 5, 1809. AHN-CD, Estado, leg. 5635, 696, no. 34.

Chapter 4

Epigraph: Luís de Onís to Enrique White, Philadelphia, February 16, 1810, UF-EFP, reel 40.

1. Onís to Garay, December 29, 1809, AHN-CD, Estado, leg. 5635, exp. 706, no. 45. Perhaps the first reports of the ship were published in the *Maryland Gazette* on November 29, 1809. The paper included an extract of a letter from Norfolk, dated November 18, which read: "The French armed schooner *Tilsit*, mounting eighteen guns, has arrived in Hampton Roads from Bayonne, in a passage of forty-three days. She is said to be a National vessel, and to bring dispatches for gen. Turreau. Four or five of her officers are in town; but I understand that they have not

any news or newspapers. The schooner is stated to be destined for Baltimore, but the wind being directly adverse, prevents her from proceeding" (*Maryland Gazette*, November 29, 1809, 66, no. 3281, MSA-ESR).

2. On December 6, 1809, the *Maryland Gazette* announced the arrival of the *Tilsit* in Baltimore, identifying the captain as Desmolands (66, no. 3282, MSA-ESR). The name appears in different forms in the historical literature. Most common is Desmolard, though it is also spelled Desmolands, Desmolards, Demoland, and Desmoland. Very little is known about him or his background. In a letter to James Madison, however, John Francis Mercer notes: "When in Baltimore a few days since, a French Emigrant of distinction gave me some details relative to a conspicuous personage lately arriv'd there from Spain, apparently in the capacity of Captain & Owner of a Privateer but who I believe holds the Commission of General in the service of Joseph Buonaparte—his Vessell is gone but he remains, having landed some Spaniards & Frenchmen who are Agents of the Buonaparte's & who have gone into our back Country, where One of them has employ'd himself in a manner that may be ultimately interesting to our Government" (John Francis Mercer to James Madison, West River, MD, February 18, 1810, *PJM*, 2:237). In 1823 a case involving a Mr. Joseph Desmoland of Baltimore was argued before the Supreme Court of the United States. It involved a commercial voyage from Baltimore to Cayenne on a ship, the schooner *Luminary*, whose cargo was partially owned by Desmoland. The legal dispute arose over questions of ownership of the vessel itself, for Desmoland subsequently directed it to New Orleans, where, either on his own behalf or as an agent of the true owner, he attempted to transfer title to Francois L'Amoureaux. In the event, this Desmoland appears in the ruling as someone prone to disguising his true citizenship and designs. Justice Story noted while writing for the Court: "We do not know his national character or his private situation." See *Reports of Cases Argued and Adjudged in the Supreme Court of the United States, February Term 1823*, vol. 21, ed. by Henry Wheaton (New York: Banks Law, 1904), 405–19.

3. Luís de Onís to Enrique White, Philadelphia, February 16, 1810, UF-EFP, reel 40.

4. Onís to Garay, Philadelphia, January 7, 1810, AHN-CD, Estado, leg. 5636, exp. 710, no. 49.

5. A clockmaker by trade, Antonini was implicated in the "French Conspiracy" that convulsed Buenos Aires for much of 1795. See Johnson, *Workshop of Revolution*, 149–50, 172–77.

6. Onís to Francisco de Saavedra, Philadelphia, January 17, 1810, AHN-CD, Estado, leg. 5636, exp. 717, no. 57.

7. Onís to Francisco de Saavedra, January 17, 1810.

8. Onís to Francisco de Saavedra, January 17, 1810. The quote is taken from Onís to Saavedra, Philadelphia, February 1, 1810, AHN-CD, Estado, leg. 5636, exp. 724, no. 66.

9. Onis to White, Philadelphia, February 1, 1810, UF-EFP, reel 40.

10. Onis to White, February 1, 1810. See also Onís to Saavedra, February 1, 1810.

11. Onís to White, February 1, 1810.

12. Onís to Vicente Emparán, Philadelphia, February 2, 1810, NA-NSL, r. 4, vol. 2A.

13. James Madison to the Senate and House of Representatives of the United States, January 10, 1811. Translation of a letter from Luis de Onis to the Captain General of the Province of the Caracas, dated Philadelphia, February 2, 1810, in *American State Papers: Documents, Legislative and Executive, of the Congress of the United States, from the First Session of the First to the Third Session of the Thirteenth Congress, Inclusive*, vol. 3, ed. Walter Lowrie (Washington: Gales and Seaton, 1832), 404.

14. Onís to White, Philadelphia, February 8, 1810, UF-EFP, reel 40.

15. Onís to Saavedra, Philadelphia, February 6, 1810, AHN-CD, Estado, leg. 5636, exp. 727, no. 70.

16. Onís to White, Philadelphia, February 16, 1810, UF-EFP, reel 40.

17. The following summary is taken from Onís to Saavedra, Philadelphia, 24 February 1810, AHN-CD, Estado, leg. 5555, exp. 4, no. 1. This document is reproduced and translated in its entirety in the appendix.

18. In fact, Onís was far off the mark when it came to the background of Francisco Antonio Peredo y Pereyra. The latter was born in Actópan, in the modern Mexican state of Hidalgo, in 1775. After taking minor orders, he ran afoul of the archbishop of Mexico, who sought an investigation into his private life. Peredo fled Mexico and ended up in Portugal after a circuitous journey that included capture by an English warship and a brief visit to the United States. In Lisbon, he assumed the guise of a bishop and somehow ingratiated himself with the Portuguese royal family shortly before the French invasion of 1807. According to a biographer, Peredo's next stop was Havana, where he again raised suspicions among the Cuban authorities. In 1808 Peredo arrived in New York, where Onís's account of his activities through January 1810 is plausible but unconfirmed. See Alejandro Villaseñor y Villaseñor, *Biografías de los héroes y caudillos de la Independencia* (Mexico: Imp. De V. Agubros, ed., 1910), 2:400–402.

19. Onís to Saavedra, Philadelphia, February 24, 1810, AHN-CD, Estado, leg. 5555, exp. 4, no. 1.

20. Onís to Saavedra, February 24, 1810.

21. "Las Instrucciones dadas por el Usurpador Josef Napoleón al Comisionado o Agente Principal que tiene en Baltimore Mr Desmolard, y a los demás, que bajo las ordenes de este han pasado a las Américas Españolas con el fin de sublevarlas," AHN-CD, Estado, leg. 5555, exp. 4, no. 2. This document is reproduced and translated in its entirety in the appendix.

22. See Onís to White, Philadelphia, February 25, 1810, UF-EFP, reel 40.

23. Onís to Mauricio de Onís, Philadelphia, March 29, 1810, in del Río, *La Misión*, 211–12. After enlisting Peredo to undertake this commission against Desmolard, Onís sent the young man to New Spain, with the promise of a significant financial reward, to warn the viceroy about the activities of the French emissaries. Peredo completed his mission in April and was then asked to carry this information to Spain. However, he was almost immediately brought before the Inquisition

on suspicion of possessing seditious and inflammatory documents. Peredo argued that this was simply the material that he had removed from Desmolard's house and was part of his original commission. Other witnesses testified that they had heard him make heretical and subversive statements in public. Charges were brought by the Inquisition on April 22, and he was subsequently found guilty of heresy, apostasy, and supporting independence. His sentence included wearing the penitential *sambenito* and a ten-year exile from Mexico and Spain, including six years imprisonment on the Marianas Islands. Transferred from prison to prison by the Inquisition, Peredo finally escaped in January 1813 and made his way to the insurgent forces of Ignacio López Rayón. Awarded the military rank of colonel, Peredo was asked to travel to the United States in March 1813 on a diplomatic mission for the Mexican insurgency. Unable to find a way out of New Spain, Peredo continued to fight with the insurgent forces before disappearing from history after 1817. Villaseñor y Villaseñor, *Biografías de los héroes*, 2:402–8.

24. List of Emissaries, AHN-CD, Estado, leg. 5555, exp. 4, no. 3. This document is reproduced and translated in its entirety in the appendix.

25. See also the summary and analysis of Joseph's proclamation in Rydjord, *Foreign Interest*, 296–98.

26. The king of Westphalia was Jerome Bonaparte, Napoleon's youngest brother. In 1803 Jerome visited Baltimore, where he met and then married Elizabeth Patterson, the daughter of a local merchant. Their son, Jerome, was born in 1805 in England. Napoleon refused to recognize the marriage and compelled Jerome to give up his wife and son. The two returned to Baltimore in 1805. For more on this family, see Charlene M. Boyer Lewis, *Elizabeth Patterson Bonaparte: An American Aristocrat in the Early Republic* (Philadelphia: University of Pennsylvania Press, 2012).

27. As Onís put it, "unánimes fueron todos del parecer que se me reconociese por Ministro del Rey, que se pagasen todas las libranzas que yo expidiese contra la Tesorería para mis comisiones." Onís to Mauricio de Onís, March 30, 1810, quoted in del Río, *La Misión*, 212.

28. Onís asked Jackson to intervene with Admiral Sir John Warren, commander-in-chief of the North American station, to ensure that Antonini and the other "traitors" be sent to Spain. Onís to Saavedra, Philadelphia, March 14, 1810, AHN-CD, Estado, leg. 5636, exp. 734, no. 82.

29. Onís to Jackson, Philadelphia, March 7, 1810, AHN-CD, Estado, leg. 5636, exp. 735, no. 83.

30. Onís to White, Philadelphia, March 9, 1810, UF-EFP, reel 40.

31. Onís listed the parish name as Ayacapiztla. He also wrote that it was rumored that Bonavita had been Napoleon's grammar teacher on Corsica. This is unlikely, however, if Onís was correct about Bonavita's age (Onís to White, March 9, 1810). While serving in Mexico, this priest did express positive views regarding the French Revolution that brought him to the attention of the Inquisition. See William B. Taylor, *Magistrates of the Sacred: Priests and Parishioners in Eighteenth-Century Mexico* (Stanford, CA: Stanford University Press, 1996), 438.

32. See Stagg, *Borderlines in Borderlands*, 54–56.

33. Onís to White, Philadelphia, March 9, 1809, UF-EFP, reel 40.

34. "Proclama de Don Josef, rey de las Españas," Madrid, October 2, 1809. Biblioteca Virtual, Biblioteca Luís Angel Arango, Bogotá, Colombia, http://www.banrepcultural.org/blaavirtual/historia/palabras-que-nos-cambiaron/proclama-don-josef-rey-de-las-espagnas.

35. "Proclama de Don Josef."

36. "Proclama dirigida al clero en general de todas sus posesiones en America," Madrid, October 3, 1809, reproduced in Rydjord, *Foreign Interest*, 300. Onís included a copy of it in a letter to Spain at the end of April 1810. See Onís to Saavedra, Philadelphia, April 30, 1810, AHN-CD, Estado, leg. 5636, exp. 744, no. 94.

37. Onís to White, Philadelphia, March 9, 1809, UF-EFP, reel 40. Based on his summary of the documents here Onís appeared to conflate the two proclamas in his own mind. He also complained that another pro-Joseph missive to Spanish Americans, this one written by an anonymous creole, had so far eluded him. John Rydjord identifies this as the *Avisos y exhortaciones de un criollo español a sus conciudadanos de América* and notes that it was discovered by the Spanish cónsul in New Orleans, Diego Morphy. See Rydjord, *Foreign Interest*, 300, note 29. It was in Onís's possession by the beginning of May. Onís to Saavedra, Philadelphia, May 2, 1810, AHN-CD, Estado, leg. 5636, exp. 752, no. 106.

38. Onís to Saavedra, Philadelphia, May 1, 1810, AHN-CD, Estado, leg. 5636, exp. 749, no. 103.

39. Onís to Saavedra, Philadelphia, April 30, 1810, AHN-CD, Estado, leg. 5636, exp. 744, no. 94.

40. Onís to Saavedra, Philadelphia, May 23, 1810, AHN-CD, Estado, leg. 5636, exp. 754, no. 108. Onís to Hormazas, Philadelphia, May 31, 1810, AHN-CD, Estado, leg. 5636, exp. 756, no. 111. See also Rydjord, *Foreign Interest*, 301–2.

41. Jaime E. Rodríguez O., *The Independence of Spanish America* (Cambridge: Cambridge University Press, 1998), 110–11.

42. Onís to Bardají, Philadelphia, July 17, 1810, AHN-CD, Estado, leg. 5636, exp. 782, no. 139.

43. Onís to Bardají, Philadelphia, July 15, 1810, AHN-CD, Estado, leg. 5636, exp. 782, no. 139.

44. Bernabeu to Smith, Baltimore, July 17, 1810, NA-NSL, r. 4, vol. 2A. Onís was so worried that American policy toward Venezuela would cause significant problems for Spain that he took the rare step of writing to Secretary Smith a personal letter one week later. Here he provided assurances that the authorities in the Venezuelan provinces of Guiana, Coro, Maracaibo, Cumaná, and Barinas had, in fact, sworn allegiance to the Spanish Regency, leaving Caracas isolated. He hoped that this news would make the administration reconsider the appointment of Lowry for fear of causing greater injury to its relations with Spain. Onís to Smith, Philadelphia, July 24, 1810, NA-NSL, r. 4, vol. 2A.

45. Onís to Bardají, Philadelphia, July 12, 1810, AHN-CD, Estado, leg. 5636, exp. 781, no. 138. The description of Lestique provided by Morphy reads: "He is about

five feet nine or ten inches tall, with an oval face and a large nose, the front long and narrow, brown eyes, dark chestnut hair, with some grey strands, a normal beard, about forty-five or fifty years old; when he speaks with intensity he raises his eyes and forms four or five wrinkles in front, his face is pleasant with good features; he has the air of an Italian, although some believe that he is Swiss."

46. Onís to Bardají, July 12, 1810.

47. Onís to Bardají, Philadelphia, July 15, 1810, AHN-CD, Estado, leg. 5636, exp. 784, no. 142. The Crown response is dated November 5.

48. Onís to Bardají, Philadelphia, August 14, 1810, AHN-CD, Estado, leg. 5636, exp. 801, no. 170. The second was an officer by the name of Ernouf, reportedly an aide to Marshal Bon-Adrien Jeannot de Moncey, the commander of one of Napoleon's army corps in Spain. It is possible that Onís confused this individual with Jean Augustin Ernouf, a French general who served as the governor of Guadeloupe until its capture by British forces in February 1810. He was taken to England, where he remained until 1811, when he returned to France.

49. Onís to Bardají, August 14, 1810.

50. Onís to Bardají, Philadelphia, August 14, 1810, AHN-CD, Estado, leg. 5636, exp. 803, no. 172. Onís sent a nearly identical letter to the captain general of Cuba on the same day. Someruelos then forwarded the warning to East Florida. Someruelos to White, Havana, October 3, 1810, UF-EFP, reel 4.

51. Someruelos to White, Havana, October 5, 1810, UF-EFP, reel 4. This is regarding the letter from Onís dated September 4, 1810.

52. Someruelos to White, October 5, 1810. Here Someruelos references a letter from Onís dated September 6, 1810. See also Onís to Bardají, Philadelphia, September 9, 1810, AHN-CD, Estado, leg. 5636, exp. 812, no. 182. This same report was sent to other colonial authorities. By the end of October, Onís reported additional evidence of a "Machiavellian plot" of Bonaparte's in the western territories: "It has been five or six days since fifteen French soldiers, some in uniform, left Baltimore in the middle of the day with their bags packed. A Frenchman, who presented himself as their leader and who had the appearance of an officer, journeyed with them by carriage. The road these emissaries have taken is the one to Kentucky, and it is simply not possible that all these Frenchmen could head out there for no other reason than to travel and see forests" (Onís to Bardají, Philadelphia, October 31, 1810, AHN-CD, Estado, leg. 5636, exp. 820, no. 193).

53. George W. Erving to James Madison, Philadelphia, September 2, 1810, *PJM*, 2:519–21. See in particular note 1.

54. Bernabeu to Smith, Baltimore, October 1, 1810, NA-NSL, r. 4, vol. 2A.

55. Bernabeu to Smith, Baltimore, October 3 and 4, 1810, NA-NSL, r. 4, vol. 2A.

56. Bernabeu to Smith, October 3 and 4, 1810.

57. Not surprisingly, Onís was furious with this turn of events. See Onís to Mauricio de Onís, New York, September 11, 1810, in del Río, *La Misión*, 215–16. He wrote: "Este juez malvado nos hizo confiscar la goleta, causando un sentimiento general a todos los federalistas, que han visto en ello una confirmación de que no ha dis-

minuido lo más mínimo la influencia de Francia, por cuya intriga se ha hecho este atentado con el objeto de impedir que vaya este socorro de armas y municiones a Maracaybo." As a consequence, he began to question the British commitment to the Spanish cause. See George W. Erving to James Madison, Boston, January 29, 1811, *PJM*, vol. 3, ed. J. C. A. Stagg et al. (Charlottesville: University of Virginia Press, 1996), 139–41. See note 1 here for further details on the case of the *Ramona.* Also Onís to Bardají, Philadelphia, January 12, 1811, AHN-CD, Estado, leg. 5637, exp. 846, no. 12.

58. Onís to Smith, Philadelphia, October 9, 1810, NA-NSL, r. 4, vol. 2A.

59. Stagg discusses the West Florida controversy and the Madison proclamation in *Borderlines in Borderlands*, 52–86. He argues that news, which spread across the United States in June, concerning the fall of the Junta Central had the same impact in Washington as it did in Caracas. For a time, Madison hoped to avoid a direct confrontation. However, by July residents of Baton Rouge had begun to organize in anticipation of the end of Spanish rule, actions that evolved toward the seizure of the city's fort on September 22 and the creation of a convention that proclaimed the independence of West Florida four days later. Convinced that the fall of Spain was imminent and that events on the ground had forced his hand, Madison concluded that American commercial and security interests, specifically the need to avoid French or British occupation of the Gulf coast, required the immediate possession of the territory. The Madison proclamation, *Respecting taking Possession of Part of Louisiana*, October 27, 1810, can be found in *PJM*, 2:595–96. See also Lewis, *The American Union*, 37–38. Onís had a different interpretation, of course. In a letter to his son he wrote about the developments in West Florida: "Se cree que este Gobierno, aunque fomenta la revolución, no lo hace directamente contra nosotros, sino que está engañado por Bonaparte con la perspectiva de que les dará las Floridas para que las reúnan a este país. La revolución es, como todas, fomentada por Bonaparte. Parece que es el partido de Burr, puesto en movimiento por el Tirano con el doble fin de segregar de este país la Luisiana, el Kentuky, Tennessee y Ohio, que unido a las Floridas, les dará la facilidad para invadir a México." Onís to Mauricio de Onís, Philadelphia, November 5, 1810, quoted in del Río, *La misión*, 216–17.

60. Onís to White, Philadelphia, December 10, 1810, UF-EFP, reel 40. He added an interesting postscript: Apparently, Bernabeu learned from the British chargé d'affairs that Minister Turreau was demanding that the US turn over West Florida to the government of Joseph Bonaparte.

61. Bernabeu to Smith, Baltimore, December 10, 1810, NA-NSL, r. 4, vol. 2A.

62. Luís de Onís [Verus, pseud.], *The passage of the President's message, which relates to the forcible occupation of West Florida* (n.p., 1810).

63. Verus, *Passage*, 16–17.

64. Verus, *Passage*, 17–18.

65. Verus, *Passage*, 19–20.

66. To add insult to injury, in September Onís received word that the Spanish government had appointed Sebastián de Lugo to the post of legation secretary. Ac-

cording to Onís, Lugos was the nephew of two notorious servants of Joseph, the result being that "yo me veré desde el día de su arribo en el caso de no escribir más o de hacerlo y copiarlo yo todo, pues no puedo ponerle a él en los secretos." Onís to Mauricio de Onís, New York, September 11, 1810, quoted in del Río, *La misión*, 215. Lugo arrived in Philadelphia on December 3, 1810.

67. Onís to Bardají, Philadelphia, January 12, 1811, AHN-CD, Estado, leg. 5637, exp. 846, no. 6. He enclosed in this correspondence an undated and untitled clipping from an American newspaper with the referenced article.

68. Onís to Bardají, January 12, 1811.

69. Onís to Bardají, Philadelphia, December 27, 1810, AHN-CD, Estado, leg. 5636, exp. 841, no. 224.

Chapter 5

Epigraph: Luís de Onís to Mauricio de Onís, Philadelphia, September 30, 1811, quoted in del Río, *La Misión*, 222.

1. He claimed that no American would risk fighting for land notorious for being unhealthy. Onís to Bardají, Philadelphia, January 10, 1811, AHN-CD, Estado, leg. 5637, exp. 843, no. 3.

2. Moreau's commitment to the cause against Napoleon was so strong that he returned to Europe in 1813 and offered his services to the Allies. He died on the battlefield at Leipzig in the company of Tsar Alexander I. See Ernest Picard, *Bonaparte et Moreau: L'entente initiale, les premiers dissentiments, la rupture* (Paris: Plon-Nourrit et cie, 1905).

3. Onís was so worried about Moreau that he took the extraordinary step of renting a summer home near the Frenchman's residence with the intention of extracting as much information as he could about the people who met there. Onís to Bardají, Philadelphia, June 28, 1811, AHN-CD, Estado, leg. 5637, exp. 940, no. 127.

4. Onís to Bardají, Philadelphia, January 12, 1811, AHN-CD, Estado, leg. 5637, exp. 846, no. 6. For more on Skipwith, see Roger G. Kennedy, *Mr. Jefferson's Lost Cause: Land, Farmers, Slavery, and the Louisiana Purchase* (Oxford: Oxford University Press, 2003), 173–75.

5. Onís to Bardají, January 12, 1811.

6. The Skipwiths were a distinguished family from southern Virginia. Two sons of William Skipwith (1707–1764), Robert and Henry, married two sisters, Anne and Tabitha Wayles, who were the daughters of John Wayles. A third child, Martha Wayles, who was a half-sister to Anne and Tabitha, married Thomas Jefferson. Fulwar's father, also named Fulwar Skipwith, was a brother to William and an uncle to Robert and Henry. Thus, Jefferson's brothers-in-law, Robert and Henry, were Fulwar's cousins. Kennedy, *Mr. Jefferson's Lost Cause*, 178–81.

7. See Speech of Governor Fulwar Skipwith to the Senate and House of Representatives of the State of West Florida, at St. Francisville, on the 29th of November, 1810 (Natchez, MT [Mississippi Territory]: Printed by John W. Winn, 1810).

8. George W. Erving to James Madison, Boston, January 29, 1811, *PJM*, 3:139–41.

In this letter to President Madison, Erving reported that he met with Onís on his way through Philadelphia. He had hoped to use this private encounter to gather information but found the ambassador "so extremely & even more than usually Extravagant" that nothing of interest could be obtained.

9. Onis to Bardají, Philadelphia, January 16, 1811, AHN-CD, Estado, leg. 5637, exp. 847, no. 7.

10. Onís to Mauricio de Onís, February 13, 1811, in del Río, *La Misión*, 221. Onís declared, "No hay duda en su autenticidad, pues está adornado de todos los sellos grabados y requisitos imposibles de falsificar aquí."

11. Onís to Bardají, Philadelphia, January 31, 1811, AHN-CD, Estado, leg. 5637, exp. 864, no. 28.

12. Onís to Bardají, Philadelphia, February 6, 1811, AHN-CD, Estado, leg. 5555, exp. 4, no. 8. The government thanked Onís profusely for uncovering the new emissary and asked him to keep track of the costs resulting from this affair. At the same time, it reminded him to economize as much as possible due to "nuestra penuria de fondos" (Bardají to Onís, Cádiz, April 30, 1811, AHN-CD, Estado, leg. 5555, exp. 4, no. 13). Onís responded that he would be sure to do so, while recognizing that "ninguna atención puede ser mas importante en el dia que la de trastornar los maquiabelicos designios del usurpador" (Onís to Bardají, Philadelphia, September 19, 1811, AHN-CD, Estado, leg. 5555, exp. 4, no. 36).

13. These documents are included in the dispatch sent by Onís to Bardají, Philadelphia, February 6, 1811, AHN-CD, Estado, leg. 5555, exp. 4, nos. 10–12, 19. While one, which provided d'Amblimont with ten thousand francs worth of travel funds and a letter of credit worth four hundred thousand dollars was signed by Denis Decrés, who served as Napoleon's minister of the navy at this time, two of the documents, dated September 17 and 24, 1810, have the signature Fleurieu. This is likely a reference to Charles Pierre Claret de Fleurieu, a celebrated hydrographer and former minister of the navy under Louis XVI. While this particular Fleurieu in fact served Napoleon as a councilor of state, he died on August 18, 1810, one month before d'Amblimont's appointment was dated.

14. Fleurieu to d'Amblimont, Paris, September 17, 1810. Transcribed letter included in Onís to Bardají, Philadelphia, February 6, 1811, AHN-CD, Estado, leg. 5555, exp. 8, nos. 10–11.

15. The first thirteen articles give d'Amblimont authority over the planning of the attack by fireboats on the British Navy at the mouth of the Tagus, assuming that he would be able to reach the United States by November 1810. Failing that, the remaining articles charge him with launching conspiracies in Spanish America. Onís to Bardají, Philadelphia, February 12, 1811, AHN-CD, Estado, leg. 5555, exp. 4, nos. 14–15.

16. Onís to Bardají, Philadelphia, March 10, 1811, AHN-CD, Estado, leg. 5555, exp. 4, no. 25. Onís was certainly correct that the US government was actively exploring ways to acquire borderlands territory. For details on one proposal, see the letter from Jonathan Russell to James Madison, January 2, 1811, in *PJM*, 3:91–93.

17. Bardají to Wellesley, Cádiz, March 30, 1811, AHN-CD, Estado, leg. 5555, exp. 4, no. 22.

18. Bardají to Venegas, Cádiz, May 12, 1811, AHN-CD, Estado, leg. 5555, exp. 4, no. 24.

19. Onís to Bardají, Philadelphia, January 31, 1811, AHN-CD, Estado, leg. 5637, exp. 864, no. 28. In November, one of Onís's sources returned from Salvador da Bahia with the news that these men, who had in fact made their way to Brazil, had been arrested by local authorities. Onís to Bardají, Philadelphia, November 6, 1811, AHN-CD, Estado, leg. 5637, exp. 1002, no. 196.

20. Onís to Bardají, Philadelphia, February 19, 1811, AHN-CD, Estado, leg. 5637, exp. 877, no. 43.

21. Onís to Bardají, February 19, 1811. Writing to his son, Mauricio, who was serving in the Spanish embassy in London, Onís wrote about his recent discoveries of these new French intrigues: "He tenido en mi mano los documentos originales y me parece imposible que sean falsos, pero aun cuando lo fuesen, están bien hilados y conviene tomar medidas de precaución" (Onís to Mauricio de Onís, Philadelphia, February 21, 1811, quoted in del Río, *La Misión*, 219).

22. See Daniel Rasmussen, *American Uprising: The Untold Story of America's Largest Slave Revolt* (New York: Harper-Collins Publishers, 2011).

23. Onís to Bardají, Philadelphia, February 19, 1811, AHN-CD, Estado, leg. 5637, exp. 878, no. 44.

24. Onís to Bardají, Philadelphia, March 25, 1811, AHN-CD, Estado, leg. 5637, exp. 892, no. 62. Onís made this point in a letter to his son, Mauricio, more than two months earlier: "En mi concepto, la toma de la Florida es proyecto de Bonaparte para revolucionar este país y servirse de estos americanos para conquistar a México. El tiempo nos hará ver si me engaño en mi pronóstico" (Onís to Mauricio de Onís, Philadelphia, January 12, 1811, quoted in del Río, *La Misión*, 219).

25. Onís to Bardají, March 25, 1811.

26. Onís to Bardají, March 25, 1811.

27. Another example was Robert K. Lowery, who was sent to Caracas as an American commercial agent at the same time. Onís to Bardají, Philadelphia, April 10, 1811, AHN-CD, Estado, leg. 5637, exp. 904, no. 77.

28. Onís to Bardají, Philadelphia, April 4, 1811, AHN-CD, Estado, leg. 5637, exp. 900, no. 73. In a letter dated January 24, Onís told his son that he was investigating these reports: ". . . y aunque no la creo, con todo, es menester verificarla, y no dudo que lo haré dentro de poco" (Onís to Mauricio de Onís, Philadelphia, January 24, 1811, quoted in del Río, *La Misión*, 219).

29. Onís to Bardají, Philadelphia, August 13, 1811, AHN-CD, Estado, leg. 5637, exp. 961, no. 149. The relationship between the United States and the rebellious colonies in Spanish America is the subject of Gordon S. Brown, *Latin American Rebels and the United States, 1806–1822* (Jefferson, NC: McFarland, 2015).

30. Onís to Bardají, Philadelphia, March 25, 1811, AHN-CD, Estado, leg. 5637, exp. 892, no. 62.

31. Onís to Monroe, Philadelphia, April 11, 1811, NA-NSL, r. 4, vol. 2A.

32. Early in April Onís informed the Spanish government that he had received intelligence about two French expeditions destined for Spanish America. According to his report, the first, which was comprised of four frigates, was headed for Buenos Aires. Six more frigates were on their way to the Caribbean, where they were to attack Caracas and Cartagena. Such rumors received support on April 4, when an American merchant ship arrived in Philadelphia. It reported that it had been stripped of its goods by three French frigates while in transit from Cádiz. The crew believed that the warships were on their way to Mauritius, but Onís thought that they might in fact be part of one of the American expeditions. He was worried enough to send warnings to the authorities in Puerto Rico, Río de Janeiro, and Havana (Onís to Bardají, Philadelphia, April 6, 1811, AHN-CD, Estado, leg. 5637, exp. 902, no. 75). Two weeks later the Spanish consul in Norfolk, Antonio Argote Villalobos, reported that a French corsair, *La revanche du cerf*, had caught fire in Norfolk harbor (Argote Villalobos to Onís, Norfolk, April 22, 1811, AHN-CD, Estado, leg. 5637, no. 85).

33. Bernabeu to Monroe, Baltimore, June 7, 1811, NA-NSL, r. 4, vol. 2A.

34. "Substance of informal remarks made by M. Monroe in an unofficial conversation between him and Mr. Bernabeu" [1811], NA-NSL, r. 4, vol. 2A. Monroe was likely alluding to the letter that Onís sent to Captain General Emparán early in 1810, which did speculate on the dismemberment of the United States. The correspondence came into the hands of American authorities; President Madison referred it to Congress in January 1811. See this volume, ch. 4, n. 14.

35. The following quotes are drawn from the letter from Bernabeu to Monroe, Baltimore, July 3, 1811, NA-NSL, r. 4, vol. 2A.

36. As Bernabeu noted to Monroe, this exchange occurred in the immediate aftermath of a minor scandal in which Onís was compelled to publicly refute a proclamation "to the Inhabitants of South America" which was printed in his name in 1810 and which named Santiago Liniers as a French agent. In "*El fraude descubierto*" Onís declared that the fraudulent publication had in fact been written by revolutionaries in Buenos Aires and transmitted all the material relating to the case to Spain. See Onís to Bardají, Philadelphia, June 3, 1811, AHN-CD, Estado, leg. 5637, exp. 930, no. 109.

37. Onís to Bardají, Philadelphia, April 27, 1811, AHN-CD, Estado, 5637, exp. 916, no. 92.

38. Likely the source of much of the information Onís relied upon in his intelligence work, Correa was very much a creature of the Spanish counterespionage system. In October 1811, the Spanish ambassador complained to Bardají that Correa had been absent from Philadelphia for the entire summer despite being charged with certain commissions that required the legation to pay out large amounts of cash. Reports came in that located Correa in "los diferentes Baños de este país, donde se reúne la gran sociedad para divertirse." Onís doubted that the agent would complete his work and worried that the press had latched onto a rumor—instigated

by two newly arrived Spaniards—that Correa intended to assassinate Napoleon (Onís to Bardají, Philadelphia, October 4, 1811, AHN-CD, Estado, leg. 5553, exp. 6, no. 37). In his response, Bardají told Onís not to worry, because no one knew anything about Correa's actual commission (Bardají to Onís, Cádiz, December 11, 1811, AHN-CD, Estado, leg. 5553, exp. 6, no. 38). In July 1812, Ambassador Serurier wrote to Monroe complaining about the presence of Correa in New York. According to the French minister, Correa had plans to travel to France in order to assassinate Napoleon. See Louis Serurier to James Monroe, July 3, 1812, Washington, DC, in *Papers of James Monroe*, vol. 1, ed. Daniel Preston (New York: Greenwood Press, 2003), 268.

39. Greffe to Gorbalán, New York, June 9, 1811, AHN-CD, Estado, leg. 5553, exp. 6, no. 36.

40. Onís to Bardají, Philadelphia, June 3, 1811, AHN-CD, Estado, leg. 5637, exp. 963, no. 109.

41. Printed extract from the Boston *Sentinel*, June 26, 1811, sent by Onís to Bardají, AHN-CD, Estado, leg. 5637, exp. 945, no. 128.

42. Onís to Bardají, Philadelphia, August 8, 1811, AHN-CD, leg. 5637, exp. 963, no. 146.

43. Onís to Bardají, August 8, 1811.

44. Onís to Bardají, August 8, 1811.

45. Onís to Bardají, August 8, 1811.

46. Council of Regency to Onís, Cádiz, November 20, 1811, AHN-CD, leg. 5637, exp. 963, no. 146.

47. Onís to Bardají, Philadelphia, August 25, 1811, AHN-CD, leg. 5637, exp. 963, no. 151.

48. Transcription of letter from the duc de Bassano to Ledrezenech, Paris, April 12, 1811, AHN-CD, leg. 5637, exp. 963, no. 151.

49. Bassano to Ledrezenech, April 12, 1811.

50. Serurier to Ledrezenech, Washington, DC, July 14, 1811, AHN-CD, leg. 5637, exp. 963, no. 151.

51. Onís to Bardají, Philadelphia, August 25, 1811, AHN-CD, leg. 5637, exp. 963, no. 151.

52. Council of Regency to Onís, Cádiz, November 21, 1811, AHN-CD, leg. 5637, exp. 963, no. 151.

53. In Serurier's letter the name appears as Zemirez. Onís believed that this was incorrect. See Onís to Bardají, Philadelphia, September 3, 1811, AHN-CD, leg. 5637, exp. 970, no. 161.

54. Transcription of letter from Serurier to Ledrezenech, Washington, DC, August 19, 1811, AHN-CD, leg. 5637, exp. 970, no. 161.

55. Serurier to Ledrezenech, August 19, 1811.

56. Serurier to Ledrezenech, August 19, 1811.

57. Onís wrote that he could not find any evidence of this person in the Lisbon Almanac or Guide to Foreigners. He did note, however, that a Josef Scabra da Silva

appeared on the list of recipients of the Grand Cross of the Order of Christ and speculated that they might be the same person. Onís to Bardaji, Philadelphia, September 11, 1811, AHN-CD, leg. 5637, exp. 977, no. 169.

58. Bassano to Luca de Scabra da Silva, Paris, April 14, 1811, AHN-CD, leg. 5637, exp. 977, no. 169.

59. Bassano to d'Amblimont, April 14, 1811. A copy also appears in AHN-CD, Estado, leg. 5555, exp. 4, no. 38.

60. Bassano to l'Exme Mgr. L'Archeveque du Mexique, Paris, April 14, 1811, AHN-CD, leg. 5637, exp. 977, no. 169.

61. Bardají to Onís, Cádiz, November 29, 1811, AHN-CD, leg. 5637, exp. 977, no. 169.

62. Onís relayed these developments in a dispatch to Spain at the end of September. This includes his summary letter to Bardají from September 28, a copy of a letter from the commander of the port of Fernandina to Governor Estrada, dated August 12, with a translation of the August 2 letter from the captain of HMS *Emulus*, a copy of Estrada's letter to Onís, the note from Onís to Ambassador Foster dated September 28, and the response from Onís to Estrada, dated September 29. See AHN-CD, leg. 5637, exp. 988, no. 180.

63. Onís to Bardají, Philadelphia, October 7, 1811, AHN-CD, leg. 5637, exp. 991, no. 184; see also Bardají to the duque del Infantado, Cádiz, December 28, 1811, AHN-CD, leg. 5637, exp. 991, no. 184.

64. Onís to Bardají, Philadelphia, October 9, 1811, AHN-CD, leg. 5637, exp. 997, no. 187.

65. Onís to Bardají, October 9, 1811.

66. Onís to Bardají, Philadelphia, November 15, 1811, AHN-CD, leg. 5637, exp. 1005, no. 199. Toledo was born in Havana in 1779. Elected in 1810 to represent Santo Domingo in the Spanish Cortes, he became a leader in the movement to promote American rights. After fleeing to the United States, he made his way to Texas where he joined the Mexican insurgent forces of Bernardo Gutierrez de Lara. After suffering a series of defeats at the hands of the royalists, Toledo returned to the United States and by 1817 proclaimed his loyalty to Fernando VII. He returned to Spain, became a diplomat, and remained a devoted servant of the monarchy until his death in 1858. See Joseph B. Lockey, "The Florida Intrigues of José Alvarez de Toledo," *Florida Historical Society* 12, no. 4 (April 1934): 145–78.

67. Onís to Bardají, Philadelphia, November 20, 1811, AHN-CD, leg. 5637, exp. 1006, no. 200.

68. Onís to Bardají, Philadelphia, November 27, 1811, AHN-CD, leg. 5637, exp. 1009, no. 203.

69. Onís to Bardají, Philadelphia, December 6, 1811, AHN-CD, leg. 5637, no. 215. See also Brown, *Latin American Rebels*, 65.

70. Onís to Estrada, Philadelphia, January 21, 1812, UF-EFP, reel 41. Coincidentally, less than a month earlier, the US envoy in Paris, Joel Barlow, wrote to President Madison that he had been approached by someone who "is charged with full powers by King Joseph to negotiate & conclude a convention of boundaries

with the French or American authorities on terms, as he thinks, so advantageous to the US that their government cannot refuse them." Barlow proceeded to assert that the time was right to make a deal with Joseph for Texas and Florida, arguing that the Bonapartist legitimacy in Madrid was no longer in doubt, that, nevertheless, the josefino government needed an immediate infusion of funds, and that both Spain and France would accept the terms of the land grant if Madison were willing to forgive the debt these countries owed to the United States. See Joel Barlow to James Madison, Paris, December 30, 1811, *PJM*, vol. 4, ed. J. C. A. Stagg et al. (Charlottesville: University of Virginia Press, 1999), 97–104.

Chapter 6

Epigraph: Orden General de 22 Abril 1810, included in *Medidas de seguridad dictado por el Superior Gobierno contra los emisarios franceses*, May 15, 1810, AGCA, A1, leg. 6112, exp. 56127.

1. Approximately half of this population was indigenous. See Carolyn Hall and Héctor Pérez Brignoli, *Historical Atlas of Central America* (Norman: University of Oklahoma Press, 2003), 92.

2. Jordana Dym, *From Sovereign Villages to National States: City, State, and Federation in Central America, 1759–1839* (Albuquerque: University of New Mexico Press, 2006), 3–32.

3. The audiencia possessed executive, legislative, and judicial power. The senior official in the colony held military authority as captain general, political power as governor, and also served as president of the audiencia. See Oakah L. Jones, *Guatemala in the Spanish Colonial Period* (Norman: University of Oklahoma Press, 1994), 37–43.

4. The Guatemalan jurisdictions in 1796 were: the alcaldías mayores of Chimaltenango, Escuintla, Sacatepéquez, Sololá, Sonsonate, Suchitepéquez, Totonicapán, and Verapaz; and the corregimientos of Chiquimula and Quezaltenango. After independence, Sonsonate became part of the nation of El Salvador. Dym, *From Sovereign Villages*, 53 and Appendix B, 269.

5. Totonicapán has received important attention in the literature of the colonial period. For a brief introduction, see W. George Lovell, *Conquest and Survival in Colonial Guatemala: A Historical Geography of the Cuchumatán Highlands, 1500–1821* (Kingston, ON: McGill-Queen's University Press, 1985).

6. Juarros cites 58,200 total inhabitants, with 55,450 Indians and 2,750 Ladinos. See Domingo Juarros, *Compendio de la historia del reino de Guatemala* (Guatemala: Editorial Piedra Santa, 1981), 39. See also Hall and Pérez Brignoli, *Historical Atlas*, 88, 90. The only communities with proportionally significant—50 percent or more—Ladino or Spanish populations were San Carlos Sija and San Luís Salcajá, both of which were designated aldeas de ladinos, as well as Huehuetenango, Chiantla, Cuilco, and Malacatancito. Even the capital, San Miguel Totonicapán, was more than 75 percent indigenous (*Historical Atlas*, 88, 90, 148).

7. *Historical Atlas*, 179.

8. John L. Stephens, *Incidents of Travel in Central America, Chiapas, and Yucatan*, vol. 2 (New Brunswick, NJ: Rutgers University Press, 1949), 168, 187–88. See especially chapters 11–13.

9. In fact, Stephens visited the nearby village of San Antonio Huista as he descended the Cuchumatanes and described it as "beautifully situated on a tableland projecting from the slope of a mountain, looking upon an immense opening, and commanding on all sides a magnificent view" (*Incidents of Travel*, 199).

10. Stacey Schwartzkopf, "Maya Power and State Culture: Community, Indigenous Politics, and State Formation in Northern Huehuetenango, Guatemala, 1800–1871," (PhD diss., Tulane University, 2008), 218–19. In the late 1800s, Yalixján was absorbed into the new municipality of Nentón.

11. Victoria R. Bricker, *The Indian Christ, the Indian King: The Historical Substrate of Maya Myth* (Austin: University of Texas Press, 1981), 80.

12. To the extent there was a historical distinction between the alcaldía mayor and the corregimiento it was based on the population of the particular province. As Dym notes, the Crown established "alcaldías mayores in the jurisdictions with Spanish cabildos and corregimientos in districts whose principal settlement was an Indian pueblo." Totonicapán, in fact, began as a corregimiento but ended up as an alcaldía mayor (*From Sovereign Villages*, 27). The intendencia was an innovation of the Spanish Bourbons, who sought to reorganize and reenergize colonial administration in the late 1700s, with mixed success. See Miles Wortman, *Government and Society in Central America, 1680–1840* (New York: Columbia University Press, 1982).

13. Juarros, *Compendio*, 39–41. As he notes, the partidos were about the same population, though Totonicapán had only seven pueblos and two aldeas, while Huehuetenango encompassed multiple communities.

14. The alcalde mayor is described by Schwartzkopf as the "physical exemplar of state authority" and "the local embodiment of the king." See Schwartzkopf, "Maya Power," 222–28, for more on the ceremonial role of this official. See also Timothy Hawkins, *José de Bustamante and Central American Independence: Colonial Administration in an Age of Imperial Crisis* (Tuscaloosa: University of Alabama Press, 2004), 30.

15. Jones, *Guatemala*, 42.

16. Municipal governance according to the Spanish tradition incorporated both the core urban space and a significant rural perimeter. See Dym, *From Sovereign Villages*, for more on the cabildo (17–24).

17. *From Sovereign Villages*, 27.

18. According to Juarros the secular parishes were Huehuetenango, Chiantla, Momostenango, San Cristobal Totonicapán, Sacapulas, Solomá, and Cuilco. The doctrinas were San Miguel Totonicapán (Franciscan), Nebaj (Dominican), Malacatán and Jacaltenango (Mercedarian) (*Compendio*, 39, 61).

19. Lovell, *Conquest and Survival*, 90–93.

20. A detailed study of these officials appears in Schwartzkopf, "Maya Power," 214–22. As he notes, they were also known as *jueces preventivos* or *tenientes*.

21. "Maya Power," 215. Not surprisingly, considering the shifting demographic

makeup of the area, not to mention more idiosyncratic reasons, theory and practice infrequently converged. Schwartzkopf reports that Huehuetenango, Cuilco, and Chiantla, each with substantial ladino populations, functioned with both a juez comisionado and an alcalde pedáneo. In Malacatán, Momostenango, and Sacapulas, the separate portfolios were merged under one official. The authorities at San Miguel Totonicapán gave San Francisco el Alto its own juez comisionado. Jacaltenango operated with one juez comisionado, while Solomá had two ("Maya Power," 215–17).

22. "Maya Power," 218–20.

23. "Maya Power," 214.

24. Hawkins, *José de Bustamante*, 33–34. See also, Jones, *Guatemala*, 211–30.

25. Juarros, *Compendio*, 39. There were approximately fifty men per company.

26. For more on the powers of the captain general, see Hawkins, *José de Bustamante*, 26–28; Jones, *Guatemala*, 40–41; and Dym, *From Sovereign Villages*, 25.

27. Juarros put the distance at thirty-eight *leguas* (38 × 2.6 miles US = 98.8 miles). See *Compendio*, 39.

28. *Real orden relativa a que se tomen medidas de seguridad contra los franceses*, decree, April 13, 1809, AGCA, A1, leg. 6093, exp. 55340; AGCA, A1, leg. 4643, fol. 154.

29. Hawkins, *José de Bustamante*, 49–52.

30. *José de Bustamante*, 56–60.

31. *Orden General*, decree, April 22, 1810, included in *Medidas de seguridad dictado por el Superior Gobierno contra los emisarios franceses*, May 15, 1810, AGCA, A1, leg. 6112, exp. 56127.

32. The letter, which was dated April 29, is included in material found in AGCA, B1.3, leg. 3, exp. 48. It caused a stir at a meeting of the *Real Acuerdo*, which included the captain general and the audiencia judges, as the subsequent response from González suggests. As an immediate consequence, the authorities determined to keep special watch on anyone arriving from Oaxaca and sent word to all regional and local commanders on May 18 with a note that strangers had been sighted in Verapaz. This led to a response from the *alcalde mayor interino* of Verapaz, Angel Valenzuela on May 29. He acknowledged receiving the *oficio* from the Real Acuerdo concerning the three *forasteros* who had arrived "en traje de campechanos." Their passports and papers were carefully examined, and they were found to be Ramon Colmenero, Pedro Sanchez, and Pedro Mongiste. The first two were Spaniards living in Veracruz and Guanajuato, the third was from Merida. The trio had left Campeche with all required travel documents. They showed no sign of being traitors; instead, "han manifestado en sus conversaciones un gran amor al Rey, a la Religion, y a la Patria, detestando y aborreciendo las miguas y pérfidas ideas del más cruel y abominable monstruo de la naturaleza Bonaparte" (Angel Valenzuela to González, Salamá, May 29, 1810, AGCA B2.7, leg. 32, exp. 781).

33. This letter of May 10 was sent to Chiapas and copied to Cózar on May 17 (see AGCA, A1, leg. 6112, exp. 56124). The letter notes that González had received new information since the April 22 Proclamation about the number, characteristics, methods, and destinations of the French emissaries. As a result of the intelli-

gence coup from Onís, the captain general could now identify Estanislao Oropesa, Ciriaco Betolaza, Fermín Esparragosa, and Juan Chagaray as French agents. See the appendix.

34. González to Cózar, May 17, 1810.

35. *Medidas de seguridad dictado por el Superior Gobierno contra los emisarios franceses*, Guatemala City, May 15, 1810, AGCA A1, leg. 6112, exp. 56127.

36. *Manifiesto promulgado por González con respecto a las actuales circunstancias de nuestra Monarquía*, Guatemala City, May 22, 1810, AGCA B1.1, leg. 1, exp. 29.

37. Its first provision confirmed the orders of May 15 with respect to foreigners or Spanish subjects with less than a two-year residency in the kingdom. The fourth reads: "Las conversaciones, o especies en que algunos muestren su execrable adhesión a los franceses, o su animo perverso de esparcir ideas contrarias a los intereses de nuestra Nación, o en descredito del Gobierno, o en trastorno del orden, o sugiriendo diferencias y divisiones de Españoles Europeos y Americanos, podrán dar suficiente margen para la pesquisa; y según lo que resultare de ella procederá este Tribunal a corregirles con proporción a su ligereza, o a procesarlos con toda formalidad si el caso fuera grave." Decree ordering the creation of the Tribunal of Loyalty, Guatemala City, May 27, 1810, AGCA, A1, leg. 66093, exp. 55344, fol. 53.

38. Prudencio de Cózar, decree, Totonicapán, May 28, 1810. Located in Medidas de seguridad dictado por el Superior Gobierno contra los emisarios franceses, Guatemala City, Mayo 15, 1810, AGCA A1, leg. 6112, exp. 56127.

39. Joaquín José Calvo to Cózar, Guatemala City, October 24, 1810, AGCA, A1, leg. 66093, exp. 55344.

40. For Bustamante's early career, see Hawkins, *José de Bustamante*, 1–21.

41. Narciso Mallol to José de Bustamante, Totonicapán, May 11, 1811, AGCA, A1, leg. 6113, exp. 56224.

42. Bustamante to Mallol, Guatemala City, June 18, 1811, AGCA, A1, leg. 6113, exp. 56216.

43. Mallol to Bustamante, Totonicapán, July 4, 1811, AGCA, A1, leg. 6113, exp. 56212.

44. Bustamante to Mallol, Guatemala City, August 2, 1811, AGCA, A1 leg. 6113 exp. 56239.

45. Bustamante to Mallol, Guatemala City, August 3, 1811, AGCA, A1 leg. 6113, exp. 56230. The descriptions follow:

> Señales de dos Sugetos muy sospechosos que han fugado del Reyno de Mexico y pueden dirigirse a Guatemala:
>
> El 1º es de regular tamaño y contextura, lleno de cara, color trigueño amarillo, ojos negros grandes, pelo crespo sin cortar y grande, cutis granoso, barbicenado: habla precipitado con el hábito de revolcar la lengua por dentro de los dientes y carrillo: velludo de muñecas: de edad como de 40 años, conduce plata en marquetas o barras con las mareas del margen y las mulas con estos fienos.
>
> El 2º es alto de cuerpo bien hecho, blanco de cara, pelo crespo castaño cortado

por delante, cara redonda, ojos medios azules, barba regular: su modo de andar doblando el cuerpo por ambos lados, de edad de 22 a 24 años.

46. Bustamante to Mallol, Guatemala City, September 9, 1811, AGCA, A1 leg. 6113 exp. 56231. The description reads:

Filiación de Mr. Greffe:

1. Tendrá de 28 a 30 años de edad; cinco o seis pies de estado
2. Color y pelo raxo
3. Usa peluquín por tener herido el Cráneo con varias cuchilladas
4. Tiene ojos vivos y azules
5. Rostro tacho y nariz afilada
6. Cuerpo bien formado entre magro y gordo
7. Habla perfectamente el Español y remeda el Andaluz

47. Bustamante to Mallol, Guatemala City, September 13, 1811, AGCA, A1, leg. 6113 exp. 56183.

48. Hermenegildo López to Narciso Mallol, Nebaj, September 21, 1811, AGCA, A1, leg. 6113 exp. 56194.

49. Nasario Argueta to Narciso Mallol, Jacaltenango, September 24, 1811, AGCA, A1, leg. 6113, exp. 56193. Argueta's performance as juez comisionado had been under review since June, when Bustamante informed Mallol that he had received complaints about Argueta. The magistrate was charged with a number of abuses against the Indians under his authority, including extortion through fines, demands for provisions, and forced labor without payment in his factories. Bustamante ordered Argueta to leave the Indians in the hands of their own alcaldes and justicias, who were responsible to Mallol (Bustamante to Mallol, Guatemala City, June 25, 1811, AGCA, A1, leg. 6113 exp. 56237).

50. Marcos Castañeda to Mallol, Solomá, October 9, 1811, AGCA, A1, leg. 6113 exp. 56139.

51. Marcos Castañeda to Mallol, October 9, 1811.

52. Bustamante, decree, Guatemala City, November 8, 1811, AGCA, A1, leg. 6113, exp. 56150. The description reads: "Es alto de cuerpo, grueso, lleno de cara, Bermejo, pelo cortado a la frente, nariz larga y abultada, ojos grandes azules, dentadura blanca complete, patilla hasta la barba = edad de 30 a 35 años, vestido de levita o franque, de paño celeste de primera, con gorrita de pico alto, cinturón negro de lustre laboreado de plata = Caballo tordillo flaco, herrado de los cuatro pies, silla brida, anquera de paño azul con fleco amarillo, estribera de plata."

53. Mallol, circular, Totonicapán, November 11, 1811, AGCA, A1, leg. 6113, exp. 56150.

54. Mont to Mallol, Chiantla, November 17, 1811, AGCA, A1, leg. 6113, exp. 56178.

55. Mallol to Bustamante, Totonicapán, December 6, 1811, AGCA, A1, leg. 6113, exp. 56209.

56. Mallol, decree, December 28, 1811, Totonicapán, AGCA, A1, leg. 6113, exp. 56149.

57. "Contra el Yndio Manuel Paz," testimony of P. Fr. Manuel Echeverria, Chiantla, December 28, 1811, AGCA, A1 leg. 6922 exp. 56945.

58. Mallol to Mont, Totonicapán, January 18, 1812; and Mallol to Audiencia of Guatemala, Totonicapán, January 18, 1812, AGCA, A1, leg. 6922, exp. 56945.

59. Manuel Paz, testimony, Chiantla, February 17, 1812, AGCA, A1, leg. 6922, 56945.

60. Oidor Fiscal González, report, Guatemala City, March 16, 1812, AGCA, A1, leg. 6922, exp. 56945.

61. Bustamante to Mallol, Guatemala City, February 3, 1812. This was inserted in a letter from Mallol to Mont, Totonicapán, February 7, 1812, AGCA, A1, leg. 6115, exp. 56356.

62. Mont to Mallol, Chiantla, February 7, 1812, AGCA, A1, leg. 6115, exp. 56349.

63. Mallol, decree, Totonicapán, September 26, 1812, AGCA, A1, leg. 6115, exp. 56383.

64. Mallol, decree, September 26, 1812.

Conclusion

1. See Hawkins, *José de Bustamante*, 115–14; Anna, *Fall of the Royal Government in Mexico City*, 98–139; and Anna, *The Fall of the Royal Government in Peru* (Lincoln: University of Nebraska Press, 1979), 53–75.

2. Scott Eastman and Natalia Sobrevilla Perea, eds., *The Rise of Constitutional Government in the Iberian Atlantic World: The Impact of the Cádiz Constitution of 1812* (Tuscaloosa: University of Alabama Press, 2015).

3. Onís to Bardají, Philadelphia, January 10, 1812, AHN-CD, leg. 5638, no. 2.

4. Onís to Bardají, Philadelphia, January 16, 1812, AHN-CD, leg. 5638, no 3. Onís assumed this was Louis Antoine Francois de Crillon-Mahon, the son of a French officer who moved to Spain, became a Spanish grandee and won renown as a general. Louis Antoine declared for Joseph Bonaparte, who appointed him viceroy of Navarre. He is not known to have traveled to the United States. In fact, Onís got a glimpse of "Crillon" and reported that he did not look like the duke but rather like another nobleman, the marqués de Salas. Onís to Bardají, Philadelphia, January 20, 1812, AHN-CD, leg. 5638, no. 5.

5. Onís to Bardají, Philadelphia, January 17, 1812, AHN-CD, leg. 5638, no. 4.

6. Onís to Bardají, Philadelphia, March 20, 1812, AHN-CD, leg. 5638, no. 34.

7. Onís to Bardají, Philadelphia, January 29, 1812, AHN-CD, leg. 5638, no. 8.

8. See Cusick, *The Other War of 1812*.

9. Onís to Bardají, Philadelphia, June 8, 1812, AHN-CD, leg. 5638, no. 75.

10. Monroe to Madison, Washington, DC, September 2, 1812 and Madison to Monroe, Montpellier, September 8, 1812, *PJM*, vol. 5, ed. J. C. A. Stagg et al. (Charlottesville: University of Virginia Press, 2004), 252–54, 287–88. See the notes to these documents by J. C. A. Stagg.

11. Brooks, *Diplomacy and the Borderlands: The Adams-Onis Treaty of 1819* (Berkeley: University of California Press, 1939), 21.

12. Wilbert H. Timmons, "Tadeo Ortiz, Mexican Emissary Extraordinary," *HAHR* 51, no. 3 (August 1971): 464–68.

13. See Elizabeth Howard West, "Diary of José Bernardo Gutiérrez de Lara, 1811–1812, I," *American Historical Review* 34, no. 1 (October 1928): 55–77; also J. C. A. Stagg, "Madison and the Problem of Mexican Independence: The Gutiérrez-Magee Raid of August 1812," editorial note, *PJM*, 5:235–45.

14. The delay seems to have resulted from Spanish refusals to recognize the American diplomat, John Erving. See Lewis, *The American Union*, 93.

15. For his own views on the treaty, see Onís, *Memoria*. It was finally ratified in 1821.

16. Emilio Ocampo, *The Emperor's Last Campaign* (Tuscaloosa: University of Alabama Press, 2009), 23–25. The larger wave of refugees is covered by Rafe Blaufarb in *Bonapartists in the Borderlands: French Exiles and Refugees on the Gulf Coast, 1815–1835* (Tuscaloosa: University of Alabama Press, 2005).

Appendix

1. Likely a reference to Tepexpan.

2. A likely reference to the alcaldía mayor of Cuatro Villas del Marquesado in south central Mexico.

3. Now Matagorda Bay, Texas.

4. Tetuan and Tepeque are likely a reference to the Isthmus of Tehuantepec.

5. Possibly a reference to Sonsonate, El Salvador.

6. A town, now known as Aguada, on the west coast of Puerto Rico.

7. This may be a reference to the Caribbean island of Trinidad. However, the islas de Sotavento, the Leeward Islands, ran from Aruba east along the Venezuelan coast up to but not including Trinidad. The latter would have generally been considered part of the islas de Barlovento, the Windward Islands.

8. A reference to Santiago Antonini.

9. This is likely a reference to the outpost known in the early 1800s as Fort Miro and later as Monroe. The Ouachita River runs from southern Arkansas and northern Louisiana through this settlement.

10. This is possibly a reference to the department of l'Artibonite in modern Haiti.

Glossary

afrancesados. Francophiles.

alcabala. Sales tax.

alcalde mayor. Spanish colonial official who served as a governor and magistrate over a district or province.

alcalde pedáneo. Spanish colonial official who served as a local magistrate. See also *juez comisionado*.

alcalde. Member of a municipal council (*cabildo*), who served as a judge of first instance; more formally, *alcalde ordinario*.

alcaldía mayor. Administrative unit at the district or provincial level, governed by an alcalde mayor.

aldea (pl. aldeas). Settlement.

antiguo régimen. Old regime; the traditional order.

audiencia. High court empowered with judicial, legislative, and administrative authority over a viceregal subdivision also known as an audiencia; for example, the audiencia of Guatemala.

ayuntamiento. Municipal council. See also *cabildo*.

cabecera. Primary administrative town, literally *head* town, of a district or province.

cabecera de doctrina. Parish seat.

cabildo. Municipal council. See also *ayuntamiento*.

camino real. Royal highway.

casta. Of mixed-race ancestry. See also *pardo*.

Chapetones. Term referring to Spaniards.

conde. Count.

cofradías. Religious brotherhoods.

Consulado de Comercio. Merchants' guild.

corregidor. Spanish colonial official who served as a governor and magistrate over a district or province.

corregimiento. Administrative unit at the district or provincial level, governed by a *corregidor*.

Cortes. Spanish parliamentary assembly.

criollos. American-born Spaniards.

diputado en jefe. Chief deputy.

donativos patrióticos. Patriotic donations.

doctrinas. Parishes.

emisario francés. French emissary.

fiscal. Crown attorney who serves on an *audiencia*.

gachupines. European-born Spaniards.

gobierno militar. Administrative unit at the district or provincial level, overseen by a military governor.

guerra patriótica. Patriotic war.

historia patria. Nationalist history.

ilustrados. Advocates of the Spanish Enlightenment who sought to draw the Hispanic world into the European cultural mainstream.

incendiarios. Troublemakers.

infidencia. Subversion or treason.

intendencia. Administrative unit at the provincial level, governed by an intendant.

josefino. Supporter of Joseph Bonaparte.

juez (pl. jueces). Magistrate or judge.

juez comisionado. Royal official who served as a local magistrate. See also *alcalde pedáneo*.

Junta Central. The supreme governing authority of Spain from 1808 to 1810.

juntas de vigilancia. Surveillance committees.

ladino. Term used commonly in Guatemala to describe Hispanicized peoples, regardless of race.

mantuanos. Members of the Creole aristocracy in Venezuela.

marqués. Marquis.

mayordomo mayor. The royal high steward.

Mercedarian. Member of the Catholic Order of Mercy, founded in thirteenth-century Spain.

ministro plenipotentiario y embajador extraordinario. Minister plenipotentiary and Ambassador extraordinary.

pardo. Term used to refer to a person of mixed-race ancestry. See also *casta*.

partidos. Districts.

patria. Country, nation, or fatherland.

peninsulars. Natives of Spain.

primer secretario. First secretary.

proclama. Proclamation or decree.
pueblo anexo. Subject town of a *cabecera.*
real orden. Royal order or decree.
regidor (pl. regidores). Member of a municipal council, i.e., *cabildo.*
reino. Kingdom.
rey deseado. Desired king, reference to Fernando VII.
rey intruso. Intruder king, reference to Joseph Bonaparte.
secretario de estado. Secretary of state; in practice, the principal minister of Spain.
valido. Royal favorite.

Bibliography

Primary Sources

Archives and Libraries

Archivo General de Centroámerica, Guatemala City, Guatemala (AGCA)
Archivo General de Indias, Seville, Spain (AGI)
Archivo General de la Nación, Buenos Aires, Argentina (AGN-BA)
Archivo Historico Nacional, Madrid, Spain:
 Correspondencia Diplomática (AHN-CD)
Library of Congress, United States:
 Thomas Jefferson Papers (LC-TJP)
Maryland State Archives:
 Early State Records Online, *Maryland Gazette* (MSA-ESR)
National Archives, United States:
 Notes from the Spanish Legation (NA-NSL)
Newberry Library, Chicago, IL:
 Ayer Collection, Papers of Alejandro Marure (AC-PAM)
Tulane University, New Orleans, LA:
 Latin American Library (TU-LAL)
University of Florida, Gainesville, FL:
 East Florida Papers (UF-EFP)
 Papeles de Cuba (UF-PC)
University of Texas, Austin, TX:
 The Bexar Archives, General Manuscript Series (UT-BA)

Contemporary Publications and Published Documents

Bonaparte, Joseph. *Mémoires et correspondance politique et militaire du roi Joseph*. Edited by A. du Casse. 10 vols. Paris, 1853–1854.

Bonaparte, Napoleon. *Correspondence de Napoléon Ier: Publiée par ordre de l'empereur Napoléon III*. 32 vols. Paris, 1864–1866.

Cevallos, Pedro. *Exposicion de los hechos y maquinaciones que han preparado la usurpación de la corona de España, y los medios que el emperador de los franceses ha puesto en obra para realizarla*. Cadiz, 1808.

Chateaubriand, F. R., vicomte de. *Congres de Vérone. Guerre d'Espagne. Négociations. Colonies espagnoles*. 2 vols. Paris, 1838.

"El aventurero conde Octaviano d'Alvimar espia de Napoleon." *Boletín del Archivo General de la Nación* 7, no. 2 (April/May/June 1936): 161–75.

Escoiquiz, Juan de. *Memorias (1807–1808)*. Seville: Editorial Renacimiento, 2007.

Grandmaison, Geoffroy de. *Correspondance du comte de La Forest, ambassadeur de France en Espagne, (1808–1813)*. 7 vols. Paris: La société d'histoire contemporaine, Alphonse Picarde et fils, 1905–1913.

Grisanti, Angel. *El informe de Palacio Fajardo a Napoleón, emperador y rey: Documento rigurosamente inédito*. Caracas: Tipografía Principios, 1961.

Hernández y Davalos, Juan E. *Colección de documentos para la historia de la guerra de independencia de Mexico de 1808 a 1821*. 6 vols. Mexico: Biblioteca de "El sistema postal de la Republica Mexicana," 1968.

Jackson, George, and Catherine Charlotte Jackson. *The Bath Archives: A Further Selection from the Diaries and Letters of Sir George Jackson, K.C.H.* London: R. Bentley and Son, 1873.

Lowrie, Walter, ed. *American State Papers: Documents, Legislative and Executive, of the Congress of the United States, from the First Session of the First to the Third Session of the Thirteenth Congress, Inclusive*. Vol. 3. Washington: Gales and Seaton, 1832.

Manning, William R., ed. *Diplomatic Correspondence of the United States concerning Independence of the Latin-American Nations*. 3 vols. New York: Oxford University Press, 1925–1926.

Murat, J. B. A., comte de. *Murat, lieutenant de l'empereur en Espagne 1808: D'après sa correspondance inédite et des documents originaux*. Paris, 1897.

Onís, Luís de. *Memoria sobre las negociaciones entre España y los Estados Unidos de América*. Madrid: Ediciones José Porrua Turanzas, 1969.

——— [Verus, pseud.]. *The passage of the President's message, which relates to the forcible occupation of West Florida*. N.p., 1810.

Outline of the Revolution in Spanish America; or, An account of the origin, progress, and actual state of the war carried on between Spain and Spanish America, containing the principal facts which have marked the struggle, by a South-American. London: Longman, Hurst, Rees, Orme, and Brown, 1817.

Preston, Daniel, ed. *The Papers of James Monroe*. New York: Greenwood Press, 2003.

Rutland, Robert A., et al., eds. *The Papers of James Madison*. Presidential Series. 8 vols to date. Charlottesville: University of Virginia Press, 1984–.

Saavedra, Francisco de. *Rebelión de las provincias en España: Los grandes días de la Junta Suprema de Sevilla, 1808–1810*. Madrid: Ediciones Alfar, 2011.

Skipwith, Fulwar. "Speech of Governor Fulwar Skipwith to the Senate and House of Representatives of the State of West Florida, at St. Francisville, on the 29th of November, 1810." Natchez, MT (Mississippi Territory): John W. Winn, 1810.

Stephens, John L. *Incidents of Travel in Central America, Chiapas, and Yucatan*. Vol. 2. New Brunswick, NJ: Rutgers University Press, 1949.

Torres, Camilo. *Representación del Cabildo de Bogotá Capital del Nuevo Reino de Gra-*

nada a la Suprema Junta Central de España, en el año de 1809. Santa Fé de Bogotá: Imprenta de N. Lora, 1832.

Vanegas Useche, Isidro, ed. *Plenitud y disolución del poder monárquico en la Nueva Granada: Documentos 1807–1819*. Bucaramanga: Universidad Industrial de Santander, Colección Bicentenario, 2010.

A View of South America and Mexico, comprising their history, the political condition, geography, agriculture, commerce, &c. of the republics of Mexico, Guatemala, Columbia, Peru, the United provinces of South America and Chili, with a complete history of the revolution in each of these independent states. New York: H. Huntington Jr., 1826.

Warren, Harris Gaylord. "Documents relating to Pierre Laffite's Entrance into the Service of Spain." *Southwestern Historical Quarterly* 44 (July 1940): 76–87.

Webster, C. K., ed. *Britain and the Independence of Latin America, 1812–1830: Select Documents from the Foreign Office Archives*. 2 vols. London: Oxford University Press, 1938.

Wheaton, Henry. *Reports of Cases Argued and Adjudged in the Supreme Court of the United States, February Term 1823*. Vol. 21. New York: Banks Law, 1904.

Secondary Sources

Adelman, Jeremy. *Sovereignty and Revolution in the Iberian Atlantic*. Princeton, NJ: Princeton University Press, 2006.

Alamán, Lucas. *Historia de Mexico desde los primeros movimientos que prepararon su independencia en el año 1808 hasta la época presente*. Vol. 3. Mexico: Instituto Cultural Helénico, Fondo de Cultura Económica, 1985.

Alderson, Robert J. *This Bright Era of Happy Revolutions: French Consul Michel-Ange-Bernard Mangourit and International Republicanism in Charleston, 1792–1794*. Columbia: University of South Carolina Press, 2008.

Amunátegui, Miguel Luís. *Los precursores de la independencia de Chile*. Santiago: Impr. de J. Nuñez, 1872.

Anna, Timothy E. *The Fall of the Royal Government in Mexico City*. Lincoln: University of Nebraska Press, 1978.

———. *The Fall of the Royal Government in Peru*. Lincoln: University of Nebraska Press, 1979.

———. *Spain and the Loss of America*. Lincoln: University of Nebraska Press, 1983.

Archer, Christon I. "Mexico en 1810: El fin del principio, el principio del fin." In *Mexico en tres momentos, 1810-1910-2010: Hacia la conmemoración del bicentenario de la Independencia y del centenario de la Revolución Mexicana: Retos y perspectivas*, vol. 1, edited by Alicia Mayer, 21–40. Mexico: Universidad Nacional Autónoma de México, 2007.

Armitage, David, and Michael J. Braddick, eds. *The British Atlantic World, 1500–1800*. London: Palgrave Macmillan, 2002.

Armitage, David, and Sanjay Subrahmanyam, eds. *The Age of Revolutions in Global Context, c. 1760–1840*. London: Palgrave Macmillan, 2009.

Artola, Miguel. *Los afrancesados y América.* Madrid: Instituto Gonzalo Fernández de Oviedo, 1949.

Bailyn, Bernard. *Atlantic History: Concept and Contours.* Cambridge, MA: Harvard University Press, 2005.

Beerman, Eric. "Spanish Envoy to the United States (1796–1809): Marques de Casa Irujo and His Philadelphia Wife Sally McKean." *The Americas* 37, no. 4 (April 1981): 445–56.

Belaubre, Christophe, Jordana Dym, and John Savage, eds. *Napoleon's Atlantic: The Impact of Napoleonic Empire in the Atlantic World.* Leiden: Brill, 2010.

Bemis, Samuel Flagg. *The Latin American Policy of the United States, an Historical Interpretation.* New York: Harcourt, Brace, 1943.

Benjamin, Thomas. *The Atlantic World: Europeans, Africans, Indians, and Their Shared History, 1400–1900.* Cambridge: Cambridge University Press, 2009.

Bergamini, John. D. *The Spanish Bourbons: The History of a Tenacious Dynasty.* New York: G. P. Putnam's Sons, 1974.

Blaufarb, Rafe. *Bonapartists in the Borderlands: French Exiles and Refugees on the Gulf Coast, 1815–1835.* Tuscaloosa: University of Alabama Press, 2005.

———. "The Western Question: The Geopolitics of Latin American Independence." *American Historical Review* 112, no. 3 (June 2007): 742–63.

Boyer Lewis, Charlene M. *Elizabeth Patterson Bonaparte: An American Aristocrat in the Early Republic.* Philadelphia: University of Pennsylvania Press, 2012.

Braudel, Fernand. *La Méditerranée et le monde méditerranéen à l'époque de Philippe II.* Paris: A. Colin, 1949.

Bricker, Victoria R. *The Indian Christ, the Indian King: The Historical Substrate of Maya Myth.* Austin: University of Texas Press, 1981.

Brooks, Philip C. *Diplomacy and the Borderlands: The Adams-Onis Treaty of 1819.* Berkeley: University of California Press, 1939.

Brown, Gordon S. *Latin American Rebels and the United States, 1806–1822.* Jefferson, NC: McFarland, 2015.

Bullón de Mendoza, Alfonso, and Gomez de Valugera. "Revolución y contrarrevolución en España y América (1808–1840)." In *España siglo XIX*, edited by Francisco Javier Parades Alonso, 71–75. Madrid: Editorial ACTAS, 1991.

Bumgartner, Louis E. *José del Valle of Central America.* Durham, NC: Duke University Press, 1963.

Bustamante, Carlos María. *Cuadro histórico de la Revolución Mexicana.* 3 vols. Mexico: Instituto Cultural Helénico, 1985.

Caillet-Bois, Ricardo. *La América Española y la revolución francesa.* Buenos Aires: Talleres gráficos Rodríguez Giles, 1940.

———. "Duclos Guyot emisario napoleónico: Una aclaración al señor Tramond." *Boletín del Instituto de investigaciones históricas* 12, nos. 47–48 (1931): 72–74.

———. "La misión de Antonini en 1808." *Boletín del Instituto de investigaciones históricas* 15, no. 53 (1932).

Carrillo Rocha, Magali. "Comienzos de una desilusión: Noticias públicas y lealismo, Nueva Granada, 1808." *Historia y sociedad* 21 (July–December 2011): 93–113.

Chambers, Sarah H. *From Subjects to Citizens: Honor, Gender, and Politics in Arequipa, Peru, 1780–1854*. University Park, PA: Penn State University Press, 1999.

Childs, Matt D. *The 1812 Aponte Rebellion in Cuba and the Struggle against Atlantic Slavery*. Chapel Hill: University of North Carolina Press, 2006.

———. "'The Revolution against the French': Race and Patriotism in the 1809 Riot in Havana." In Belaubre, Dym, Savage, *Napoleon's Atlantic*, 119–38.

Cortada, James W., ed. *Spain in the Nineteenth-Century World: Essays on Spanish Diplomacy, 1789–1898*. Westport, CT: Greenwood Press, 1994.

Costeloe, Michael P. *Response to Revolution: Imperial Spain and the Spanish American Revolutions, 1810–1840*. Cambridge: Cambridge University Press, 1986.

Cusick, James G. *The Other War of 1812: The Patriot War and the American Invasion of Spanish East Florida*. Gainesville: University Press of Florida, 2003.

Delumeau, Jean. *La Peur en Occident, XIVe–XVIIIe siècles: Une cité assiégée*. Paris: Fayard, 1978.

Dessens, Nathalie. *From Saint-Domingue to New Orleans: Migration and Influences*. Gainesville: University Press of Florida, 2007.

———. "Napoleon and Louisiana: New Atlantic Perspectives." In Belaubre, Dym, Savage, *Napoleon's Atlantic*, 63–77.

Diccionario Biográfico Español. 50 vols. Madrid: Real Academia de la Historia, 2009–2013.

Dubois, Laurent. *A Colony of Citizens: Revolution and Slave Emancipation in the French Caribbean, 1787–1804*. Chapel Hill: University of North Carolina Press, 2006.

Dym, Jordana. *From Sovereign Villages to National States: City, State, and Federation in Central America, 1759–1839*. Albuquerque: University of New Mexico Press, 2006.

Dym, Jordana, and Christophe Belaubre, eds. *Politics, Economy and Society in Bourbon Central America, 1759–1821*. Boulder: University Press of Colorado, 2007.

Eastman, Scott. *Preaching Spanish Nationalism across the Hispanic Atlantic, 1759–1823*. Baton Rouge: Louisiana State University Press, 2012.

Eastman, Scott, and Natalia Sobrevilla Perea, eds. *The Rise of Constitutional Government in the Iberian Atlantic World: The Impact of the Cádiz Constitution of 1812*. Tuscaloosa: University of Alabama Press, 2015.

Elliott, J. H. *Empires of the Atlantic World: Britain and Spain in America, 1492–1830*. New Haven, CT: Yale University Press, 2006.

Esdaile, Charles J. *Fighting Napoleon: Guerrillas, Bandits, and Adventurers in Spain, 1808–1814*. New Haven, CT: Yale University Press, 2004.

Ferrer, Ada. *Freedom's Mirror: Cuba and Haiti in the Age of Revolution*. New York: Cambridge University Press, 2014.

Fischer, John R., Allan J. Kuethe, and Anthony McFarlane, eds. *Reform and Insurrection in Bourbon New Granada and Peru*. Baton Rouge: Louisiana State University Press, 1990.

Fitz, Caitlin. *Our Sister Republics: The United States in an Age of American Revolutions*. New York: Liveright, 2016.

Furstenberg, Francois. *When the United States Spoke French: Five Refugees Who Shaped a Nation*. New York: Penguin Press, 2014.

Gandia, Enrique de. *Napoleón y la independencia de América*. Buenos Aires: Editorial Antonio Zamora, 1955.

Gaspar, David Barry, and David P. Geggus, eds. *A Turbulent Time: The French Revolution and the Greater Caribbean*. Bloomington: Indiana University Press, 1997.

Gates, David. *The Spanish Ulcer: A History of the Peninsular War*. New York: Norton Press, 1986.

Geggus, David P. *The Impact of the Haitian Revolution in the Atlantic World*. Columbia: University of South Carolina Press, 2001.

———. "Slave Rebellion during the Age of Revolution." In *Curacao in the Age of Revolutions, 1795–1800*, edited by Wim Klooster and Gert Oostindie, 23–56. Leiden: Brill, 2011.

Greene, Jack D., and Philip D. Morgan. *Atlantic History: A Critical Appraisal*. Oxford: Oxford University Press, 2009.

Griffin, Charles C. *The United States and the Disruption of the Spanish Empire, 1810–1822*. New York: Columbia University Press, 1937.

Guardino, Peter. *Peasants, Politics, and the Formation of Mexico's Nation State: Guerrero, 1800–1857*. Stanford, CA: Stanford University Press, 1996.

Guedea, Virginia, ed. *La independencia de México y el proceso autonomista novohispano, 1808–1824*. Mexico City: Universidad Nacional Autónoma de México and Instituto Mora, 2001.

Guerra, François-Xavier. *Revoluciones hispánicas: Independencias americanas y liberalism español*. Madrid: Editorial Complutense, 1995.

Hall, Carolyn, and Héctor Pérez Brignoli. *Historical Atlas of Central America*. Norman: University of Oklahoma Press, 2003.

Hamill, Hugh. "Royalist Counterinsurgency in the Mexican War for Independence: The Lessons of 1811." *Hispanic American Historical Review* 53, no. 3 (August 1973): 470–89.

Hamnett, Brian R. "Mexico's Royalist Coalition." *Journal of Latin American Studies* 12, no. 1 (May 1980): 55–86.

———. *La politica Española en una época revolucionaria, 1790–1820*. Mexico: Fondo de Cultura Económica, 1985.

———. *Revolución y contrarevolución en México y el Perú: Liberalismo, realeza y separatismo (1800–1824)*. Mexico: Fondo de Cultura Económica, 1978.

Hanger, Kimberly S. "Conflicting Loyalties: The French Revolution and Free People of Color in Spanish New Orleans." In *A Turbulent Time: The French Revolution and the Greater Caribbean*, edited by David Barry Gaspar and David P. Geggus, 178–203. Bloomington: Indiana University Press, 1997.

Harvey, Robert. *Liberators: Latin America's Struggle for Independence*. New York: Overlook Press, 2000.

Hawkins, Timothy. *José de Bustamante and Central American Independence: Colonial Administration in an Age of Imperial Crisis*. Tuscaloosa: University of Alabama Press, 2004.

———. "La subversion napoléonienne et la défense impériale espagnole en Amérique Centrale, 1808–1812." In *Napoléon et les Amériques: Histoire atlantique et empire napoléonien*, edited by Christophe Belaubre, Jordana Dym, and John Savage. Collection Méridiennes de l'UMR Framespa (Université de Toulouse II), 2009.

———. "El mito del terror bustamantino." In *La época de las Independencias en Chiapas y Centroamérica: Procesos sociales y politicos*, edited by Aaron Pollack. Mexico City: Instituto Mora, 2013.

———. "A Research Note: The Narrative of Spanish-American Independence and the Kingdom of Guatemala." *Latin Americanist* 57, no. 3 (September 2013): 83–98.

Herr, Richard. *The Eighteenth-Century Revolution in Spain*. Princeton, NJ: Princeton University Press, 1958.

Hill, Peter P. *Napoleon's Troublesome Americans: Franco-American Relations, 1804–1815*. Washington, DC: Potomac Books, 2005.

Hilt, Douglas. *The Troubled Trinity: Godoy and the Spanish Monarchs*. Tuscaloosa: University of Alabama Press, 1987.

Houdaille, Jacques. "Frenchmen and Francophiles in New Spain from 1760–1810." *The Americas* 13, no. 1 (July 1956): 1–29.

———. "Gaetan Souchet d'Alvimart, the Alleged Envoy of Napoleon to Mexico, 1807–1809." *The Americas* 16, no. 2 (October 1959): 109–31.

———. "La Mission de Monsieur Greffe, 1810." *Revista de historia de América*, no. 50 (December 1960): 475–83.

Ibarra, Antonio. "Crimenes y castigos politicos en la Nueva España borbónica." In *Las guerras de independencia en la América española*, edited by Marta Terán and José Antonio Serrano Ortega, 255–72. Morelia: El Colegio de Michoacán, 2002.

Johnson, Lyman L. *Workshop of Revolution: Plebeian Buenos Aires and the Atlantic World, 1776–1810*. Durham, NC: Duke University Press, 2011.

Jones, Oakah L. *Guatemala in the Spanish Colonial Period*. Norman: University of Oklahoma Press, 1994.

Joyaux, Georges J. "De Beaujour's Views of America at the Beginning of the Nineteenth Century." *Modern Language Journal* 39 (1955): 165–73.

Juarros, Domingo. *Compendio de la historia del reino de Guatemala*. Guatemala: Editorial Piedra Santa, 1981.

Kaufmann, William W. *British Policy and the Independence of Latin America, 1804–1828*. New Haven, CT: Yale University Press, 1951.

Kennedy, Roger G. *Mr. Jefferson's Lost Cause: Land, Farmers, Slavery, and the Louisiana Purchase*. Oxford: Oxford University Press, 2003.

Kinsbruner, Jay. *Independence in Spanish America: Civil Wars, Revolutions, and Underdevelopment*. 2nd ed. Albuquerque: University of New Mexico Press, 2000.

Klooster, Wim. *Revolutions in the Atlantic World: A Comparative History*. New York: NYU Press, 2009.

Klooster, Wim, and Gert Oostindie, eds. *Curaçao in the Age of Revolutions, 1795–1800*. Leiden: Brill, 2011.

Kraus, Michael. *The Atlantic Civilization: Eighteenth-Century Origins*. Ithaca, NY: Cornell University Press, 1949.

Landavazo, Marco Antonio. "La sacralización del Rey Fernando VII, la insurgencia novohispana, y el derecho divino de los reyes." *Revista de Indias* 61, no. 221 (January–April 2001): 67–90.

Landers, Jane G. *Atlantic Creoles in the Age of Revolutions*. Cambridge, MA: Harvard University Press, 2010.

Langley, Lester D. *The Americas in the Age of Revolution, 1750–1850*. New Haven, CT: Yale University Press, 1996.

Lasso, Marixa. *Myths of Harmony: Race and Republicanism during the Age of Revolution, Colombia 1795–1831*. Pittsburgh: University of Pittsburgh Press, 2007.

Laughlin, Robert M. *Beware the Great Horned Serpent: Chiapas under the Threat of Napoleon*. Albany: University of Albany Press, 2003.

Lefebvre, Georges. *The Great Fear of 1789: Rural Panic in Revolutionary France*. New York: Pantheon Books, 1973.

Lerdo de Tejada, Miguel. *Apuntes históricos de la heróica ciudad de Vera-Cruz: Precedidos de una noticia de los descubrimientos hechos en las islas y en el continente americano, y de las providencias dictados por los reyes de España para el gobierno de sus nuevas posesiones, desde el primer viaje de Don Cristobal Colón, hasta que se emprendió la conquista de Mexico*. Vol. 2. Mexico City: Imprenta de Vicente García Torres, 1857.

Lewis, James E. *The American Union and the Problem of Neighborhood: The United States and the Collapse of the Spanish Empire, 1783–1829*. Chapel Hill: University of North Carolina Press, 1998.

Lockey, Joseph B. "The Florida Intrigues of José Alvarez de Toledo." *Florida Historical Society* 12, no. 4 (April 1934): 145–78.

Lovell, W. George. *Conquest and Survival in Colonial Guatemala: A Historical Geography of the Cuchumatán Highlands, 1500–1821*. Kingston, ON: McGill-Queen's University Press, 1985.

Lynch, John. *Bourbon Spain, 1700–1808*. Oxford: Basil Blackwell, 1989.

———. *The Hispanic World in Crisis and Change, 1598–1700*. Oxford: Blackwell Press, 1992.

———. *Simón Bolívar: A Life*. New Haven, CT: Yale University Press, 2006.

———. *The Spanish-American Revolutions, 1808–1826*. New York: W. W. Norton, 1973.

Magill, John T., Pamela D. Arceneaux, and John H. Lawrence. "Between Colony and State: Louisiana in the Territorial Period, 1803–1812." *Historic New Orleans Collection Quarterly* 26, no. 4 (Fall 2009): 2–28.

May, Robert E. *Manifest Destiny's Underworld: Filibustering in Antebellum America*. Chapel Hill: University of North Carolina Press, 2002.

Mayer, Alicia, ed. *Mexico en tres momentos, 1810-1910-2010: Hacia la conmemoración del bicentenario de la Independencia y del centenario de la Revolución Mexicana: Retos y perspectivas*. Vol. 1. Mexico City: Universidad Nacional Autónoma de México, 2007.

McMichael, Andrew. *Atlantic Loyalties: Americans in Spanish West Florida, 1785–1810*. Athens: University of Georgia Press, 2008.

Michelena, Carmen L. *Luces revolucionarias: De la rebelión de Madrid (1795) a la rebelión de La Guaira (1797)*. Caracas: Fundación Centro de Estudios Latinoamericanos Rómulo Gallegos, 2010.

Mitre, Bartolomé. *Historia de Belgrano y de la independencia argentina*. Buenos Aires: Ediciones Estrada, 1960.

Ocampo, Emilio. *The Emperor's Last Campaign*. Tuscaloosa: University of Alabama Press, 2009.

Onís, José de. "Don Valentín de Foronda en los Estados Unidos." *Cuadernos Hispanoamericanos* 207 (March 1967): 448–64.

———. "Valentín de Foronda's Memoir on the United States of North America, 1804," *The Americas* 4 (1947–1948): 351–62.

Pagden, Anthony. *Lords of All the World: Ideologies of Empire in Spain, Britain, and France, c. 1500–1800*. New Haven, CT: Yale University Press, 1995.

Paladines, Carlos. *Juicio a Eugenio Espejo*. Quito: Casa de la Cultura Ecuatoriana, 2007.

Parades Alonso, Javier, ed. *España siglo XIX*. Madrid: ACTAS, 1991.

Parra Pérez, Caracciolo, ed. *Bayona y la politica de Napoleon en America*. Caracas: Tip. Americana, 1959.

———. *Historia de la primera República de Venezuela*. Caracas: Tip. Americana, 1939.

Peralta Ruiz, Víctor. "From Indiano Bureaucrats to Afrancesado Politicians in the Spanish Bonapartist State: The Cases of Azanza and Mata Linares." In Belaubre, Dym, Savage, *Napoleon's Atlantic*, 173–91.

Perrone, Sean T. "The Formation of the Spanish Consular Service in the United States, 1795–1860." In *Consuls et services consulaires au XIXe siècle/Die Welt der Konsulate im 19. Jahrundert/Consulship in the 19th Century*, edited by Jorg Ulbert and Lukian Prijac. Hamburg: DOBU-Verlag, 2010.

———. "The Role of Spanish Consuls in the United States, 1795–1898." In *Nation and Conflict in Modern Spain: Essays in Honor of Stanley G. Payne*, edited by Brian D. Bunk, Sasha D. Pack, and Carl Gustaf Scott, 81–102. Madison: Parallel Press, 2008.

———. "Spanish Consuls and Trade Networks between Spain and the United States, 1795–1820." *Bulletin for Spanish and Portuguese Historical Studies* 38, no. 1 (2013): 75–94.

Phaf-Rheinberger, Ineke. *The "Air of Liberty": Narratives of the South Atlantic Past*. Amsterdam: Editions Rodopi B. V., 2008.

Philip, Mark, ed. *Resisting Napoleon: The British Response to the Threat of Invasion, 1797–1815*. Aldershot, England: Ashgate Press, 2006.

Picard, Ernest. *Bonaparte et Moreau: L'entente initiale, les premiers dissentiments, la rupture*. Paris: Plon-Nourrit et cie, 1905.

Polasky, Janet. *Revolutions without Borders: The Call to Liberty in the Atlantic World*. New Haven, CT: Yale University Press, 2015.

Racine, Karen. *Francisco de Miranda: A Transatlantic Life in the Age of Revolution*. Wilmington, DE: Scholarly Resources, 2003.

Rasmussen, Daniel. *American Uprising: The Untold Story of America's Largest Slave Revolt*. New York: Harper-Collins Publishers, 2011.

Rippy, J. Fred. *The Rivalry of the United States and Great Britain over Latin America (1808–1830)*. Baltimore: Johns Hopkins Press, 1929.

Río, Angel del. *La misión de Don Luís de Onís en los Estados Unidos (1809–1819)*. Barcelona: Talleres Novagrafik, 1981.

Robertson, William Spence. *France and Latin-American Independence*. Baltimore: Johns Hopkins University Press, 1939.

———. "The Juntas of 1808 and the Spanish Colonies." *English Historical Review* 21, no. 124 (October 1916): 573–85.

Rodríguez O., Jaime E. *The Independence of Spanish America*. Cambridge: Cambridge University Press, 1998.

———, ed. *Mexico in the Age of Democratic Revolutions, 1750–1850*. Boulder, CO: Lynne Rienner, 1994.

———. *"We Are Now the True Spaniards": Sovereignty, Revolution, Independence, and the Emergence of the Federal Republic of Mexico, 1808–1824*. Stanford, CA: Stanford University Press, 2012.

Rosas Lauro, Claudia. *Del trono a la guillotina: El impacto de la Revolución Francesa en el Perú (1789–1808)*. Lima: Institut français d'études andines, Embajada de Francia en el Perú, Fondo Editorial de la Pontificia Universidad Católica del Perú, 2006.

Rubio Mañé, J. I. "Juan (Emilio) Gustavo de Witt, emisario del Ministro M. J. de Azanza, al servicio de José Bonaparte, que llegó a Yucatán en el año de 1810." *Boletín del Archivo General de la Nación* 15, no. 3 (July–September 1944).

Rydjord, John. *Foreign Interest in the Independence of New Spain*. Durham, NC: Duke University Press, 1935.

———. "The French Revolution in Mexico." *Hispanic American Historical Review* 9, no. 1 (1929): 60–98.

———. "Napoleon and the Independence of New Spain." In *New Spain and the Anglo-American West: Historical Contributions Presented to Herbert Eugene Bolton*, edited by Charles W. Hackett. 2 vols. Los Angeles: Lancaster Press, 1932.

———. "British Mediation between Spain and her Colonies: 1811–1813." *Hispanic American Historical Review* 21, no. 1 (1941): 29–50.

Schwartzkopf, Stacey. "Maya Power and State Culture: Community, Indigenous Politics, and State Formation in Northern Huehuetenango, Guatemala, 1800–1871." PhD diss., Tulane University, 2008.

Sevilla Soler, Rosario. "Las repercusiones de la Revolución Francesa en el Caribe español: Los casos de Santo Domingo y Trinidad." *Cuadernos Americanos de Historia Nueva Época* 17, no. 5 (September–October 1989). Mexico: Universidad Nacional Autónoma de México, 126–30.

Silva, René, and Victor M. Uribe. "Spanish American Royalism in the Age of Revolution." *Latin American Research Review* 49, no. 1 (2014): 271–81.

Socolow, Susan Migden. *The Bureaucrats of Buenos Aires, 1769–1810: Amor al Real Servicio*. Durham, NC: Duke University Press, 1987.

Soriano, Cristina. "Revolutionary Voices: The Presence of Visitors, Fugitives and Prisoners from the French Caribbean in Venezuela (1789–1799)." *Storia e Futuro, Rivista di Storia e Storiografia* no. 30 (November 2012).

Stagg, J. C. A. *Borderlines in Borderlands: James Madison and the Spanish-American Frontier, 1776–1821*. New Haven, CT: Yale University Press, 2009.

———. "Madison and the Collapse of the Spanish-American Empire: The West Florida Crisis of 1810 (Editorial Note)." In *Papers of James Madison*, Presidential Series, vol. 2, edited by J. C. A. Stagg et al., 305–20. Charlottesville: University of Virginia Press, 1992.

———. "Madison and the Problem of Mexican Independence: The Gutiérrez-Magee Raid of August 1812, 1 September 1812 (Editorial Note)." In *Papers of James Madison*, Presidential Series, vol. 5, edited by J. C. A. Stagg et al., 235–45. Charlottesville, University of Virginia Press, 2004.

———. *Mr. Madison's War: Politics, Diplomacy, and Warfare in the Early American Republic, 1783–1830*. Princeton, NJ: Princeton University Press, 1983.

Stein, Barbara H., and Stanley J. *Crisis in an Atlantic Empire: Spain and New Spain, 1808–1810*. New York: Johns Hopkins University Press, 2014.

———. *Edge of Crisis: War and Trade in the Spanish Atlantic, 1789–1808*. New York: Johns Hopkins University Press, 2009.

Taylor, William B. *Magistrates of the Sacred: Priests and Parishioners in Eighteenth-Century Mexico*. Stanford, CA: Stanford University Press, 1996.

Terán, Marta, and José Antonio Serrano Ortega, eds. *Las guerras de independencia en la América española*. Morelia: El Colegio de Michoacán, 2002.

Timmons, Wilbert H. "Tadeo Ortiz, Mexican Emissary Extraordinary." *Hispanic American Historical Review* 51, no. 3 (August 1971): 463–77.

Tutino, John. *From Insurrection to Revolution in Mexico: Social Bases of Agrarian Violence, 1750–1940*. Princeton, NJ: Princeton University Press, 1986.

Uribe-Uran, Victor M., ed. *State and Society in Spanish America during the Age of Revolution*. Wilmington, DE: Scholarly Resources, 2001.

Van Young, Eric. *The Other Rebellion: Popular Violence, Ideology, and the Mexican Struggle for Independence, 1810–1821*. Stanford, CA: Stanford University Press, 2001.

Vázquez Cienfuegos, Sigfrido. "*Víboras en nuestro seno*: Franceses y afrancesados en Cuba durante la Guerra de la Independencia." In *El comienzo de la Guerra de la Independencia*, edited by José Luis Martínez Sanz and Emilio de Diego, 1–13. Madrid: Congreso Internacional del Bicentenario, 2008.

Vicuña MacKenna, Benjamín. *La revolución de la independencia del Perú desde 1809 a 1819*. Lima: Imprenta del Comercio por J. M. Monterola, 1860.

Villamar, Claudio Mena. *El Quito rebelde (1809–1812)*. Quito: Abya-Ayala, 1997.

Villanueva, Carlos A. *Historia y diplomacia: Napoleon y la independencia de America*. Paris: Garnier, 1911.

Villaseñor y Villaseñor, Alejandro. *Biografías de los héroes y caudillos de la Independencia*. Vol. 2. Mexico: Imp. de V. Agubros, ed., 1910.

Weber, David J. *Bárbaros: Spaniards and Their Savages in the Age of Enlightenment*. New Haven, CT: Yale University Press, 2005.

West, Elizabeth Howard. "Diary of José Bernardo Gutierrez de Lara, 1811–1812, I." *The American Historical Review* 34, no. 1 (1928): 55–77.

Whitaker, Arthur P. *The United States and the Independence of Latin America, 1800–1830*. Baltimore: Johns Hopkins University Press, 1941.

Whitcomb, Edward A. *Napoleon's Diplomatic Service*. Durham, NC: Duke University Press, 1979.

Wortman, Miles. *Government and Society in Central America, 1680–1840*. New York: Columbia University Press, 1982.

Zeiler, Thomas W. "The Diplomatic History Bandwagon: A State of the Field." *Journal of American History* 95, no. 4 (March 2009): 1053–73.

Index

Page numbers in italics refer to illustrations.

Abascal, José Fernando de, 148
Achard, Monsieur, 117
Adams, John, 46
Adams, John Quincy, 98
Adams-Onís Treaty, 153
afrancesados, 1, 28, 32, 36, 57, 65, 175–76n24
Aguacatán, 129, 139, 142
alcalde mayor, duties of, 129–31, 206n14
alcalde pedáneo, duties of, 130. *See also* juez comisionado
alcaldía mayor, 125–26, 129, 206n12
Aldana, Juan, 34
Allende, Ignacio de, 34
Amar y Borbón, Antonio, 37–38
Amelia Island, 49; and filibusters, 151; and French emissaries, 79, 120
Andrés, as suspected emissary, 136
Annales school, 10–11
Antonini, Santiago, 27, 85, 175–76n24; in the United States, 77–78, 89
Aranda, conde de (Pedro Pablo Abarca de Bolea), 20, 59
Argueta, Nasario, 138, 209n49
Armero, Francisco, 110
Atlantic World, 4, 18, 123, 149; historiography of, 10–11, 171n10
Ayerbe, marqués de (Pedro María Jordán de Urríes y Fuenbuena), 61
Azanza, Miguel José de. *See* Santa Fe, duque de
Azara, Pio, 117
Bahamas, and French emissaries, 87
Bailén, Battle of, 53, 65
Baltimore, 42, 52, 75, 86, 112; and French emissaries, 76, 83, 93, 104
Bardají Azara, Eusebio, 90–91, 105–6, 108–9, 116, 119–20, 123, 150; at Bayonne, 61, 64
Barlow, Joel, 106
Bassano, duc de (Hugues-Bernard Maret), 117, 119–20
Baton Rouge, 33, 44, 50–51, 95, 150; as base for US intervention against Spanish empire, 115; and West Florida revolt, 96–97, 105
Bayonne, 101; overthrow of Spanish Bourbons in, 2, 4–5, 15, 19, 28, 31, 37, 39, 43, 50, 58, 61–62, *63*, 64, 66, 124, 148. *See also* Carlos IV; Fernando VII; Godoy, Manuel; Napoleon I; Onís, Luís de; Statute of Bayonne
Bayonne Constitution. *See* Statute of Bayonne
Beaujour, Felix, 53
Belmont, Francisco, 89
Bernabeu, Juan, 52, 76–77, 155; and communications with Monroe, 111–13; as Onís's representative before the US government, 72–74, 90, 94, 96; and *Ramona* case, 95. *See also* Madison administration; Monroe, James; Onís, Luís de; Smith, Robert; Spanish legation
Bogotá (Santa Fé de Bogotá), 24, 84, 150;

diplomatic outreach to the United States, 110; reaction to Bayonne coup, 37–39
Bolívar, Simón, 12, 149
Bonaparte, Joseph. *See* José I
Bonaparte, Napoleon. *See* Napoleon I
Bonavita, Antonio, 87, 195n31
Borgas de Barsos, Domingo, 107
Bourbon Reforms, 18, 20, 126, 177n2
Bourbons, Spanish, 2, 4, 5, 17, 31, 47, 51, 55, 57, 62, *63*, 66, 77, 88, 124, 131. *See also names of individual rulers*
Branciforte, marqués de (Miguel de la Grúa Talamanca), policy toward French expatriates, 23
Brazil, 89, 107
Brouard, Monsieur, 104
Buenos Aires, 2, 9, 11, 18, 26–27, 45, 77; British invasion of, 5, 29, 60, 81; diplomatic outreach to the United States, 122; 1810 revolt in, 3, 102, 150; as target of French emissaries, 84–85, 150. *See also* Río de la Plata
Bustamante, José de, and counterinsurgency measures, 136–44, 148, 209n52
Bustos, José Antonio, 132

Caballero, Juan, 106
cabecera de doctrina, 130
Cabral de Noroña, Miguel, 122–23
Cabrera, Ventura, 87
Calleja, Felix María, 148
camino real (Guatemala), 128–29
Campeche, and French emissaries, 98, 137
Campo Alange, duque de (Manuel José de Negrete de la Torre), 48; contact with Foronda, 53–54, 65
Campomanes, conde de (Pedro Rodríguez), 20
Cantalapiedra, 58
Caracas, 18; diplomatic outreach to the United States, 110–11; revolt in, 3, 9, 89–90, 95, 102, 120; support for Fernando VII, 35; and threat of French subversion, 106, 115, 118. *See also* Bolívar, Simón; Emparán, Vicente de; Miranda, Francisco de; Venezuela
Carbonell, Pedro, 25
Carlos III (king of Spain), 18, 20, 59
Carlos IV (king of Spain), 19, 41, 43, 51, 59, 65, 81, 147; and Aranjuez abdication, 31, 35, 39, 47, 61; and Bayonne abdication, 50, 64, 132
Carondolet, baron de (Francisco Luís Héctor de Carondolet), 23
Cartagena, 24, 38, 118
Casa Calvo, marqués de (Sebastián Calvo de la Puerta y O'Farrill), 87
Casa Irujo, marqués de. *See* Irujo, Carlos Martínez de
Casas, Juan de, 35–37
Castañeda, Marcos, 138–39
Catholic Church: counterrevolutionary measures, 21; French targeting of clergy, 88–89, 120, 138; and provincial governance, 130
Central America, isthmus of, 124–25. *See also* Guatemala
Cevallos, Ciriaco de, 32–33, 73, 192n42
Cevallos, Pedro, 61, 64; post-Bayonne career, 65–66
Chacon, Pablo, 111
Champagny, comte de (Jean-Baptiste de Nompère): at Bayonne, 62, 64; instructions to Serurier, 114
Charleston, 42, 68, 72, 84, 120; as base for French emissaries, 79, 85, 87, 108
Chiantla, 127, 129, 137, 139–42
Chiapas, 2, 125, 129, 134; unrest in, 132
Chile, Captaincy General of: and French Revolution, 26; as target of French emissaries, 84–85. *See also* Peru; Santiago
Ciudad Real, 128
Claiborne, William, 51, 152; and occupation of West Florida, 95, 104
colonial bureaucracy. *See* Spanish colonial bureaucracy
Constitution of 1812, 149
Correa, Diego, 113–14, 202n38
Cortes, 149
Council of Regency, 90, 106, 109, 149; proposed expedition to New Spain, 118; warnings about French emissaries, 116, 120–21

counterinsurgency policies, 5–6, 15, 35, 78, 92, 98, 142–43, 148, 169n3. *See also* Spanish colonial bureaucracy
Cózar, Prudencio de, and defense of Totonicapán, 132–36
Crillon, duque de, 150, 210n4
Cuba, Captaincy General of, 80, 150; commercial interests in, 94; and French community, 22, 181n53; and French Revolution, 21; reaction to Bayonne coup, 28–31; and threat from French emissaries, 76, 79, 85, 91–93, 106–9, 113–19, 121–22. *See also* French émigrés; Havana
Cuchumatán Mountains, 126, 128, 139, 142. *See also* Guatemala; Totonicapán

d'Alcantara, Pierre, 117
Dallas, Alexander, 111
d'Alvimart, Gaetan Souchet, 33–34, 176–77n25, 182n62
d'Amblimont, Jacques Athanase, 104–6, 116–20, 176–77n25, 200nn12–13. *See also* d'Amblimont Instructions
d'Amblimont Instructions, 105–7, 116
Declaration of the Rights of Man and Citizen, 21, 24
Desmolard, Joseph, 176–77n25; arrival in the United States, 75–76, 193n2; communications with José I, 86; disappearance of, 89; list of French emissaries, 83–85, 134, 164–67; operations of, 77–79, 88; recruitment of Peredo, 83, 156–57. *See also* Desmolard Instructions
Desmolard Instructions, 16, 84, 89, 116, 156–58, 161–64
doctrinas, 130
Domás y Valle, José, 23–24
dos de mayo revolt, 57, 64
Duclos Guyot, Alexandre, 26–27, 81, 85

East Florida, 28, 43, 48–49, 71, 78–79, 82, 98; as contested territory, 44, 151; French residents in, 29, 181n53; and threat from French emissaries, 120. *See also* Cuba; Florida; Madison administration; St. Augustine; West Florida; White, Enrique

Echeverría, Manuel, 141–42
Embargo Act, 49, 51
emisario francés. *See* French emissary
Emparán, Vicente de, 37, 79–80, 182n76; overthrow of, 89–90, 110
England. *See* Great Britain
Enlightenment, 18
Ensenada, marqués de la (Zenón de Somodevilla), 20
Eppes, John Wayles, 80
Erskine, David, 52
Erving, George W., 67, 104
Escoiquiz, Juan de, 61–62
Esparragosa, Fermín, 87
Estrada, Juan José de, 120, 123

Family Compact, 18
Fatio, Felipe, 82, 84
Felipe V (king of Spain), 20
Fernando VII (king of Spain), 1, 8, 19, 31–32, 34, 39, 53, 67, 72, 90, 92, 113, 121, 153; and Bayonne coup, 61–64, 132; false proclamations from, 76, 81; recognition of, 28–29, 33, 35–37, 55, 57, 147–48, 152
Florida, 28; foreign interest in, 44, 53, 56, 94–98, 108, 110, 115, 123, 151; loss to England, 18; security after Bayonne, 29–30; as target of French emissaries, 87, 93, 100, 103, 106. *See also* East Florida; West Florida
Floridablanca, conde de (José Moñino y Redondo), 20, 59, 65; counterrevolutionary measures, 21
Folch, Vicente, 30, 33
Foronda, Valentín de, 15, 43, 69, 156, 184n4, 187n38; duties as chargé d'affaires, 41–42; and Jefferson administration, 47; and Madison administration, 50–56. *See also* Campo Alange, duque de; Onís, Luís de
Fosso, Carlos, 100
Foster, Augustus, 115
France: influence in North America, 45; influence on Spain, 20; invasion of Hispaniola, 5; invasion of Spain, 2, 64–66; legation in the United States, 69, 77, 88, 114–15, 117–19; relations with the United States, 46; revolutionary alliance

with Spain, 19, 62. *See also* Francophobia; French émigrés; French emissary; French Revolution; Great Fear; José I; Napoleon I

Francophiles. *See* afrancesados

Francophobia, 2–3, 17–40. *See also* Great Fear

French émigrés, 121, 178n7; in Cuba, 22, 29–31, 86, 178n13, 180n42; in Louisiana, 23, 30–31, 73; in New Spain, 23, 178–79n17; in Puerto Rico, 22–23; in South America, 24–27, 179n33

French emissary, 1–3, 5, 7–9, 30, 55, 71, 123; Desmolard list of French emissaries, 85, 164–67; in Guatemala, 133–44, 207–8n33; as historical agent, 145–48; historiography of, 13–15, 173–74n21, 175–76n24; identifications of, 76, 78–81, 86–87, 91–93, 100, 103–7, 113–16, 122, 208–9n45; means of avoiding detection, 82, 108, 121; operations of, 77, 79, 88, 102–3, 109, 118–19, 156–59; on *Tilsit*, 74–75. *See also* d'Amblimont Instructions; Desmolard Instructions; Ledrezenech Instructions; *and names of individuals*

French Revolution, 59; and global politics, 45–46, 54; impact on Spanish empire, 4–5, 19, 22–27, 55. *See also* France; Francophobia

French subversion. *See* French emissary; José I; Napoleon I; Napoleon's shadow

Frías, duque de (José García León y Pizarro), 149

Gallatin, Albert, 79

Galzevan, Ventura. *See* Cabrera, Ventura

Garay, Martín de, 66, 72

Garibay, Pedro de, 32

Genêt, Edmond Charles, 46

German Coast Uprising, 108. *See also* Louisiana

Gil de Taboada y Lemos, Francisco, 25

Godoy, Manuel, 19, 23–24, 26, 31, 47, 60; and conspiracy of El Escorial, 61

Gómez Labrador, Pedro, 61

González, José, 79–80

González Saravia, Antonio: antisubversive regulations, 133–36, 207–8n33; response to imperial crisis, 132

Gorbalán, Antonio. *See* Correa, Diego

Granpré, Carlos de, 33

Great Britain, 101; alliance with Spain, 54–55, 68, 97; and Amelia Island, 49; assistance in campaign against French emissaries, 86, 93, 106, 120; as enemy of Spain, 5, 19, 60; and *Ramona* case, 95; relations with the United States, 69, 102, 115, 123, 150–51. *See also* Buenos Aires; Río de la Plata

Great Fear, 3, 16, 144, 146, 148, 177n4

Greffe, Monsieur (a.k.a. Le Grefe), 176–77n25; in Guatemala, 137–39, 209n46; in the United States, 100, 113–14

Guadalcázar, marqués de (Rafael António Alfonso de Sousa), 61

Guadeloupe, 32; as base for French emissaries, 79

Guatemala, Kingdom of: and camino real, 128; colonial authorities and response to Bayonne coup, 124, 132; description of, 125–26, *127*; and French Revolution, 23–24; and French threat, 84–85, 87, 113, 133–44, 207n32; political and military organization, 129–31. *See also* Bustamante, José de; French emissary; González Saravia, Antonio; Guatemala City; New Spain; Totonicapán

Guatemala City, 11, 24, 126, 128–29, 142, 148; antisubversive measures in, 132, 137; militia forces in, 131

Gutierrez de Lara, José Bernardo, 152. *See also* Gutierrez-Magee expedition; Texas

Gutierrez-Magee expedition, 152. *See also* Texas

Habsburgs, 17

Haiti, 22, 27, 45; French invasion of, 19. *See also* Haitian Revolution

Haitian Revolution, 22, 24–25; as model for subversion, 79

Havana, 11, 22, 28, 91–93, 106, 109, 113, 121–22; and expulsion of French community, 30. *See also* Cuba

Hidalgo, Miguel, 12, 141, 149; and associa-

tion with French emissary, 9, 34. *See also* Hidalgo Revolt; New Spain
Hidalgo Revolt, 9, 35, 100, 102, 108, 152. *See also* Hidalgo, Miguel; New Spain
Hispaniola, 27, 45, 71, 79; French occupation of, 5, 147. *See also* France; Haiti
Holy Office. *See* Inquisition
Huehuetenango, 127, 129, 137. *See also* Guatemala; Totonicapán

ilustrados, 20, 24
imperial crisis. *See* Spanish imperial crisis
Infantado, duque del (Pedro de Alcántara), 61–62
infidencia, 1, 34, 132, 141
Inquisition, 28; in Mexico, 23; in Peru, 25; in Spain, 21. *See also* Catholic Church
intendencias, 126
Internal Provinces: French emissaries in, 92, 119; San Antonio uprising, 108–9, 113. *See also* New Spain; Texas
Irujo, Carlos Martínez de, 41, 183n1
Iturrigaray, José de, 31–32, 34

Jacaltenango, 127, 129, 138; as cabecera de doctrina, 130
Jackson, Francis J., 67–69, 71, 86, 191n31
Jefferson, Thomas, 41, 43, 80; and Florida, 45, 110; and France, 47; suspected links to Napoleon, 52, 55, 108, 114–15; and West Florida revolt, 103–4. *See also* Jefferson administration; Napoleon I; Skipwith, Fulwar
Jefferson administration: and France, 46; and Spain, 45, 51. *See also* Foronda, Valentín de; Jefferson, Thomas; Louisiana; Madison, James; Madison administration; Spain; United States
José I (Joseph Bonaparte, king of Spain), 2, 9, 32, 38, 47, 50, 53, 55, 57, 77, 102, 114, 148; assumption of Spanish throne, 64–65; Desmolard Instructions and list of French emissaries, 161–67; emissaries of, 74–75, 81–84, 86–87, 92, 98, 105, 107, 150, 157–58; exile in the United States, 153; proclamations to Spanish America, 88–89, 91; Russian recognition of, 66; US diplomacy and, 52, 68. *See also* French emissary; Napoleon I; Onís, Luís de; Spain
josefinos. *See* afrancesados
Joseph Napoleon. *See* José I
juez comisionado, 206–7n21; duties of, 130–31; role in counterinsurgency operations, 133–44. *See also* alcalde pedáneo
Junta Central, 7, 37–38, 49–50, 57–58, 84, 91; collapse of, 89; decrees from, 132; foreign recognition of, 67–69, 75; formation of, 65–66, 189n19; legitimacy of, 51–55
Junta de Seguridad y Buen Orden (New Spain), 34
juntas de vigilancia (Cuba), 30–31
Junta Suprema of Seville, 28, 31, 36–38, 188n15

Kingdom of Guatemala. *See* Guatemala

La Guaira, 35, 90, 106, 120
Lamanon, Paul de, 35
Las Casas, Juan Bautista de, 108
Lastra, Pedro de la, 110
Latin American independence, 150; foreign agency and, 9, 11, 147; historiography of, 2, 12–15, 169n4, 171nn6–7, 172n16, 173–74n21
Ledrezenech, Louis Jean Marie, 116–19. *See also* Ledrezenech Instructions
Ledrezenech Instructions, 117–19
Le Grefe, Monsieur. *See* Greffe, Monsieur
Lestique, Monsieur, 91
Lima, 25, 84. *See also* Peru
Liniers, Santiago, 27, 81. *See also* Buenos Aires; Río de la Plata
Lizana y Beaumont, Francisco Javier, 120
López, Hermenegildo, 138
Louis XVI (king of France), 19, 45
Louisiana: as contested territory, 44–45, 51, 80, 95; French émigrés in, 30–31, 46; and German Coast Uprising, 108; Louisiana Purchase, 43, 55, 104, 108; privateers and Spanish commerce, 94; as Spanish colony, 23, 87; as stage for French conspiracies, 68–69, 72–73, 85–87, 92–93, 102–3, 109, 113, 157; transfers between France

and Spain, 18–19, 45, 60, 96; as US state, 33. *See also* Claiborne, William; France; Jefferson, Thomas; Morphy, Diego; Napoleon I; New Orleans
L'Ouverture, Toussaint, 22
Lowry, Robert K., 90

Madison, James, 12, 67–68, 150, 152; and negotiations over East Florida, 151; as secretary of state, 41, 50; suspected links to Napoleon, 78–80, 85, 96, 99, 101, 103, 108. *See also* Madison administration; Napoleon I; Onís, Luís de; United States
Madison administration, 11, 15; diplomacy with Spanish America, 90, 109–11, 122, 150, 174–75n22, 196n44; and East Florida, 123; and French legation, 115; and loyalist Spain, 51–55, 99, 112–13, 117; recognition of Onís, 8, 67–68, 74, 146, 152, 190n26; and West Florida, 94–98, 104, 151. *See also* French emissary; Monroe, James; Napoleon I; Onís, Luís de; Smith, Robert
Madrid, 129, 152; *dos de mayo* revolt in, 57, 64; occupation by French, 61, 102, 149. *See also* Fernando VII; José I; Spain
Magee, Augustus, 152
Mallol, Narciso, counterespionage measures of, 136–44
Maracaibo, 35, 95, 121. *See also* Venezuela
Mathews, George, 151
Mazarredo Salazar, José de, 87
Mendinueta, Pedro, 24
Mexico. *See* New Spain
Mexico City, 2, 110, 128; as base for French emissaries, 86; French community in, 23; political unrest in, 31–32. *See also* New Spain
Miranda, Francisco de, 5, 9, 36, 74, 149, 184n6. *See also* Caracas; Venezuela
Mobile, 44; US occupation of, 115, 151. *See also* Claiborne, William; West Florida
Monroe, James, 69, 122; communications with Spanish legation, 111–13; coordination with French legation, 115; and negotiations over East Florida, 151. *See also* Madison administration
Mont, Joaquín, 137, 140–42
Monteiro, José Dionisio, 106
Montevideo, 26. *See also* Río de la Plata
Moreau, Jean Victor Marie, 102–3, 199nn2–3. *See also* Louisiana; Napoleon I
Morphy, Diego, 68, 72, 91, 108, 122, 152. *See also* New Orleans; Onís, Luís de; Spanish legation
Mouliat, Pedro, 106
Moxó, Leandro, 72–73
Murat, Joachim, 61. *See also* Napoleon I

Nacogdoches, 11, 33, 152
Napoleon I (Napoleon Bonaparte): and Bayonne coup, 62, *63*, 64, 67, 124; communication with Spanish colonies, 48; Desmolard Instructions and list of French emissaries, 161–67; 1812 European campaign, 149; Emperor of France, 77; espionage network, 76–83, 87–88, 102, 117, 119–20; global ambitions of, 19, 55; and historiography of Latin American independence, 12–14; interest in Louisiana, 86, 96, 102–4, 108–9; invasion of Spain, 53, 65; recognition of Fernando VII, 152; relations with the United States, 46, 52, 54, 69, 71, 77; and subversion of Spanish empire, 1–11, 22, 28–40, 68, 72–74, 84–85, 89–93, 97–101, 105–7, 113–16, 121, 132–44, 146–48, 150, 156–60, 170n5, 173–74n21, 175–76n24, 197n52. *See also* France; Francophobia; French emissary; Great Fear; Jefferson, Thomas; José I; Latin American independence; Madison, James; Napoleon's shadow; Statute of Bayonne
Napoleonic emissary. *See* French emissary
Napoleonic empire, 49, 101–2, 149. *See also* Napoleon I
Napoleon's shadow, 2–3, 10–11, 87–88, 102, 121
Nariño, Antonio, 24
Natchitoches, 150, 152
Navarro, Ramón, 94
Navarro de Andrade, Sebastian, 107
Navarro de Andrade, Vicente, 107
Nebaj, 127, 130, 138
Neirera de Sousa, Juan, 107
New Diplomatic History, 13
New Granada, Viceroyalty of, 125; and

French Revolution, 24; reaction to Bayonne coup, 35–39, 183n80. *See also* Bogotá; Quito; Venezuela
New Orleans, 42, 44, 51, 68, 96, 108; as base for French emissaries, 85–86, 91, 100, 106; as base for US intervention against Spanish empire, 115, 152; and French Caribbean refugees, 30–31, 46, 185n13; as stage for French-led conspiracies, 69, 72–73, 122, 150. *See also* Louisiana; Morphy, Diego
New Spain, Viceroyalty of, 80; connection with Guatemala, 126, 28; defense of, 118, 148, 150; and French Revolution, 23; reaction to Bayonne coup, 31–35; rebellion in, 5, 9, 100, 141, 144, 149–50; support for Onís, 86; and threat from French emissaries, 76, 85, 87, 89, 91–92, 98, 106–8, 113–14, 116–19, 175n23; and threats of invasion from the United States, 56, 68–69, 73, 87, 123, 152. *See also* French émigrés; French emissary; Hidalgo Revolt; Internal Provinces; Louisiana; Texas
New York City, 42, 89, 112; arrival of Onís in, 67, 82; as base of suspected Franco-American campaigns against Spanish America, 71, 74, 80–81, 104, 107, 110, 113, 120
Nierode, Baron de, 107–8
Non-Intercourse Act, 51, 54, 120
Nording de Witt, Juan Gustavo, 98
Norfolk, 75–76, 78, 91

O'Higgins, Ambrosio, 26
Omaña, Nicolas Mauricio de, 110
Onís, José de, 58
Onís, Luís de, 7–8, 10–11, 15, 27, 55–56, *59*; Adams-Onís Treaty, 153; appointment as US ambassador, 65–66; arrival in the United States, 67, 189nn22–23; background and early diplomatic career, 58, 60; at Bayonne, 61, 64; campaign against French subversion, 68–69, 72–73, 75–81, 87, 92–93, 98–100, 108–9, 114–16, 120–23, 146–48, 197n52, 202n32; communication with Monroe, 111–12; concerns over US foreign policy, 71, 74, 104, 110; concerns over US territorial expansion, 94–95, 115, 150–52, 198n59; and d'Amblimont Instructions, 105–7; Desmolard Instructions and list of French emissaries, 82–86, 155–67; impact of warnings in Guatemala, 125, 133–44, 207–8n33; and Ledrezenech Instructions, 117–19; obsession with Napoleon, 101–2; and proclamations from José I, 88–89, 91; reaction to Caracas revolt, 90; and West Florida annexation, 96–97, 103. *See also* Bayonne; Foronda, Valentín de; French emissary; Great Fear; Madison administration; Napoleon I; Spanish colonial bureaucracy; Spanish legation
Orea, Telesforo de, 122
Ortiz, Tadeo, 151–52

Paris Peace Treaties, 43
Paz, Manuel, 140–42
Peace of Amiens, 19
Pensacola, 44, 94, 150
Pepe Botellas. *See* José I
Peredo, Francisco, 194n18, 194–95n23; as undercover agent, 82–84, 86, 155–57. *See also* Desmolard, Joseph; Desmolard Instructions; Onís, Luís de
Pereira, Jacques, 117
Peru, Viceroyalty of: and impact of French Revolution, 25; and threat of French subversion, 79, 84, 148, 150. *See also* French émigrés; French emissary; Lima
Pétion, Alexandre, 74. *See also* Haiti
Philadelphia, 7–8, 42, 70, 96, 112, 118, 146, 153; arrival of Onís, 69; as base for Franco-American campaign against Spanish empire, 115; and suspected French emissaries, 72, 104–5, 107, 109, 150
Pike, Montgomery, 69
Portugal, 60, 62, 149
Príncipe de la Paz. *See* Godoy, Manuel
Puerto Rico: French émigrés in, 22–23; and threat of French emissaries, 87, 118, 121

Quasi-War, 46
Quito, audiencia of: rebellion in, 38–39; response to French revolutionary unrest in, 24; as target of French emissaries, 79, 84. *See also* New Granada

Ramírez, Antonio Xavier. *See* d'Amblimont, Jacques Athanase
Ramona, 95, 99
Rentería, Antonio, 86
Revillagigedo, conde de (Juan Vicente de Güemes), 23
rey deseado, 57, 152. *See also* Fernando VII
rey intruso, 32, 54, 57, 87. *See also* José I
Río de la Plata, Viceroyalty of: and British invasions, 5, 29, 60, 81; and French Revolution, 26–27; rebellion in, 3, 5; as target of French emissaries, 79. *See also* Antonini, Santiago; Buenos Aires; French emissary
Rodríguez, Luís, 86
Rodríguez Alemán de Peña, Manuel, 91–92
Rosario, 129
Roux, Monsieur, 115–16

Saavedra, Francisco de, 77, 79, 89; and Desmolard letter from Onís, 155–60
Sacapulas, 127, 129
Saint Barthélemy, 78–79
Saint-Domingue. *See* Haiti
Salcedo, Manuel María de, 108
Salcedo, Nemesio, 92
San Antonio de Béxar: and Gutierrez-Magee expedition, 152; uprising in, 108–9. *See also* Internal Provinces; New Spain; Texas
San Carlos, duque de (José Miguel de Carvajal), 61
Sánchez, Felix, 106
San Martín, José de, 9, 12
San Martín Cuchumatán, 140–41
San Miguel Acatán, 127, 139
San Miguel Totonicapán, 126, 128–29, 136
San Pedro Solomá, 127, 138
San Salvador, 126, 140–41
San Sebastian Coatán, 127, 129, 139
Santa Ana Huista, 129–30
Santa Cruz y Espejo, Javier Eugenio de, 24
Santa Fe, duque de (Miguel José de Azanza), 48, 65, 98
Santiago, 150. *See also* Chile
Santiago Chimaltenango, 129
Santo Domingo, 71, 74. *See also* Hispaniola
Savary, Anne-Jean-Marie-René, 61
Scabra da Silva, Lucas, 119
secretario de estado (secretary of state), 21, 23, 61, 66, 90. *See also names of individuals*
Serurier, Louis Charles, 114–15, 117–19
Seven Years' War, 18, 43, 45
Shaler, William, 109–10, 152
Skipwith, Fulwar, 199n6; and West Florida revolt, 103–4. *See also* Jefferson, Thomas; Louisiana; West Florida
Smith, Robert, 110–11; and Bernabeu, 73–74, 90, 94, 96; and Foronda, 51–53, 55; and Onís, 67–69, 72, 95. *See also* Jefferson administration; Madison administration; Spanish legation
Someruelos, marqués de (Salvador de Muro), 33, 92–93, 181n55; and post-Bayonne unrest, 28–30, 48–49
Spain: alliance with Great Britain, 54–55, 68, 97; and American Revolution, 18–19; Bayonne coup, 61–64; Bonapartist government of, 48, 52–54; eighteenth-century revival of, 18, 20; and loyalist resistance to Napoleonic invasion, 2, 6, 28, 57, 65–66, 102, 149; and relations with revolutionary France, 18–19, 27, 59–60; and relations with the United States, 8, 41–43, 51–56, 67, 95–98, 102, 115, 150–53, 171–72n11; xenophobia in, 20. *See also* Bayonne; Bourbons; Carlos III; Carlos IV; Council of Regency; Fernando VII; José I; Junta Central; Napoleon I; Spanish colonial bureaucracy; Spanish imperial crisis
Spanish America: and fear of French subversion, 1–3, 6–7, 21–28, 107, 143, 149; and migrants from French colonies, 22–25; potential for revival, 150; rebellions in, 4–5, 102, 120, 150; threat from the United States, 44, 115, 121. *See also* Chile; Cuba; Florida; French emissary; Great Fear; Guatemala; Hispaniola; Latin American independence: historiography of; Louisiana; Napoleon I; New Granada; New Spain; Peru; Puerto Rico; Quito; Río de la Plata; Spanish Americans; Spanish colonial bureaucracy; Venezuela
Spanish Americans: conflict between Eu-

ropean Spaniards and American Spaniards, 34; diplomatic outreach to the United States, 110–11; loyalty of, 3, 6–7, 38–39, 55, 72, 90, 92, 106, 113, 141–42. *See also* Great Fear; Spain; Spanish America
Spanish colonial bureaucracy: and antisubversive warnings from Onís, 72, 76, 78, 84, 91–93, 98–99, 106–9, 113, 115–16, 120–22; and campaign against French subversion, 1–3, 5–7, 9–10, 15, 21–39, 55, 102, 118, 133–44, 148–49; contact with Bonapartist regime, 53–54; organization of, 7–8, 126, 129–31, 206n12; preservation of order after Bayonne, 48–49, 124–25; support for Onís, 86, 146–47. *See also* Foronda, Valentín de; Onís, Luís de; Spanish legation
Spanish Crown, 129, 147; legitimacy of, 3, 47–48, 58; warnings about French agents, 23. *See also* Carlos III; Carlos IV; Cortes; Council of Regency; Fernando VII; Junta Central; Spain; Spanish imperial crisis
Spanish empire. *See* Spanish America
Spanish imperial crisis, 2–4, 11, 17, 19, 34, 60–67, 130, 132, 147. *See also* Great Fear; Napoleon I; Spain; Spanish Crown
Spanish legation (United States), 15, 83, 185–86n22; campaign against French emissaries, 75–89, 91–93, 100, 105, 118, 121–22; defense of Onís, 111–12; and Foronda, 50–56; and Onís, 68, 72, 102; operations of, 41–42, 118, 183–84n2; protests against US foreign policy, 90, 109–10, 114–15. *See also* Bernabeu, Juan; Chacon, Pablo; Foronda, Valentín de; Morphy, Diego; Onís, Luís de; Spanish colonial bureaucracy
Statute of Bayonne, 2, 38, 54, 64, 98, 188n13. *See also* Bayonne; José I; Napoleon I
St. Augustine, 11, 28, 48, 148, 180n47; proclamation of Fernando VII, 29. *See also* East Florida
Stephens, John Lloyd, 128

Talleyrand, Charles Maurice de, 46, 102
Texas: French emissaries in, 100, 113; and Gutierrez-Magee expedition, 152; security of, 103, 150; unrest in, 108–9. *See also* Internal Provinces; New Spain
Tilsit, French emissaries and, 74–78, 82, 92, 99, 155, 192–93n1. *See also* Antonini, Santiago; Desmolard, Joseph; French emissary; Onís, Luís de
Tineo, Juan, 87
Todos Santos Cuchumatán, 127, 129, 140
Toledo, José Álvarez de, 122–23, 152, 204n66
Torres, Camilo, 38–39
Totonicapán, 11, 128; alcaldía mayor of, 125–28, *127*; political and military organization of, 129–31; and threat of French subversion, 132–44
Treaty of Basle, 27
Treaty of Madrid, 45
Treaty of San Ildefonso (1800), 44
Tribunal of Loyalty (Guatemala), 135–36, 208n37
Turreau, Louis Marie, 69, 77, 88

United States, 4, 8, 11; as base for French emissaries, 8, 78, 88, 92, 104, 111; commerce with Spanish America, 81–82; emergence as major power, 43; foreign policy of, 44–47, 50–56, 77, 90; and French immigrant population, 30–31; interest in Spanish territory, 95–98, 102, 115, 150–53, 171–72n11, 204–5n70; official diplomacy with Spanish America, 90, 109–10, 122, 171–75n22; and official treatment of Onís, 67–68, 99, 112–13, 190–91n28; and partisan divide over Spain, 79–80, 85–86, 117, 159–60; public support for Spanish American revolutions, 121; and relations with Great Britain, 115, 123, 150–51; suspected subversive operations against Spanish America, 69, 71–74, 94–95, 107–9. *See also* Jefferson administration; Madison administration; Napoleon I; Onís, Luís de
Urquijo, Mariano Luís de, 65, 188n14

Vaillant, 32–33
Valero, José Mariano, 132
Venegas, Francisco Javier, 106, 148
Venezuela, Captaincy General of, 80, 95; First Republic, 120, 149; impact of

French Revolution on, 24–25; reaction to Bayonne coup, 35–37; rebellion in, 3, 5, 89–90; as target of French emissaries, 79, 84–85, 93, 106, 121. *See also* Caracas; Emparán, Vicente de; French emissary; Miranda, Francisco de; New Granada
Veracruz, 34, 73, 92, 113, 118, 150; anti-French uprising in, 32–33. *See also* New Spain
Verus (a.k.a. Luís de Onís), and West Florida annexation, 96–97. *See also* Madison administration; Onís, Luís de; West Florida
Viar, José de, 52
Vilches, Agustín, 132
Villariezo, conde de (Valentín Belbis), 61

War of 1812, 150–51
War of Jenkins's Ear, 18
Washington, George, 46, 85, 159–60
Wellesley, Arthur (Viscount Wellington), 149
West Florida, 28, 30, 43; American annexation of, 95–98, 100, 102, 105, 111, 151; Anglo-American revolt of, 103–4, 113, 198n59; as contested territory, 44, 94; French emissaries in, 33. *See also* Claiborne, William; Florida; Folch, Vicente; Louisiana; Madison administration; Mobile; West Florida
White, Enrique, 29, 48–49, 71, 78–79, 82, 87, 89, 95. *See also* Cuba; East Florida; Someruelos, marqués de; St. Augustine
Wilkinson, James, 56, 69

Yalixján, 129, 139
Yucatan, 98